COSMOPOLITAN IMAGINATION IN THE NINETEENTH CENTURY: VISIBLE CITY, INVISIBLE WORLD

This book tells a story about the transformation of mid-Victorian urban writing in response both to London's growing size and diversity, and to Britain's shifting global fortunes. Tanya Agathocleous departs from customary understandings of realism, modernism, and the transition between them, to show how a range of writers throughout the nineteenth century – including William Wordsworth, Charles Dickens, William Morris, Henry James, Arthur Conan Doyle, and Joseph Conrad – explored the ethical, social, and political implications of global belonging. Showcasing a variety of different genres, Agathocleous uses the lens of cosmopolitan realism – the literary techniques used to transform the city into an image of the world – to explain how texts that seem glaringly dissimilar actually emerged from the same historical concept, and in doing so she presents startlingly new ways of thinking about the meaning and effect of cosmopolitanism.

TANYA AGATHOCLEOUS is Assistant Professor of English at Hunter College, City University of New York.

D1556541

CAMBRIDGE STUDIES IN NINETEENTH-CENTURY
LITERATURE AND CULTURE

General editor

GILLIAN BEER, *University of Cambridge*

Editorial board

ISOBEL ARMSTRONG, *Birkbeck, University of London*
KATE FLINT, *Rutgers University*
CATHERINE GALLAGHER, *University of California, Berkeley*
D. A. MILLER, *University of California, Berkeley*
J. HILLIS MILLER, *University of California, Irvine*
DANIEL PICK, *Birkbeck, University of London*
MARY POOVEY, *New York University*
SALLY SHUTTLEWORTH, *University of Oxford*
HERBERT TUCKER, *University of Virginia*

Nineteenth-century British literature and culture have been rich fields for inter-disciplinary studies. Since the turn of the twentieth century, scholars and critics have tracked the intersections and tensions between Victorian literature and the visual arts, politics, social organization, economic life, technical innovations, scientific thought – in short, culture in its broadest sense. In recent years, theoretical challenges and historiographical shifts have unsettled the assumptions of previous scholarly synthesis and called into question the terms of older debates. Whereas the tendency in much past literary critical interpretation was to use the metaphor of culture as "background," feminist, Foucauldian, and other analyses have employed more dynamic models that raise questions of power and of circulation. Such developments have reanimated the field. This series aims to accommodate and promote the most interesting work being undertaken on the frontiers of the field of nineteenth-century literary studies: work which intersects fruitfully with other fields of study such as history, or literary theory, or the history of science. Comparative as well as interdisciplinary approaches are welcomed.

A complete list of titles published will be found at the end of the book.

URBAN REALISM AND THE COSMOPOLITAN IMAGINATION IN THE NINETEENTH CENTURY

Visible City, Invisible World

TANYA AGATHOCLEOUS

CAMBRIDGE
UNIVERSITY PRESS

CAMBRIDGE UNIVERSITY PRESS
Cambridge, New York, Melbourne, Madrid, Cape Town,
Singapore, São Paulo, Delhi, Mexico City

Cambridge University Press
The Edinburgh Building, Cambridge CB2 8RU, UK

Published in the United States of America by Cambridge University Press, New York

www.cambridge.org
Information on this title: www.cambridge.org/9781107663695

First published 2011
First paperback edition 2013

A catalogue record for this publication is available from the British Library

Library of Congress Cataloguing in Publication Data
Agathocleous, Tanya, 1970–
Urban realism and the cosmopolitan imagination in the nineteenth century : visible city,
invisible world / Tanya Agathocleous.
p.   cm. – (Cambridge studies in nineteenth-century literature and culture)
ISBN 978-0-521-76264-9 (Hardback)
1. London (England)–In literature.   2. English literature–19th century–History and criticism–
Theory, etc.   3. City and town life in literature.   4. Cosmopolitanism in literature.   5. Great
Britain–Civilization–19th century.   I. Title.   II. Series.
PR468.L65A73 2010
820.9´32421–dc22
                                                                                              2010023059

ISBN 978-0-521-76264-9 Hardback
ISBN 978-1-107-66369-5 Paperback

Contents

Illustrations

Acknowledgments

Financial support for the writing and publication of this book came from the Griswold Junior Faculty Research Grant; the Morse Fellowship in the Humanities Grant; and the Hilles Publication Grant at Yale University. An earlier version of the Wordsworth section of Chapter 2 appeared in *Genre* 36 (Fall/Winter 2003); a version of Chapter 3 appeared in *Nineteenth-Century Contexts* 26: 2 (June 2004); and short sections of the Preface and Introduction appeared in an article on "Cosmopolitanism and Literary Form" in *Literature Compass* 7:6 (June 2010).

The project grew out of a dissertation written at Rutgers University under the guidance of Carolyn Williams, George Levine, Barry Qualls, and Bruce Robbins. I continue to be astonished, years later, at the good fortune I had to have worked with all these brilliant, kind people simultaneously – I am profoundly grateful to them for their mentoring and friendship. Special thanks are due to Carolyn Williams, who was my director and who has been a source of inspiration and insight ever since.

I would also like to acknowledge all those from graduate school and beyond whose friendship and intellect have contributed immeasurably to my work – in particular Joseph Chaves, Erik Dussere, Sarah Ellenzweig, and Lisa Lynch, who were there from start to finish. For direct input, encouragement, well-timed words of wisdom, and various other forms of invaluable aid, I thank also Dohra Ahmad, Kristie Allen, Ann Dean, Regenia Gagnier, Lisa Gitelman, Karin Gosselink, Jonathan Grossman, John Jordan, Vincent Lankewish, Sebastian Lecourt, Kathleen Lubey, Kristin Mahoney, Vanessa Manhire, Dan Novak, Matthew Parry, Tanya Pollard, Ray Ricketts, Elda Rotor, Mike Rubenstein, Purvi Shah, Rachel Sherman, Jonah Siegel, Kate Stanton, and Karen Strassler.

Many individuals I met while at Yale University offered me guidance, feedback, and enthusiasm for this project. I owe special thanks to Jennifer Baker, Tim Barringer, Janice Carlisle, Wai Chee Dimock, George Fayen, Langdon Hammer, Amy Hungerford, Pericles Lewis, Morna O'Neill,

Lloyd Pratt, and Nicole Rice. I am particularly grateful to Richard Maxwell and Katie Trumpener for reading the whole manuscript and for so much else, and terribly saddened by Richard's death shortly before the publication of this book, which owes so much to his work and encouragement. Most of all, I can't imagine how I would have written this book without Shameem Black, who provided meticulous commentary on countless drafts, as well as unflagging support – she has been a wonderful interlocutor and friend throughout this process. I also thank Denis Ferhatovic for his help with all the details. The Beinecke and British Art Center at Yale, treasure troves of information and images, became indispensable to me over the course of my research, and I owe thanks to Elizabeth Fairman, Kevin Repp, Maria Singer, and Timothy Young for their expertise and largesse.

One of the benefits of this project has been the opportunity to engage with scholars whose work I greatly admire, all of whom have been unfailingly generous with their time and ideas. I am indebted to Amanda Anderson, Nancy Armstrong, Jim Buzard, Elaine Freedgood, Lauren Goodlad, Kurt Koenigsberger, Caroline Levine, and Gage McWeeny for their incisive feedback on various stages of the manuscript and to Rebecca Walkowitz and an anonymous reviewer at Cambridge University Press for reading and commenting on the whole. I am also grateful to those who contributed to the special issue of *Victorian Literature and Culture* on "Victorian Cosmopolitanisms" that I co-edited with Jason Rudy, as well as to the journal's editors, Adrienne Munich and John Maynard. The excellent essays we featured in that issue inspired and influenced me as I finished this book. Among the many fruitful outcomes of that collaboration was a close friendship with Jason Rudy, for which I will always be grateful.

In connection with this book's publication, I thank Gillian Beer for supporting this project, as well as Linda Bree, my editor at Cambridge, and Elizabeth Hanlon, who has been incredibly patient, kind and helpful.

Lastly, I would like to thank my family who, in their various ways, have inspired my affinity for cities and utopias. I am happy to owe a lifelong debt to Chris O'Brien, who in every way made this possible, and to Zora, who put it in perspective.

Preface

The metropolis of Britain, and of the world, is a literary mine, which a
round number of workers with head and hand have been long quarry-
ing out to the public advantage, and, it is to be hoped, to their own.
Charles Manby Smith, *The Little World of London: or,*
Pictures in Little of London Life.[1]

In the introduction to his 1856 social study "The Great World of
London," Henry Mayhew contends that London is best understood as a
"world" rather than a city because of the vastness and diversity of its
population. Producing a flurry of statistics to make the case for London's
unprecedented scale, Mayhew sums them up by stating: "in every thousand of the aggregate composing the immense human family, two at least
are Londoners."[2] References to astronomy bolster the scientism and
grandeur of his assertions. Comparing the capital city to a "planetoid,"
Mayhew imagines the Earth exploding and London spinning off as a
world in its own right: "If . . . by some volcanic convulsion . . . the great
Metropolis were to be severed from the rest of the globe, London is quite
large enough to do duty as a separate world" (7). As well as seeing London
as a planet, Mayhew projects its social geography on to the world's
physical geography so that "Belgravia and Bethnal Green become the
opposite poles of the London sphere – the frigid zones, as it were, of
the Capital; the one icy cold of its exceeding fashion, form, and ceremony;
and the other wrapt in a perpetual winter of withering poverty" (4).

For Mayhew, London's size is matched only by its sociological complexity, for it is "made up of different races like a world" (4). As he often
does in his better-known work of urban sociology *London Labour and the
London Poor* (1851), Mayhew reads class difference through the lens of
the racial categories employed by Victorian anthropologists. "As regards
the metropolitan people," he states, "the polite Parisian is not more
widely different from the barbarous Botecudo, than is the lack-a-daisical
dandy at Almack's from the Billingsgate 'rough'" (4).[3] But class is not the

only variable he uses to see London as an "aggregate of *various nations*" (4) – religious and linguistic differences also contribute to his account of the city's anthropological variety. The eccentricities of "the Bight of Benin, who have a lizard for their particular divinity," he notes, are no more outlandish than the Mormonism and spiritualism practiced by individuals in the British capital. Global philological diversities, too, can be compared to those within London for they are "hardly more manifold than the distinct modes of speech peculiar to the various classes of Metropolitan society" (5).

Through these comparisons of London to the world as a whole, Mayhew underscores the magnitude of his own project. "The Great World of London" was initially conceived of as an encyclopedic collection of sketches that would encompass all major elements of London society.[4] Mayhew's elaborate introduction, however, implies an even grander venture: if London, via his imagery, takes on planetary dimensions, his local observations acquire universal resonances, providing insight into the operations of society across a global landscape.

Mayhew's reading of London as not only *a* world but *the* world is characteristic of Victorian city writing. In 1851, a journalist in *Table Talk* wrote that "London is not a poetical place to look at; but surely it is poetical in the very amount and comprehensiveness of its enormous experience of pleasure and pain ... It is one of the great giant representatives of mankind, with a huge beating heart."[5] The grandiose adjectives he used to describe the city – "comprehensive," "enormous," "great," "giant," and "huge" – suggest how unfathomably vast London appeared to Victorian observers.

Proffering an "enormous experience of pleasure and pain," London's sublime ambivalence made it an appealing literary ("poetical") subject – as did the notion that it was representative of "mankind." Henry James also stressed London's representativeness: "London is indeed an epitome of the round world, and just as it is a commonplace to say that there is nothing one can't 'get' there, so it is equally true that there is nothing one may not study at first hand."[6] For James, London is both a way to imagine a global whole ("the round world") and to consume it, both materially ("getting") and mentally, through exposure to boundless knowledge.

From metaphors such as these to entire novels by writers from Charles Dickens to William Morris, a significant range of writings use London as a way to apprehend global modernity. This book shows how urban realism, the chief mode used to represent the British capital in the nineteenth century, brought the modern idea of the world-city into being.

As Britain's capital and economic center, London was, of course, a symbol of the nation and the "heart of the empire." But with the new and fast-expanding networks of trade, finance, post, steamship, telegraph, print, and immigration that took shape over the course of the nineteenth century, it became unmistakably linked to the world beyond the nation as well. This unprecedented level of connectivity produced both dreams and nightmares, giving shape to a city literature as richly evocative as it was deeply equivocal.

How did the city come to represent both the pre-eminence of the English nation and the world as a whole? In early to mid-nineteenth-century fiction, the countryside *is* the country, as Raymond Williams famously wrote.[7] Novels such as Jane Austen's, in his account, focus primarily on knowable communities situated in provincial landscapes; the bounded social networks delineated by these works stand in metonymically for social relations in the nation at large. Yet, by mid-century, the city came into prominence as a literary subject and the scale of imagined community changed dramatically. While Austen's geographies, according to Edward Said, extend beyond the English countryside to the imperial peripheries, she nonetheless focuses on a bounded and coherent community: "this particular web," as George Eliot puts it in *Middlemarch*.[8] The city, by contrast, was imagined as a complex, incoherent web of interconnections that spanned the entire globe. In works by authors ranging from William Wordsworth and Charles Dickens to Arthur Conan Doyle and Henry James, London stands for human society conceptualized at the national *and* the global level simultaneously.

The city's global dimensions, moreover, were not always understood in imperial terms. Critics such as Joseph McLaughlin and Ian Baucom have argued that the city posed a negative challenge to English identity because, as Baucom puts it, London represented an "imperial 'without' inside the national 'within.'"[9] Writers like Mayhew, he contends, "rewrite the map of the city as a map of English and imperial space."[10] While indebted to these critics in my understanding of the role of empire in the imagination of urban space, I emphasize the double valence of the Victorian urban vision: the city did provoke a turn to the country as the site of authentic Englishness, but it also inspired attempts to sublimate its threatening plurality into an image of global community. The dislocating effect of the city, in other words, was not only viewed negatively as a sign of otherness but positively, as a spur to visions of collectivity.

Tracing the depiction of the city in literature from the mid-nineteenth century to the early twentieth, I show that two forms drawn from visual culture – the sketch and the panorama – allowed Victorian writers to move between the fragmentary view from the street and a distant, all-encompassing overview. I call this melding of city and world *cosmopolitan realism*. Employing shifts in perspective from *polis* to *kosmos* and back again, realist writing produced both a sense of detailed, accumulative local knowledge and an ideal of totality. Together, these different scales allowed for a sense of human community designed to give shape and meaning to the inconceivable complexity of the modern world: a world made newly visible by the alienating forces of imperialism, capitalism, and technology at work in the city. Writers did not merely reflect a new global consciousness, then, but used the city to shape it – and to relate it to quotidian experience.

This global consciousness, I argue, is critical to our understanding of Victorian realism. It also sheds light on literature's contribution to secularization. If secularism, as scholars such as Vincent Pecora contend, is not simply a critique of religious paradigms but a transformation of them, cosmopolitan realism represents one of the concrete forms of secularism's alchemical work.[11] From the saintly iconography that influences the journalistic sketch tradition to the Renaissance allegories that inform the novelistic schemas of writers from Dickens to William Morris, religious paradigms permeate the texts of cosmopolitan realism, functioning not just as the residue of older forms but as a means to imbue urban narratives with moral meaning. While it is not controversial to claim that realist writing was indebted to religious epistemologies as well as to scientific ones, my contention is that by secularizing religious paradigms writers sought not merely to universalize the moral meanings of their texts but to *globalize* them, locating them within a historicized vision of the contemporary world.

The scientific specificity of urban realism, with its attention to particular locales, class, or ethnicity, anchored and differentiated the abstractions of universalism in order to situate them in the "real world" of capitalist modernity. If cosmopolitan realism sought to conceptualize human community at a worldwide level, it did so with the perplexing and recalcitrant inequities of urban existence as a symbol for what would have to be overcome globally. The visible world of the *polis*, in all its grim materiality, was a constant reproach to the invisible, idealistic world of the *kosmos*.

Cosmopolitan realism, therefore, was both utopian and dystopian in outlook. It was a realist*ic* cosmopolitanism, critical of those forms which preceded it. While Enlightenment cosmopolitanism, in Kant's seminal articulation, was optimistic in its correlation of international economic exchange with the coming of "perpetual peace," the Victorians, from mid-century onwards, tended to be less sanguine about the progress of globalization.[12] In one of the period's most famous and trenchant critiques of capitalism, *The Communist Manifesto* of 1848 by Karl Marx and Friedrich Engels, the "cosmopolitan character of production and consumption in every country" is inseparable from the malign effects of the bourgeois "exploitation of the world market." Yet even the *Manifesto* insisted on a utopian side to this development: "National one-sidedness and narrow-mindedness become more and more impossible, and from the numerous national and local literatures, there arises a world literature."[13] This profound ambivalence about cosmopolitanism, and hence about Western progress, is echoed in each of the texts I examine, which struggle in different ways to read the visible face of the city as the sign of an invisible world of solidarity to come.

The Communist Manifesto's conditions of production are as relevant to cosmopolitan realism as its ideological stance. Published in several languages and addressed to an international audience, the work was itself an example of the new *Weltliteratur* heralded by Marx and Engels. As such, the *Manifesto* helps to explain why cosmopolitan realism emerged when it did. Mass population shifts in London had radically changed the scale and composition of the city by mid-century. This, together with the new global networks of communication and travel, and a burgeoning culture of urban spectacle – brought to the forefront of national consciousness with the 1851 Great Exhibition – inspired literature's global turn. But writers were also self-consciously reproducing and shaping their own conditions of production. British writers, in particular, were operating in an increasingly global literary marketplace; moreover, they were publishing in a city competing with Paris to position itself as the center of a "world republic of letters" (in Pascale Casanova's influential phrase) and had access to new and growing markets in the colonies.[14] Texts concerned with cosmopolitanism as an idea, in other words, were written in a public sphere defined by cosmopolitanism as a material condition. For Marx, the internationalization of literature represents an opportunity for political progress – one of the ways in which capitalism will sow the seeds of its own demise. But for authors less assured about the trajectory of globalization, yet more invested in the material success of their writings, such as Dickens and Conrad, this widening purview is at once a threat to the national culture they both held sacred and a bewitching opportunity to speak both for, and *to*, the modern world as a whole, rather than merely Britain. A heightened consciousness of global space, therefore, helps to shape their conceptions of the novel's ever-broadening boundaries.

The globalization of the literary marketplace and a sense of the inter-penetration of national and international space only intensified in the twentieth century, but modernist city writers, in forfeiting the unifying perspectives of cosmopolitan realism, struggle to imagine the city as a site of community. While urban cosmopolitanism has been more readily associated with modernism than with Victorian literature, I show that modernist writers turn from the dislocating spaces of the city to new forms of temporality to imagine community. The experimental ways in which modernist and postmodernist writings depict cosmopolitan cities have been the subject of a number of recent studies; this book expands these narratives to show how Victorian literature helped to make the now-familiar connection between city and world feel organic to urban living and its ongoing narratives.

Today it is commonplace for all kinds of narratives, from novels to films to non-fiction, to draw intricate connections between metropole and periphery in the service of a global ethos. A 2008 news story, for instance, connects demand for coltan – a rare metal used to manufacture Sony Playstations – with the exploitation of children and civil war in the Congo, where the metal is mined, in order to draw attention to the hidden costs of Western consumerism.[15] I seek to illustrate how our ability to tell stories such as this one, which connects micro-level concrete detail (a small piece of a gaming device) to a macro-level map of global capital and international politics, is bound up with the history of urban literary realism.

In analyzing the internal contradictions and flawed utopianism of cosmo-politan realism, this book tells a story about the transformation of mid-Victorian urban writing in response to London's growing size and diversity and Britain's shifting global fortunes. Its argument unfolds in two sections, one focused on mid-century and the other on the *fin de siècle*. Part One historicizes cosmopolitan realism, taking the moment of the Great Exhibition and London's subsequent canonization as world-city as its central axis. Part Two moves from the tentative cosmopolitanism of mid-century writers to its efflorescence at the turn of the century, when the word appeared with increased frequency in literary and journalistic writing.

Because it charts the rise and fall of cosmopolitan realism – a form of writing linked to Britain's role in the world – *Urban Realism and the Cosmopolitan Imagination* departs from customary understandings of realism, modernism, and the transition between them. While many studies of urban realism emphasize the canonical novels produced between 1850 and 1870, such as those of Charles Dickens, Elizabeth Gaskell, and William Makepeace Thackeray, my broad definition of realism expands its temporal parameters. I treat as "realistic" works that rely on visual and empirical modes of knowledge to represent urban life but that are also invested in the invisible world beyond the city. I therefore see texts at either end of the century, such as Wordsworth's *The Prelude* and General William Booth's *In Darkest England*, as part of the same epistemological project. My emphasis on cosmopolitanism, however, shifts realism's center of gravity to the end of the century, for I argue that the proliferation of narrative styles at this time – Doyle's detective novel, James' naturalism, Morris' romance-allegory – can be read as efforts to address urban writing's sense-making capacities to an ever-widening terrain.

Diachronically, the chapters of this book trace the development of cosmopolitanism as a formal endeavor from the 1850s to the end of the nineteenth century and into the twentieth in order to show how urban realism was instrumental in shaping a global imaginary. Synchronically, each chapter looks closely at two or more contemporaneous texts that are generically disparate but formally similar. The chapter structures showcase a range of different genres – poetry and prose (*The Prelude* and *Bleak House* in Chapter 2), high and popular literature (*The Princess Casamassima* and *A Study in Scarlet* in Chapter 3), and fiction and non-fiction (*News from Nowhere* and *In Darkest England* in Chapter 4) – but demonstrate how each pair of texts, in using the city to imagine the world, employs similar formal juxtapositions. Thus both Wordsworth and Dickens use the sketch and the panorama as verbal-visual modes; both James and Doyle use an aestheticist version of realism along with novelistic romance; and both Morris and Booth use a combination of allegory and ethnography to construct socialist utopias. The lens of cosmopolitan realism, then, helps to explain why texts that seem glaringly dissimilar emerge from the same historical context.

The Introduction situates the argument I outline here historically and within current critical debates. Chapter 1 begins the story of cosmopolitan realism by tracing the wide range of ways the word *cosmopolitan* and its variants were used in the period and foregrounding the role of different cultural forms – in this case, the Great Exhibition and the middle-class periodical – in codifying and circulating the word's different meanings. Subsequent chapters look at how the disparate scales of realist writing are leveraged to contend with specific notions of cosmopolitanism and the singular balance between local and global that each requires. At mid-century, the sketch and the panorama are used in tandem to view the world as a unified human family. Chapter 2 examines the generic origins of cosmopolitan realism in this formal combination. Through a reading of William Wordsworth's *The Prelude* (1850), among other texts, I argue that the fragmentary view of the street and the worldwide view from above allow authors to register the anxieties of difference without abandoning a sense of solidarity with humankind. With their intrinsic contest between local and global perspectives, the sketch and the panorama laid the foundation for cosmopolitan realism.

Over the course of the century, the antithetical scales of urban writing were adapted by increasingly radical and disenchanted writers to fit their more explicit engagement with ideals of global community. The second half of the book focuses closely on individual texts to trace the fate of realist convention in the hands of these writers. Each chapter in this section shows how the disparate scales of sketch and panorama became exaggerated and attenuated over the course of the century. While the *fin de siècle* is traditionally seen as the death-knell of realism, my emphasis on scale allows us to see literature's formal changes as the intensification rather than ossification of realist representation. Thus the sketch tradition becomes more explicitly scientific and ethnographic in the works of Arthur Conan Doyle, William Booth, and William Morris, such that the degree of difference revealed threatens to pull the city apart. In order to restore a sense of unity to their urban portraits, *fin-de-siècle* writers self-consciously use older and more robust – though less convincingly realistic – modes of imagining shared meaning, such as romance and allegory. The contradictions of realism, in its attempt to chronicle details and distinctions yet discern from those observations the means of tran-scending difference (through humanist or Christian universals), are more readily visible in these later works.

Chapter 3 examines aesthetic writing to demonstrate how the sketch of the urban type gives way to the microscopically detailed perspective of the refined aesthete: a figure who is more interested in individual sensory impressions than in the shared encyclopedic systems to which sketches belonged. At the same time, global space is no longer held together by the panoramic overview of the realist narrator – whose conciliatory vision is unviable in the fragile, divisive urban landscape of *fin-de-siècle* literature – but by the less realistic plot devices of conspiracy and romance. Despite their obvious stylistic differences, then, both Arthur Conan Doyle's

A Study in Scarlet (1887) and Henry James' *The Princess Casamassima* (1886) have similar formal concerns. Their urban investigators shun the explicit discourse of political reform visible in earlier city writing and assume the distanced aesthetic pose of the Wildean dandy. This stance, however, does not signify political disengagement because it depends upon the ability of the aesthete figure in each novel (Holmes and Hyacinth) to maintain a global perspective: both novels make the case that the sublimity of urban space, with its infinite connections to life elsewhere, is the ultimate source of aesthetic experience. Yet they both also retreat from the radical implications of that vision and use hackneyed romance tropes to overlay the difficult ethical and existential questions they open up with more familiar, less disorienting forms of narrative.

Socialist internationalism had a far more explicitly political vision than aestheticism, for its practitioners imagined a world united by a new egalitarian order. But even the most radical versions of socialist thought drew upon the sociological discourses of urban reform that took shape earlier in the period. In Chapter 4, I show how the spatial dynamics of city mapping were adapted to the narrative visions of socialist internationalists to create new forms of cosmopolitan realism. In 1890, General William Booth, the founder of the Salvation Army, published a treatise that called for the spread of Christian work communes from London to the entire world. A pull-out map accompanying his work shows a heavily allegorized London spilling out on to the globe; the map draws on the religious iconography of Renaissance emblem books to depict the sins of the city and the salvation that lies beyond it. Unexpectedly, William Morris, whose anti-colonialism and secularism made him Booth's ideological opposite, uses similar techniques in the utopian novel he published in the same year as Booth's work. If religious allegory is the panoramic perspective that unites the worlds of Booth and Morris, the cartographic "sketches" of their texts map them squarely on to late-Victorian London. The antithesis between local and global in the work of these two very different socialists is starker and more contradictory than those in earlier texts of the period.

By the twentieth century, modernist city writing associates cosmopolitanism predominantly with the unifying but oppressive power of global capitalism, international power politics, and an accompanying sense of worldwide calamity. Chapter 5 examines two influential urban modernist novels, *The Secret Agent* (1907) and *Mrs. Dalloway* (1925), to show how the concept of subjective time and the end of time counters the homogenizing effects of "official," globalized time, replacing the dyadic visual paradigms of Victorian city writing. Individualized time is connected in both novels to urban anonymity and the disintegration of community in the city, but is also figured, more positively, as an antidote to time standardization in allowing for moments of expanded sympathy towards strangers. Both novels evoke a post-human future in which nature has reclaimed city and nation, thereby positing a new biological concept of human kinship that must be asserted in the face of its tangible vulnerability. By contrasting the cosmopolitan visions of Victorian and early twentieth-century writers, this chapter sheds new light on the formal experiments of modernism, while stressing the uniquely Victorian utopianism of urban realism. The genres of modernism can be attributed at least in part to the way that its practitioners sought to critique or reject the Victorian novel's spatial imagination of social cohesion.

The conclusion explores the legacy of Victorian cosmopolitan realism in contemporary visual spectacles such as the London Eye and urban cinema. That recent urban texts are staged against a global landscape is undisputed; I argue, however, that the formal experiments and disparate scales of realist representation re-emerge in the depiction of that landscape. Works such as Zadie Smith's *White Teeth* (2000) and Stephen Frears' film *Dirty Pretty Things* (2002) take up the nineteenth-century fascination with the city in their exploration of multi-cultural community and globalization but shift the central point of view from the urban investigator to previously marginalized figures, such as refugees, struggling immigrants, and, in the case of Patrick Keiller's *London* (1994), disaffected queer intellectuals. Though fragmentation is taken for granted in the postmodern text, the urban fictions I examine emphasize connection alongside disconnection in order to situate the experience of radically disparate city-dwellers within the context of globalization and postcolonial history. In doing so, they throw into relief the limited perspectives of Victorian cosmopolitanism but also illuminate the utopian visions of community that realism still enables.

Introduction
Cosmopolitan realism

Cosmopolitanism has a very different cast when you think of it in terms, not so much of political theory, but of social experience and particularly in terms of the social experience of cities ... Once you actually take an institution like the city, the link between cosmopolitan and cosmopolitanism is obviously a very particular one.
Richard Sennett, "Cosmopolitanism and the Social Experience of Cities"[1]

THE DIALECTICS OF COSMOPOLITANISM

Cosmopolitanism and the genres and goals of urban realism overlapped in mutually constitutive ways from the mid-nineteenth to the early twentieth century, and the legacy of their symbiosis persists into our own moment. This book is thus concerned both with *cosmopolitanism*, a discourse discernible across a range of nineteenth-century writings, and *cosmopolitan realism*, a mode of literary representation that arose in conjunction with that discourse. While I examine these as distinct phenomena, I also stress the relationship between them and hence that between discourse and literary form.

But why focus on *cosmopolitanism* at all, given the many other terms connected with global paradigms? Criticism that addresses globalization and its history has by now affected the discipline of literary studies as a whole, including Victorian studies. A variety of new paradigms have entered the literary-critical lexicon as a result. Christopher Gogwilt, for instance, uses the term *geopolitical* to investigate the literary impact of Britain's extensive range of influence in the late Victorian and modernist periods; Amanda Claybaugh's *The Novel of Purpose* employs the notion of a transatlantic genre to show how nineteenth-century British and American discourses of social reform were in explicit conversation; and Paul Young focuses on a global historical event – the Great

Exhibition of 1851 – to analyze the creation and evolution of what he calls "the Victorian New World Order."[2]

"Internationalism" has also become a key term. Margaret Cohen and Carolyn Dever's anthology *The Literary Channel* uses both *inter-national* and *cross-channel* as ways of conceiving the British–French dialogue that influenced the development of the novel tradition on both sides of the Channel. Lauren Goodlad and Julia Wright, in their introduction to a journal issue on "Victorian Internationalisms," argue that while cosmopolitanism, Orientalism, and geopolitics are central to the construal of their key term, *internationalism* might best "situate literature's aesthetic, ethical, political – even geopolitical – insights in productive ways."[3] In light of this, and the fact that so many other related terms have proven useful to the analysis of Victorian literature and culture, a focus on cosmopolitanism requires explanation.

As I will demonstrate in Chapter 1, cosmopolitanism has a particular value for Victorian studies because of its complex usages in the period; many of the meanings and uses of cosmopolitanism today can be traced to the nineteenth century. Unlike a number of other terms used in contemporary literary studies to transcend a focus on the nation and nationalism, such as *transnational, geopolitical, global,* and *postcolonial,* cosmopolitanism and its variants were used frequently by Victorians. The tensions between its different meanings thus provide insight into the wide range of responses to early globalization that characterized the period. In turn, these responses help us to understand the relationship between cosmopolitan thought and its varied formal incarnations in realism.

While discussions of cosmopolitanism first gained traction in the eighteenth century, the term began to circulate more widely in the Victorian era, appearing in a broad range of venues, from advertisements and political speeches to novels and periodicals.[4] Its contradictory and overlapping meanings can be loosely divided into two strands. Cosmopolitanism was used in the period to name the condition we now call *globalization:* "the compression of the world and the intensification of consciousness of the world as a whole," in Roland Robertson's helpful definition.[5] This connotation was closely connected to the spread of global capital – as in John Stuart Mill's oft-cited phrase, "capital is becoming more and more cosmopolitan."[6] However cosmopolitanism was also used in a more idealistic Kantian mode to evoke the ideals of "perpetual peace" and "universal brotherhood" that might accompany economic globalization. These often conflicting affiliations and meanings were hard to disentangle. In 1851, for instance, cosmopolitanism-as-globalization was burnished with the language of human interconnection and used to promote the Great Exhibition. This neo-Kantian ideal celebrated Britain's imperial and global economic power but intersected with other discourses that did not: namely, abolitionist and socialist forms of cosmopolitanism.[7]

Even though the term is used more self-consciously today, tensions and slippages between utopian and dystopian views of cosmopolitanism persist. Theorists such as Simon Gikandi, Tim Brennan, and Pheng Cheah, for instance, take a critical stance towards cosmopolitanism.[8] Showing how it is inextricably linked to the uneven development of capitalist globalization, they attribute many of its positive connotations to the false consciousness of liberal academics and writers. Others, perhaps most famously Amanda Anderson, Kwame Anthony Appiah, Bruce Robbins, and Rebecca Walkowitz, embrace these positive connotations and argue for the value of various qualified universalisms: articulations of human solidarity that seek to balance or modify universalism with particularism.[9] Rather than framing cosmopolitanism as an apology for globalization, these approaches visualize it as a potential antidote to the anomie of contemporary capitalism. Anderson argues, for example, that "the cosmopolitan tradition usefully complicates the idea of an insular Western modernity, and, moreover, may provide resources for the critique of modernity within modernity itself."[10]

Though nuanced and illuminating, these competing ways of identifying and judging cosmopolitanism make for a contentious and potentially confounding contemporary debate.[11] Given the complexity that has accrued to the term over time, it is hard either to pin it down as an object of study or to wave it as a banner of solidarity. In both the Victorian conversation and our own, cosmopolitanism is alternately seen as a phenomenon and an ideal, an ideology and an ethos. Furthermore, even though most critics agree that there are "good" as well as "bad" kinds of cosmopolitanisms, they generally stress the primacy of one over the other.

The problem with accounts that emphasize "good" over "bad" cosmopolitanisms or vice versa, however, is that they provide an incomplete picture of cosmopolitan practices in any given period. In order to do justice to cosmopolitanism's historical manifestations, I emphasize the bifurcated nature of its resonances. Rather than as a unitary concept, cosmopolitanism is best understood as a discourse engaged in an internal dialectic between the symptoms of globalization and their critique: one continually in the process of becoming. This definition allows us to understand how multiple versions might coexist simultaneously; to analyze how one form of cosmopolitanism comes to dominate others at particular moments; and to see how some versions of cosmopolitanism might be both "good" and "bad" simultaneously. As explained in the Preface, my chapter sequence explores how cosmopolitanism changes over time, while individual chapters compare different forms of cosmopolitanism synchronically to show how ideologically dissimilar writers make analogous formal decisions in their attempts to imagine global unity. Conceived in dialectical terms, cosmopolitanism allows for a nuanced view of historical change and for a sense of how discourses about globalization function at a particular historical moment.

If cosmopolitanism is engaged in an internal dialectic between complicit and critical views of globalization, it is also engaged in an external dialectic with nationalism. Cosmopolitanism and nationalism are often understood antithetically but they were frequently seen as symbiotic in Enlightenment and Victorian writings.[12] Until recently, however, many influential works of criticism have focused exclusively on the nationalist frame of literature. Benedict Anderson's *Imagined Communities*, for instance, famously identifies the imaginary space of the novel with the boundaries of the nation. On the level of form, the novel "provided the technical means for re-presenting the kind of imagined community that is the nation" through its evocation of "simultaneity-across-time," whereby different people's activities across the nation were shown to be coextensive with each other. On the level of content, novels evoke national community through their use of representative detail. The classic nineteenth-century novel, according to Anderson, depicts "the movement of a solitary hero through a sociological landscape that fuses the world inside the novel with the world outside."[13]

While Anderson's anthropological outlook gave his book a relatively broad historical and geographical focus, literary critics have since looked closely at the interaction between the nation and the novel at different stages of the novel's development and in relation to distinct generic formations.[14] James Buzard's *Disorienting Fiction*, an important contribution to this growing body of knowledge, reads the novel's nationalism in relation to the new global consciousness that I see as vital to cosmopolitan realism.[15] Like Anderson, Buzard emphasizes the relation between literary and national form, but complicates Anderson's view of the "representative details" which map the novel's space on to the nation by seeing them as part of an autoethnographic project: one erected as a defense against the vast and formless "metropolitan anticulture" generated by imperialism, globalization, and Enlightenment universalism.[16] Over and against an "unmappably vague universe, lacking in coordinates," the novel describes a bounded English culture: "a demarcated place capable of founding and sustaining collective and individual identities."[17] It does so by developing narrative techniques that foreshadow the Participant Observation of twentieth-century anthropologists, wherein cultural knowledge is produced by the mediation between outside and inside perspectives. Oscillating between the metropolitan viewpoint of an unplaced narrator and the specific locales of its central characters (between the omniscient narrator of *Bleak House* and the narrative of Esther, for instance), the Victorian novel *dislocates* British culture in order that it might be "repatriated, restored or 'returned'" to its people.[18]

By pointing to the self-consciousness with which the British novel scrutinizes its own culture, Buzard effectively contests the claims of Said and other critics who argue that Britain functioned as a "blank metaculture" during the imperial era while only *other* cultures served as objects of knowledge.[19] He also qualifies Said's notion that "[w]henever a cultural form or discourse aspired to wholeness or totality, most European writers, thinkers, politicians, and mercantilists tended to think in global terms" by claiming that "the English novelist's *way* of thinking in global terms was to hold the category of the global at bay by reinvesting and focusing detail-rapt attention upon the *national*."[20] *Disorienting Fiction* is thus a salutary corrective to earlier theories about the relation of imperialism to the novel and a valuable addition to debates about how the novel shapes community. I share Buzard's view that the novel is shaped by its consciousness of global and metropolitan space and mediates between totality and detail in representing collectivity, but make a different argument about the *scale* of collectivity by questioning the fundamental assumption of much recent criticism that the nation is the only significant form of community to which Victorian realism gives shape, and drawing attention to both the city and globe as important alternative paradigms of human collectivity in urban realism.[21] To put it differently, the metropolis not only symbolized an *anticulture* against which the nation must define itself; it also served as the embodiment of a *multiculture* that is part of, but different from, the rest of the country.[22]

In examining the cosmopolitan strain of Victorian literature, then, this book necessarily traces its engagement with nationalism as well. I show how mid-century works such as *Bleak House* generate the totalizing techniques that would allow later authors a holistic view of the world even as they remain wedded to a national outlook, and analyze the ways in which this later cosmopolitan vision is often vexed by the self-evidence of the national frame. But unlike critics who see the nation as the only totality to which realism aspires, I emphasize the more fragile global whole also discernible in a wide range of nineteenth-century texts. Wordsworth's *The Prelude*, for example, which contrasts the identifiably English places of the countryside with the unreadable spaces of the metropolis, is much more readily associated with nationalism than cosmopolitanism. As Ian Baucom has argued, Wordsworth's poems often convey the lesson that "metropolitan culture, rather than revolutionary France, is now the enemy of Englishness, primarily because the city induces a forgetfulness of precisely the skill the poems teach – the skill of reading and valuing England's memorial places."[23] Yet in my interpretation, Wordsworth's vision of the city in Book VII also proffers utopian moments in which metropolitan space is vital to the poet's world-encompassing perception of the "unity of man." Though sublime and unstable, the narrator's panoramic view of London delineates a horizon that encircles the globe in a self-consciously democratic gesture. Wordsworth's worldly overview, like other examples of cosmopolitan realism I analyze, is an imaginative effort to turn the city into a vision of human collectivity: an effort of transcendence in the face of the dehumanizing global forces that London so dramatically brought into view.

Other critics have argued for a similarly recuperative view of Victorian cosmopolitanism, most notably Amanda Anderson in her influential *The Powers of Distance*.[24] Though she takes into account critiques of cosmopolitanism that link it to histories of racism and imperialism, she insists also on its progressive potential and takes seriously the ways in which individual writers participate in a "reflective interrogation of cultural norms" through a stance of cosmopolitan disinterest.[25] Defying the "hermeneutic suspicion" of literary critics who see Victorian forms of universalism as inherently fallacious, she strives instead to see them as "self-consciously pluralistic" and politically "enabling."[26] In defining cosmopolitanism as the "*aspiration* to a distanced view," she signals the degree to which the impossibility, or undesirability, of perfect distance is acknowledged by nineteenth-century writers themselves.[27]

While I draw on Anderson's use of cosmopolitanism to name a distanced stance and an investment in ideas of universal humanity, I place more emphasis on the discourse's constitutive ambivalence, giving equal weight to its pernicious elements alongside its more progressive ones: those moments when cosmopolitanism serves the goals of empire (as in the case of General William Booth); when it results in political stasis (as in the ending of *The Princess Casamassima*); and when it is fundamentally self-contradictory (as in William Morris' mix of biological essentialism and socialist internationalism in *News from Nowhere*). Rather than focusing on the philosophies of individual authors, I look at the ways texts use verbal and visual versions of the sketch and panoramic mode to produce alternately distanced and close-up perspectives that turn the space of narrative into that of a global whole.[28] If Anderson's work allows us to see how critical stances, both then and now, attempt to navigate between particulars and universals, this book analyzes the formal maneuvers which enable that navigation.

CITY, UTOPIA, COSMOPOLIS

Victorian city literature includes some of the darkest and most despairing work of the period; it seems counterintuitive, therefore, to argue for its idealism. Joseph McLaughlin and Jonathan Schneer, among others, have amply demonstrated the degree to which London was thought to be irrevocably contaminated by its imperial reach.[29] As Ian Baucom notes in *Out of Place*, the city "seemed, uncannily, to situate the imperial 'without' inside the national 'within'" and was therefore seen as a threat to "England's authentic places of belonging."[30]

This book makes a case, nonetheless, for the importance of the category of utopia to a fuller understanding of city literature and cosmopolitan realism. Disenchanted with the forces that were bringing the world together, cosmopolitan writers attempted to *re*-enchant it by subjecting it to the alchemical power of the imagination. In doing so, they relied upon that "symbol of conscious design in society": the city.[31] Those who wrote about the city, after all, were necessarily engaging with its long and diverse literary history as the space of utopian community. Pointing to ancient texts such as Plato's *Republic*, Northrop Frye notes that "[t]he utopia is primarily a vision of the orderly city and of a city-dominated society," while Fredric Jameson makes a similar point vis-à-vis science fiction utopias, arguing for "the city ... as a fundamental form of the Utopian image."[32] Louis Marin, in his theoretical study of utopic imaginaries, argues not so much for the ideal coherence of the city as the possibilities generated by its *in*coherence: "The city map is a 'utopic' insofar as it reveals a plurality of places whose incongruity lets us examine the critical space of ideology."[33] In his account, cartographic and visual forms of knowledge are not inevitably allied with modern regimes of rationalization and imperial ideologies but can lend themselves to the re-imagining of social space.

Celebrating the utopian promise of global cities, a number of urban planners, geographers, and sociologists concur with this view, noting that the cosmopolitan populations and endless shape-shifting of cities make them impossible to homogenize or control.[34] Saskia Sassen's work, for example, which uses economic analyses and sociological studies of immigrant communities, upholds Marin's more text-based analysis. While Sassen focuses on the way global economic systems shape the local spaces and politics of modern cities in ways that result in gross inequalities, she also argues that cities allow for the emergence of new identities and transnational politics (as in the rise of queer politics and their international coordination in various urban events, such as LGBT parades). Materializing the contradictions of global capital, urban spaces become "strategic sites for disempowered actors."[35] Yet another version of the contemporary utopian city can be found in Jacques Derrida's short but suggestive essay "On Cosmopolitanism," in which he argues that the city might serve as an alternative to the state. "Cities of refuge," in his view, might allow for a kind of hospitality that addresses the exclusions of the state and the modern problem that Hannah Arendt identified as that of the displaced person.[36]

Notwithstanding these more hopeful analyses of the intersection of utopias and cities, the totalizing perspectives that I associate with nineteenth-century urban utopianism have been justifiably regarded with suspicion. Michel Foucault's famous analysis of the overview of Bentham's panopticon, for example, has become emblematic of our understanding of the institutionalized, society-wide nature of modern disciplinary power, and has been convincingly aligned with the viewpoint of the omniscient narrator of the realist novel.[37] Kurt Koenigsberger, in keeping with Foucault's critique of power, specifically connects the proliferation of Victorian forms that attempted to produce a sense of totality (such as the menagerie, the exhibition, and the novel) with the ideology and management of British imperialism.[38]

Taking into account both the positive potential of utopian thought and the coercive possibilities of totality, I argue that cosmopolitan realism involves a version of what Fredric Jameson has famously called "cognitive mapping."[39] Jameson defines this as "the coordination of the existential data (the empirical position of the subject) with unlived, abstract conceptions of the global totality," pointing out that "we all necessarily ... cognitively map our individual social relationship to local, national, and international class realities."[40] The work of totalizing, then, does not necessarily lead to totalitarianism in Jameson's account, as it does for other theorists. He sees cognitive mapping as an acceptance of the fact that capitalism, as "the fundamental rule of the world," has set "absolute barriers and limits to social changes and transformations undertaken in it"; but while the imaginative work of thinking of the world as a whole acknowledges the delimiting forces that draw it together, it can do so in the hope of transcending them.[41]

By illustrating how London might stand in for a utopian vision of the world, cosmopolitan realism gives shape to the otherwise invisible and fragmented totality of a global system.[42] It thus participates both in literal mapping (the work of documenting and organizing the city that draws on visual knowledge) and in cognitive mapping (a reckoning with the invisible that attempts to imagine the world as a geopolitical totality and potentially as a shared community).[43] The latter is an activity that Jameson regards as crucial to the construction of an alternative political and social reality, citing its "Utopian power as the symbolic affirmation of a specific historical and class form of collective unity."[44]

Jameson associates cognitive mapping with the late capitalism of the modern and postmodern periods, arguing that it is in this period that imperialism and global capitalism contribute to a sense that the economy of the nation is no longer situated within its geographical boundaries. But in doing so, he misses the significance of cosmopolitan realism for what he calls a "geopolitical aesthetic." As I argue below, there are a number of historical and literary rationales for seeing the nineteenth century as the starting-point of the imperial and metropolitan imaginary that Marxists like Jameson and Raymond Williams locate in the modern period. Through the synecdochal substitution of London for the world, imaginative works engage in an early form of cognitive mapping that must be recognized as such if we are to properly understand its later incarnations.

ANTHROPOLOGY AND UTOPIA: THE PROBLEM OF NONCOEVALNESS

In imagining the world-city as a microcosm of humanity and attempting to provide a unified vision thereof, writers had to contend with the fact that the very notion of universal humanity was under debate in the emergent discipline of anthropology: a discipline defined, early on, by its efforts to determine the nature and extent of human differences.[45]

At mid-century, many ethnologists held a "monogenist" position which "described the genesis of all races from the single creative source in Adam." This was pitted against an alternative, polygenist account "according to which theory different races had sprung up in different places, in different 'centers of creation.'" As the anatomists who propagated these theories would have it, people from disparate parts of the world probably belonged to different species. This view more self-evidently elevated human differences over commonalities, but both positions supported the notion of European racial superiority, for the monogenist position "saw different races as having fallen unevenly from the perfect Edenic form incarnated in Adam."[46]

Post-Darwinian theories of human development complicated the picture further. From its publication in 1871 onwards, E. B. Tylor's account of human evolution, *Primitive Culture*, helped to shape the anthropological debate. Like the monogenists, Tylor saw human civilization as a single narrative but, unlike them, explained human differences by hypothesizing that different groups had evolved at different rates. While the human mind had equal capabilities across cultures, Tylor argued, some cultures were more evolved than others.

Each of these anthropological theories created an implicit hierarchy within the concept of humanity, participating in what Johannes Fabian calls a "denial of coevalness." Fabian defines this denial as "*a persistent and systematic tendency to place the referent(s) of anthropology in a Time other than the present of the producer of anthropological discourse*" (his emphasis).[47] In the nineteenth century, he contends, this gesture allowed anthropology to contribute "above all to the intellectual justification of the colonial enterprise."[48] Indeed, the idea that Europe, and particularly Britain, was in the vanguard of human development influenced not only imperial ideology but many other realms of social thought as well, such as political economy. Despite the rhetoric of equality and cosmopolitanism at the Great Exhibition, for example, Britain was clearly positioned as the nation with the most evolved economy: a gracious host inviting the world in to follow her example. As Paul Young puts it, "the Great Exhibition articulated the concept of a British imperial mission to raise up the non-European world after the image of the Victorian metropolis."[49]

At the end of the century, theories of degeneration and the increased scientism and proliferation of racial discourses made egalitarian or universal views of human community even harder to fathom, or articulate convincingly. The idea that evolution, rather than charting a uniform course for mankind, could backtrack and produce atavistic types (primarily to be found among working-class and imperial subjects), permeated a range of discourses, and steadily undermined the progressive telos of earlier evolutionary thinking which, even if it placed European cultures in the vanguard, at least allowed for the possibility that other countries and races might eventually catch up.[50] By the *fin de siècle*, however, writers had ever less recourse to the notion of a common "brotherhood of man" in their depiction of global space.

Twentieth-century anthropological thinking created an even more inhospitable environment for such notions. As James Buzard and Joe Childers have argued, the Victorian view of human civilization as a single narrative (with Britain in the lead) was replaced in the modern period by the notion of discrete cultures:

> writers finally began adding an 's' to the end of Tylor's term [culture], subsuming the developmental ideas associated with it (*Bildung*, evolution) in a new conception of object-like, mappable, and incommensurable social totalities. The transition entails not merely the perception or recording of differences among people ... but the packaging and spatial organization of differences under the headings of separate cultures.[51]

How did cosmopolitan texts imagine London as a figure for global human community if dominant theories of human development situated other cultures and races as geographically marginal and temporally backward? In charting the different populations of the city, cosmopolitan realism inevitably engaged with ideas about the racial or cultural atavism, or underdevelopment, of various ethnicities and classes – hence the tendency of urban investigators such as Mayhew and Booth to discuss class in terms of race. But these writers also sought to overcome the frightening spectacle of difference that they saw in the city with a compensatory utopianism. By identifying London as a microcosm of the globe, writers were able to imagine the world within a shared space; by using various literary devices – such as the urban sublime, romance narrative, and allegory – that remove London from historical time and imagine it in an ideal future or a parallel ideal present, they obviate the problem of asynchronous development raised by anthropological theory. These self-consciously fictional, utopian versions of London were an important component of the realist endeavor.

COSMOPOLITAN REALISM AS LITERARY FORM

I have argued that the term cosmopolitanism is appealing because it allows for a complex view of Victorian attitudes towards globalization. But it also offers insight into the generic challenges of representing the global, for the word itself evokes the contrasting social spaces of the world and the city, as well as the role of the individual in forging a link between them: the *cosmopolitan* (citizen of the world) inhabits, or embodies, the *cosmopolis* (world city). In analyzing the relationship between city and world, this book necessarily engages questions of scale and perspective intrinsic to literary form. By making cosmopolitan realism rather than cosmopolitan discourse the main focus of this study, I draw attention to how these scalar questions help to shape the development both of cosmopolitan thought and of literary realism.

If cosmopolitanism is best understood as a dialectical concept, an emphasis on cosmopolitan form allows us to see the relationship between cosmopolitanism and literature as dialectical as well: cosmopolitan realism sheds light on literature, demonstrating how it often transcends or challenges the parameters of national life. The study of literature, correspondingly, sheds light on cosmopolitanism by illuminating the specific incarnations it takes over time and by identifying its circulation among authors and along global literary routes. By giving cosmopolitanism imaginative form, realism had a profound effect on its evolution and dispersal.

The *Oxford English Dictionary* defines the word "form" as "shape, arrangement of parts," and I use it here, in this loosest of senses, as a way of naming those aspects of texts that literary critics are specifically trained to analyze, such as genre, mode, language, style, and media.[52] Whether construed as a juxtaposition between citizen and world, city and world, or – more generally – the particular and the universal, cosmopolitanism offers itself up as a representational challenge, thus making it especially congenial to the work of literary critics. Examining the way that cosmopolitanism is incarnated in form, I argue, broadens the conversation about literature and cosmopolitanism, allowing us to bring our particular strengths as literary critics to bear on a fundamentally interdisciplinary conversation. Cosmopolitan realism – a term that construes cosmopolitanism as a formal problem as well as an ideological or philosophical concept – also allows for the consideration of writers not commonly identified with cosmopolitanism. Wordsworth and Dickens, for example, are associated with a valorization of the countryside and nation over the city and world, yet they grapple with the new kind of planetary consciousness that accompanied London's astonishing growth in the nineteenth century just as stolidly and significantly as the indisputably cosmopolitan figures of Henry James and Joseph Conrad.

Urban Realism and the Cosmopolitan Imagination, then, asks how literary texts construct a sense of global totality while creating a detailed, realistic sense of local geographies; in doing so, the book strives to chart

the nuances of cosmopolitanism's historical incarnations and to emphasize the representational challenge of balancing opposing scales that
cosmopolitan literature necessarily takes on. Without ignoring the problems of cosmopolitan ethics, I hope to move beyond the impasse between
recuperative and skeptical views of cosmopolitanism by posing more
open-ended questions: how do various texts create cosmopolitanism as a
literary effect? What formal techniques were used to create the sense of
global space? How has literature shaped our sense of the global over time?

In an essay on "Strategic Formalism," Caroline Levine argues that
literary critics should re-embrace formal modes of critique because this
will strengthen, rather than detract from, our ability to comment on social
and political life alongside literature.[53] Since "social hierarchies and institutions can themselves be understood as forms," we can use the tools of
literary formalism to analyze these structures and interpret the interaction
of literature and culture. This interaction is not predictable, however.
Indeed, it is "in the strange encounters among forms, even those forms
that are deliberate outcomes of dominant ideologies," Levine notes, " . . .
that unexpected, politically significant possibilities emerge."[54] Bearing out
Levine's argument, my analysis of cosmopolitan realism demonstrates the
surprising affinities of works by writers as diverse in political outlook as
Booth and Morris, James and Doyle, Conrad and Woolf, and thus the
unpredictable ideological outcomes of formal experimentation.

Lauren Goodlad is another Victorianist who has emphasized the political import of a renewed attention to form. Calling for "a cosmopolitan
Victorianist practice that attends geopolitics as well as ethos, and structure
as well as standpoint," she argues that "Marxist criticism provides fecund
ground for a Victorianist practice that sees literature's formal plasticity as
chronotopically marking the movement of actually existing cosmopolitanisms." Yet, as she goes on to demonstrate, "influential Marxists like
Jameson hinder that end by diminishing the critical status of realism." In
a useful analysis of Georg Lukacs and Frederic Jameson, she shows how
their readings of the realist novel rely on two outdated assumptions:
(1) "that mid-Victorian Britain was the scene of an insular and static
national culture" (Lukacs), and (2) "that the disconnect between metropolitan experience and imperial structure begins (like modernism), in the
late nineteenth century – with the full-blown emergence of the New
Imperialism" (Jameson).[55]

As I will demonstrate below, and as Goodlad contends as well, there is
ample historical and literary evidence now to challenge these older views
of realism. What I would like to stress here, however, is that I see the

notion of cosmopolitan realism as one way to engage in the kind of cosmopolitan Victorianist practice that Goodlad seeks to promote. My dialectic vision of the discourse of cosmopolitanism assumes that it encodes at once "geopolitics as well as ethos," while the concept of cosmopolitan realism – understood as the formal attempt to balance antithetical scales and perspectives – allows us to analyze the literary encoding of "structure and standpoint." By giving form to the world – by rendering it *as* form – Victorian urban writers tested the abstractions of Enlightenment cosmopolitanism against the ethical quandaries and material realities of everyday life, thereby exposing both its problems and possibilities. A formalist approach is peculiarly well suited to the study of cosmopolitanism because it is through the particulars of language and genre that cosmopolitan writers seek to qualify the universalisms that they espouse by grounding them in the textures of difference.

THE REALISTIC SECULARITY OF COSMOPOLITANISM

Why was cosmopolitanism a concern of realist writers? What is the relationship between cosmopolitanism and realism? Like cosmopolitanism, realism has been understood in a variety of ways. I refer here to its common usage in Victorian studies and Victorian literary criticism where it is associated broadly with "truth of observation and a depiction of commonplace events, characters, and settings" and a moral agenda. As René Wellek puts it, "Realism is didactic, moralistic, reformist. Without always realizing the conflict between description and prescription it tries to reconcile the two in the concept of 'type.'"[56]

This effort of reconciliation is of particular interest to this study for two reasons. First, as I will argue in Chapter 2, the notion of the type has formal significance for cosmopolitan realism. Types become "realistic" when they are derived from the social observation of individuals in particular settings; in realist literature, types are most often depicted in sketch form by urban investigators (such as Mayhew or "Boz") who use close-up observation and visual detail to convey their "view from the street." This view takes on moral and social import, however, through a different realist mode – the panorama – whereby the subject of the sketch is shown to operate within a specific world in which she or he takes on "typical" significance. While the interdependence of sketch and panorama might be seen as characteristic of realism in general, it is especially vital to cosmopolitan realism in its endeavor to connect city and world and to situate the urban type in a global community.

Second, realism's effort to combine description and prescription helps to explain its intersection with cosmopolitanism. Realism has long been understood as simultaneously secular and moral. George Levine, for instance, argues that realism is defined by a "sense that dogmas are obsolete" but also by "a new and universal quest for a fully coherent vision, in which body and soul, matter and morality, coalesce." The writers he examines in *The Realistic Imagination* turn from God to science and nature in pursuit of this universal quest. George Lewes and George Eliot, for example, transfer a sense of unity "from God to organism, an entity that implies continuity and growth, through evolution, inter-dependence, and therefore self-denial, love, morality, and mystery."[57]

The connection between the utopian strand of nineteenth-century cosmopolitanism and the kind of empirical thinking that Lewes and Eliot were invested in is nowhere better demonstrated than in Alexander von Humboldt's magisterial five-volume work *Cosmos* (1845–62) – a ground-breaking scientific work that employed astronomy, geology, biology, and anthropology to show the interconnectedness of all natural phenomena and all peoples without references to a creator. Humboldt's scientific cosmopolitanism is encapsulated in his elucidation of his title: "I use the word *Cosmos* in conformity with the Hellenic usage of the term ... It is the assemblage of all things in heaven and earth, the universality of created things constituting the perceptible world."[58]

The literature of cosmopolitan realism, however, turns to a man-made evolving organism – London – rather than the natural world for a sense of unity. Imagined as an interconnected whole, the cosmopolis serves as a way to conceptualize the totality of human society in a global age. Realist literature and cosmopolitanism came together in certain texts because both involved a desire for a sense of unity that might mitigate their post-Enlightenment skepticism.

The attempt of cosmopolitan realist texts to mediate between a scien-tific and redemptive view of the world is reflected in their movement between visible and invisible sources of knowledge.[59] If the world as a whole could not be seen, it could be brought before the mind's eye through the observation of the city, conceived of as a world in miniature. Many cultural theorists have stressed the vital role of the visual in the social-scientific epistemologies that influenced urban writing, and indeed, Western culture as a whole.[60] With specific reference to nineteenth-century literature, for example, Jonathan Arac contends that "the chaos of urban experience fostered a wish for a clarifying overview."[61] His work sees the panoramic perspective as integral to the realist project because it brought private lives and public institutions, sociological detail and social whole, together: "A spatializing power to locate and relate the peripheral to the central was needed to integrate an imaginative view of the city."[62] Visual forms were as influential on the global as on the urban imagination, however, not least because the two were often related: panoramas, dioramas, magic lantern shows, and stereoscopic slides offered views of international cities from the beginning of the century onwards, as did early cinematic reels by the end of it.[63] Exhibition culture was also instrumental in shaping the way that Victorians perceived the world and their role in it.[64] Influenced by the visual arts, the literary forms of sketch and panorama – whose interrelation I chart over the course of the century – demonstrate the importance of visibility to cosmopolitan realism.

Non-empirical epistemologies were just as vital to the urban imagination, however. Richard Maxwell's *The Mysteries of Paris and London* highlights the predominance of modes such as allegory in urban writing precisely because of the inadequacy of the visual alone for the task of depicting the city's immensity and complexity. Using John Ruskin's realist philosophy as an example, Maxwell shows how the relationship between visible and invisible undergirds the realist novel's natural supernaturalism: "Since the visible world is saturated with divine truth, to grasp it whole is to participate in that truth." Allegory is a useful tool for this endeavor because it was "originally a technique for using enigmatic figures to reveal an invisible world."[65]

Both Maxwell and Arac influence my understanding of the strategies employed by urban writers as they attempted to comprehend the city and project a sense of coherence on to the community therein. In focusing on how writers adapted realist techniques to an increasingly international vision over the course of the century, though, I re-read these strategies as part of a larger unifying project in which global cohesion takes shape alongside visions of urban and national totality. Images of the city – the detail-encrusted portraits for which realism is famous – were supplemented by non-empirical imaginative modes such as allegory, not only to unify the city but to situate it within the invisible world beyond.

At the height of the realist novel at mid-century, the "invisible world" to which the details of realism allude is often a religious realm of meaning in which the mundane takes on sacred significance. In *Bleak House*, the smallpox that festers in Tom-All-Alone's, kills Jo, and crosses class boundaries to threaten Esther, serves as a referent to the real-life epidemics that beleaguered Victorian London (and the East End in particular). However, in the context of the novel's moral schema, it also recalls the

Biblical plagues and hence the divine judgments that befall rich and poor alike. It thus gestures at an allegorical frame that erases social boundaries to unify the city, just as the novel's plot does. While the writers I focus on at the end of the century follow Dickens in making use of allegorical and religious tropes to create the sense of a common framework, most do so in the service of explicitly secular concepts such as universal humanity and the brotherhood of man, rather than Christian kinship. William Morris, for instance, uses John Bunyan's allegory *Pilgrim's Progress* and the typographical form of medieval religious manuscripts to make the case for the benevolence of international socialism. In cosmopolitan realism, the invisible world is less often a transcendent realm than a secular cosmos: a planetary rather than heavenly space. By coupling tropes borrowed from religious and romantic discourses (such as the sublime, allegory, and epiphany) with those belonging to the emergent sciences of sociology, anthropology, and natural history, cosmopolitan realism attempted to redeem urban anxieties by reading the city as a figure for a world at once globalized *and* communitarian. While the unities it conjured up through these uneasy configurations were tentative and fundamentally uneven, they nonetheless constitute a utopianism within Victorian urban writing that has historically been overshadowed by the darker London associated with Dickens' fogs and dustpiles, James Thomson's dreadful night, and Robert Louis Stevenson's Hyde.

The ways that cosmopolitan realism functions as a secularizing form is illuminated by recent work that stresses secularism's use of religious tradition. In Vincent Pecora's *Secularism and Cultural Criticism*, for instance, secularism is associated with "an autonomous mind possessing a worldly, cosmopolitan perspective."[66] But while the secularist is skeptical of all "official" constraints, she appropriates and internalizes traditional structures even while opposing them: "secularism, in constantly redefining and reenergizing itself by reference to outworn religious traditions, is finally a way of preserving, at a more rarefied and rationally persuasive level of awareness, precisely what it seeks to destroy."[67] Distinguishing himself from those who see secularism as the antithesis of religion, Pecora argues that we should see it as the transfiguration, rather than overturning, of religious paradigms: one that might result in dystopian as well as utopian collective possibilities. Citing nationalism and socialism as the two great sublimations of religion, Pecora argues that "the society that produces Enlightenment never fully outgrows its desire for religious sources of coherence, solidarity and historical purpose, and continually translates, or transposes, them into ever more refined and immanent, but also distorted and distorting, versions of its religious inheritance."[68]

My analysis of cosmopolitan realism follows the implications of this argument to see cosmopolitanism, alongside nationalism and socialism, as another of modernity's great sublimations of religion.[69] This, after all, is one of the reasons cosmopolitanism has been treated with suspicion by postcolonialists.[70] Citing the work of Talad Asad, Pecora notes that global ideals, such as those outlined in the Universal Declaration of Human Rights, are in fact "a secular emanation of Christian culture" and thus their claim to a "cosmopolitan transcendence of specificity" is subject to critique as a "too-convenient political fiction."[71]

While cosmopolitanism is not as visible a discourse as nationalism or socialism, partly because it cannot be contained within the form of the state, it is no less complex in terms of its historical effects and no less prone to both positive and negative utopian articulations – particularly at our own moment of heightened global consciousness.[72] The ways in which urban realism drew upon Biblical imagery to depict the city as both the New Jerusalem and the modern Babylon have been well documented.[73] But by analyzing the ways in which city literature appropriates various religious forms and tropes (such as type, allegory, and eschatology) as a mode of apprehending, and ultimately transcending, the material effects of globalization, I show how representations of the city as alternately heavenly and demonic contributed to cosmopolitanism's historical appeal.

THE CHRONOLOGY OF COSMOPOLITAN REALISM

An understanding of the global outlook of Victorian city literature offers a new view of the investments and experiments of realist forms and of the modernist and postmodern ones that succeeded them. While realism did not display the self-conscious avant-gardism of modernism, it was no less a response to the new scale and scope of the city. To make this claim, however, is to challenge the long-standing tendency of literary critics to see modernism as the period when the effects of globalization and imperialism are first visible at the level of literary form.[74] In his essay on "Metropolitan Perception," for instance, Raymond Williams says of the modern city: "It was the place where new social and economic and cultural relations, beyond both city and nation in their older senses, were beginning to be formed."[75] Georg Simmel's seminal work on modern consciousness also emphasizes the city's transnational sphere of influence. Describing the relationship between urban life and the vertiginous autonomy of the modern subject, he argues that:

> It is not only the immediate size of the area and the number of persons which ... has made the metropolis the locale of freedom. It is rather in transcending this visible expanse that any given city becomes the seat of cosmopolitanism ... The sphere of life of the small town is, in the main, self-contained and autarchic ... it is the decisive nature of the metropolis that its inner life overflows by waves into a far-flung national or international area.[76]

Both Williams and Simmel identify the early twentieth century as the moment when the city's "far-flung" role begins to affect artistic form and modes of subjectivity. It was not until then, Williams contends, that "artists and intellectuals of this movement" led cosmopolitan lives and identified themselves with "the changing cultural milieu of the metropolis."[77] Williams questions the uniqueness of this vision to the modern period, though, for a central goal of his essay is to challenge the self-universalizing tendencies of modernism by showing "how relatively old some of these apparently modern themes are" (39). Most of his examples of urban themes in literature, therefore, are taken from the Victorian period and he identifies the period of metropolitan expansion as "the second half of the nineteenth century and the first half of the twentieth century" (44). Significantly, he separates the effect of "metropolitan perception" into content and form, arguing that it manifests only in the *themes* of Victorian literature and does not become an effect of *form* until the twentieth, when the "increasing mobility and social diversity" of the metropolitan center led to "a new consciousness of conventions" (45–6).

Yet almost all the cosmopolitan texts that I treat here (except for those examined in the Conclusion) circulated between 1850 and 1925 and therefore challenge the now-familiar association of cosmopolitan literature with modernism by demonstrating the vital importance of the city to both the content *and* form of Victorian realism. Rather than seeing cosmopolitan discourse – or content – as anterior to cosmopolitan form, as Williams does, I show how the generic questions writers faced in attempting to give shape to the city helped to give form to the new kind of perception that Williams calls "metropolitan."

The time-frame of this book, then, is determined by realism's search for a holistic vision that would give form and meaning to the cosmopolis. While its narrative reaches back to the eighteenth century and looks forward to our current moment, most of the material it addresses was produced between 1850 and 1925. In literary terms, these years mark the high points of the realist and modern periods and represent the publication dates of *The Prelude* and *Mrs. Dalloway* respectively. But this was also a period that saw a number of significant changes in Britain's role in the world that contributed to the vision of London as a cosmopolis.

Situated at the hub of modern railways, steamship routes, and cable lines that were producing a new sense of worldwide interconnection, London readily lent itself to a global imaginary. With its diverse populations, its commercial and technological modernity, and its rich exhibition culture, in which "the world" as an idea was constantly on view, London symbolized both the world's compressions and its new visibility *qua* world.[78] While my argument about the phenomenon of cosmopolitan realism relies chiefly on literary evidence, what follows is a brief overview of three interrelated historical developments that help to contextualize the time-frame of the book and its focus on London. These have to do with (i) population; (ii) media and technology; and (iii) empire and globalization.

Population

London's reputation as "the world's metropolis" was due in part to its unprecedented population growth over the second half of the nineteenth century, when its ranks swelled from 3 million to 4.5 million people. Commentators were struck not only by its magnitude but by its apparent diversity in the wake of these changes; in 1867 *The Times* remarked that "There is hardly such a thing as a pure Englishman in this island."[79] In reality, the vast majority of the city's new inhabitants were migrants from within the nation rather than immigrants from outside it. Thus social and ethnic rifts within the nation – the Welsh and Scots versus the English; industrialists and workers versus southern gentility and agriculturalists – were as much a preoccupation of those representing the city as anxieties about racial and national contamination. As other critics have noted, intranational and international conflict became connected in the literature of the city, and sociologists, poets, and novelists alike took on a global frame of reference to describe the changing urban population, mapping the imperial dichotomy of East and West on to the East and West Ends of London.[80]

Yet despite the fact that the city's immigrants were smaller in number than its population of rural migrants, they made London notably more international than any other part of England. The Jewish and Irish populations in London were the largest immigrant presences, and the ones that most often inspired writers to read the city in the hierarchical and racializing language of empire. Irish immigration expanded significantly between 1845 and 1850 after the Famine, so that the 1851 census revealed a large Irish presence in the East End; Mayhew noted that the Irish made up a third of all costermongers in the capital.[81] Meanwhile, the Jewish population increased from 25,000 to 120,000 between 1815 and 1900 (spurred partly by 1881 Russian pogroms in Poland and Rumania).[82] Investigative works such as Mayhew's revealed the importance of the new immigrants to the British economy, but also circulated fears about their economic and ethnic unassimilability into mainstream society. Anti-Irish and anti-Semitic sentiment existed much more overtly as well, discernible everywhere from the pages of newspapers to parliamentary debates.[83]

As well as these sizable populations, other smaller but significant immigrant groups consolidated in the nineteenth century and affected the urban imaginary. People of African descent were brought to England from the West Indies as slaves in the seventeenth and eighteenth centuries. After 1833, once slavery had become illegal in both Britain and its colonies, Africans came to London from America, seeking asylum.[84] Chinese seamen arrived after China's defeat in the Opium Wars of 1842–60. Italian, Polish, and Spanish political refugees immigrated from the 1820s to the 1850s, fleeing absolutism on the continent; Italian street-entertainers in particular are noted in the writings of Dickens, Mayhew, and George Sala. From mid-century onwards, German clerks also appeared on the scene, in search of employment in commercial houses. In the last two decades of the century, their presence inspired anxieties about the displacement of British labor and exacerbated the sense of industrial and commercial competition with Germany. In 1887, a special committee assigned to carry out an inquiry into the problem found that "upwards of 40 per cent of the staffs of many London offices were foreigners, the majority being Germans."[85]

South Asian immigrants also became more prominent in London over the course of the century. Indian sailors known as "lascars" were noted by urban investigators and used to add exoticism and atmosphere to *fin-de-siècle* novels such as *The Picture of Dorian Grey* (1890). Antoinette Burton writes that:

in addition to lascars, domestic servants, and a community of South Asian urban poor, there was a small but culturally and politically active Indian middle class in Victorian London (as well as in other British cities), many of whom were connected with Oxford, Cambridge, and various medical schools and colleges or, after July 1889, with the British Committee of the Indian National Congress in London.[86]

By the early twentieth century, three South Asians had been elected to represent London constituencies in parliament.[87]

Along with these different nationalities, a number of political refugees came to London from Europe and Russia, fleeing persecution. As David Glover argues, the 1903 Report of the Royal Commission of Alien Immigration was partly a reaction to the purported radicalism of these émigrés and the perceived threat they posed to national stability (Conrad's *The Secret Agent* bases its plot on this particular form of xenophobia). The visibility and diversity of the immigrants who settled in London over the course of the century, although not large in number, helps to explain why so many Victorian writers described the city as cosmopolitan.[88]

Media and technology

As well as being cosmopolitan in population, London was also the center of what we would now call a media and technology revolution: one in which forms as diverse as the panorama, the Crystal Palace, and the novel (with its increasingly international circulation) partook. In their introduction to a special issue of *Nineteenth-Century Contexts* on "Global Formations," Keith Hanley and Greg Kucich locate the origin of our contemporary global consciousness in the nineteenth century, arguing that the "stunning advances" in nineteenth-century networks of transportation and communication, such as railways, steamship, and the telegraph, led to a new sense of "worldwide interconnectedness."[89]

Richard Menke's book on new media technologies emphasizes the paradigm-shifting nature of Victorian connectivity as well. The annihilation of time and space via such media contributed to a growing sense of the world as a network: "For Victorian scientists, sages, and novelists alike, the network becomes a figure that organizes the real interchanges, the unseen or imperfectly visible systems of connections and disconnections, that underlie the everyday world."[90] Certainly Sherlock Holmes, who compares himself to a spider in the middle of a web as he receives information by telegraph from America in *A Study in Scarlet*, reflects this view. His location in London, furthermore, is crucial to his being able to think this way for, as Menke notes, "London ... is the principal center of the Telegraphic enterprise in the world."[91]

London was also the center of the publishing world, which was substantially affected by telegraphy. Thomas Tobin's quantitative analysis of news circulation in the second half of the nineteenth century shows how the compressed sense of time and space that Menke points to affected the circulation and consumption of news. After mid-century, periodicals that had relied on mail service for news from far-flung places increasingly received information by telegraph and thus "[r]eaders of British newspapers in 1832 had a very different idea of the size, scope, and interconnectedness of the countries of the world than did readers in 1872." Tobin's analysis of articles published in a range of influential periodicals also reveals that "the percentage of international versus local news in most British periodicals increased over the course of the century" as did the timeliness of that news.[92]

It is not surprising, in light of these systemic changes, that Victorian literature was preoccupied with London's cosmopolitanism and its implications. I am not arguing, however, that this heightened sense of world-belonging necessarily led to an embrace of global ideals. Indeed, as Benedict Anderson argues, modern forms of media and technology were crucial to ideals of *nationalism* because the displacements that these forms effected helped both to reify a sense of place and to underscore its importance: "It was ... through print moving back and forth across the ocean that the unstable imagined worlds of Englishnesses and Spanishnesses were created ... It was beginning to become possible to see 'English fields' in England – from the window of a railway carriage."[93] What I *am* arguing is that the notion of a vast interconnected global network, constituted by the railway, the telegraph, by publishing, and by imperial trade and administration, demanded form, and London – so easy to imagine as the network's central node – lent itself to that form.

Empire and globalization

London's role as the premier world-city of the nineteenth century stemmed, most obviously, from its locus at the symbolic and geographic center of a newly consolidated empire.[94] Capitals such as Paris and Vienna were also important world cities in the nineteenth century, of course, but London's symbolic, administrative, and economic centrality to the steadily increasing sprawl of empire made it uniquely positioned to function as a synecdoche of the globe.[95] The events that cemented London's role as "heart of the empire" began in the mid-eighteenth century with the growing importance of the British presence in South Asia and the steadily accumulating mass of imperial territories.[96] Between 1760 and 1830, Duncan Bell argues, the British empire became "truly global in reach, encompassing territories in south and southeast Asia, N. America, Australasia, much of the middle east, and southern

Africa."[97] After the 1849 annexation of the Punjab and the Indian Rebellion of 1857, however, the empire transitioned from a system that was essentially mercantile to one based on military and political domination.[98] The imagination of the world as a bounded and interconnected space was a natural accompaniment to this political and ideological shift, for imperial territories, in particular the settler colonies, were increasingly seen as a physical extension of the nation. The idea of a "Greater Britain," wherein Britain and its Anglo-Saxon satellites would function as "a single transcontinental political community, even … a global federal state," had significant traction in the second half of the century.[99]

As well as being at the imaginative center of a growing empire, London was the hub of a network of trade and commerce even wider in scope: "Between 1800 and 1850 the volume of world trade grew by about two and a half times; over the next sixty years it increased tenfold as a truly multilaterial network of world trade emerged for the first time … the extent of British economic influence in the world in the nineteenth century always ranged far beyond the boundaries of sovereign control."[100] Britain was seen as the natural leader of "a European consortium of nations" that served as the basis for a new internationalism: "Commercial treaties provided a new form of 'international compact,' with the potential to unite the peoples of Europe."[101]

While the rhetoric of empire and that of economic globalization were related, they did not always go hand-in-glove, as is often assumed.[102] Instead, the tensions between imperialism and free-trade cosmopolitanism shed light upon the complexity of the Victorian discourse of cosmopolitanism. On the one hand, the globalization of capitalist ventures often served as a justification for empire. As Paul Young demonstrates, events such as the Exhibition underscored the idea of Britain's economic vanguardism and thus its mission to lead the rest of the world into modernity. Exhibition commentators produced "an authoritative and forceful account of the way in which the industrial capitalist penetration of non-Europe would engender its regeneration. A strong sense of a Victorian imperial mission emerged at the Crystal Palace."[103]

On the other hand, the discourse of globalization was neither hegemonic nor unitary. Those in favor of free trade (who harnessed the Great Exhibition as a propaganda device) did not achieve a real political breakthrough until the 1846 repeal of the Corn Laws: thus the triumphalist rhetoric of global capitalism was relatively new and still embattled at midcentury.[104] Moreover, some free trade advocates saw their interests as being in conflict with empire, either practically or ideologically or both.

Practically, imperial concerns could detract from the imperatives of free trade: "Freer trade was necessary to encourage imports which would come largely from Europe and the United States rather than the Empire."[105] Ideologically, free trade had – since the eighteenth-century writings of Kant and Adam Smith, among others – been associated with an internationalist vision of universal peace that was frequently anti-imperialist. Kant's writings on "Perpetual Peace," for example, were explicitly so, as were those of many nineteenth-century free trade advocates such as Anti-Corn Law Leaguer Richard Cobden. For thinkers like these, the end-goal of trade *and* its precondition was peace, not war. When the empire began to demand the accumulation and deployment of military forces, free trade proponents "posed the issue of ends and means – to what extent did the goal of increasing trade legitimate the use and extension of state military power?"[106]

Between the high point of the free trade optimism of the Crystal Palace and the end of the century, however, attitudes towards economic globalization and empire shifted. When Britain began to lose ground in economic competition with Western countries in the second half of the century, imperial trade blocs and protectionism were increasingly favored over free trade policies, while military control of the colonies replaced British economic influence – a transition symbolized by the crowning of Victoria as Empress of India in 1876. Racial discourses of the period increasingly undermined the notion of the world as a "Family of Man" that had predominated at the Great Exhibition and justified the use of force in colonial administration; events such as the 1857 Indian Rebellion did too. For many Britons, resistance to empire on the subcontinent functioned as evidence that "Indians had rejected policies of Western assimilation" and thus as a sign of insurmountable civilizational differences.[107] If the Great Exhibition might be seen as the crowning moment of free trade cosmopolitanism, a focus on imperial rather than "world" exhibitions at the end of the century signals the degree to which British geopolitical priorities had changed by that point:

from the 1880s the exhibitions became explicitly imperial and remained so until the Glasgow Empire Exhibition of 1938 . . . their message was that the British, as a world-wide family of white settler territories and colonies, should stick together in a supposedly complementary economic system.[108]

In the early twentieth century, however, the political and economic rivalries that prefigured and followed the First World War, together with the rise of anti-colonial movements across the empire, began the end of

British global hegemony and, correspondingly, of the totalizing frame-work of cosmopolitan realism. If, in modernist literature, London no longer serves as a sign of totality but reflects a world in fragments, the London of the late twentieth and early twenty-first centuries is not at the center of the world – fragmented or otherwise – at all, reflecting Britain's declining fortunes. Rather, it figures as one among many nodes in a decentralized geographic network. In postcolonial texts such as *White Teeth* and *The Satanic Verses* and films like *Dirty Pretty Things* and *London*, the city still brings different diasporas together in new forms of community, but these communities take neither the utopian shape of heaven nor the dystopian one of hell: instead they are more like purgatories. London is not the center or even the destination for the immigrant subjects of these texts – it is simply somewhere one finds oneself along the way.

If it has often seemed perverse to make the case for the utopianism of Victorian city writing, I have also been struck by the irony of writing about the global imagination of realism while using an archive that remains fairly national in scope, for my interest in London's unique role in the literary history of cosmopolitanism makes British literature and British authors an inevitable focus of this book. But its range of reference, I hope, shows that these very categories ("British" literature and authors) do not adequately describe the kinds of writing produced in, or about, Britain during this period. William Morris sought to relocate the novel to "Nowhere," while the editor of the journal *Cosmopolis* attempted to decentralize its location and national identity by publishing in multiple cities and multiple languages simultaneously. William Wells Brown, one of the most enthusiastic chroniclers of the Great Exhibition, was an African-American abolitionist; Henry James and Joseph Conrad, renowned cosmopolitans, were both insiders and outsiders to the British literary scene; Virginia Woolf famously proclaimed that as a woman she had no country; and the authors and texts analyzed in the conclusion demonstrate how capacious the category of "English" literature and cul-ture has become. Indeed, the engagement of contemporary writers such as Salman Rushdie and Zadie Smith in the project of cosmopolitan realism demonstrates its central paradox: that the Victorian cosmopolis of London threatened the coherence of British identity even as it epitomized British power.

PART ONE

The Emergence of Cosmopolitan Realism

The Palace and the periodical: The Great Exhibition, Cosmopolis, and the discourse of cosmopolitanism

"Draw but a little circle above the clustering housetops and you shall have within that space everything, with its opposite extreme and contradiction close by."

Charles Dickens, *Master Humphrey's Clock*[1]

How did Victorians understand cosmopolitanism? To what extent did they think in global terms and nurture global ideals? The literary mode that I call "cosmopolitan realism," wherein London was used as a way to comprehend global modernity, is best analyzed in light of a vibrant discourse of cosmopolitanism which informed the way that Victorian writers thought about their relationship to the rest of the world.

Before turning to an investigation of the formal means by which realist narrative equated urban with global space, then, I devote this chapter to examining the meanings of "actually existing cosmopolitanism" in the Victorian context.[2] The multiple ways in which the term was used demonstrate how Enlightenment ideals of cosmopolitanism were adapted to a broader range of political contexts in the nineteenth century, ranging from socialism to imperialism, and including such strange hybrids as William Booth's socialist imperialism. In order to unravel the complexities of Victorian cosmopolitanism, I consider two important contexts in which both the term *cosmopolitanism* and the idea of global community were explicitly and repeatedly evoked: the Great Exhibition of 1851 and the Victorian miscellaneous journal.

These contexts are significant not only because they offer sustained instances of appeal to a discourse of cosmopolitanism but also because they showcase positive uses of the term. Though critics such as Amanda Anderson have drawn attention to positive versions of cosmopolitanism in the period, the negative nineteenth-century usages of *cosmopolitan* and *cosmopolitanism* are still the most renowned. For instance, in an article on Trollope, Lauren Goodlad states that

Trollope's works remind us that from a Victorian perspective, the word *cosmopolitan* was more likely to evoke the impersonal structures of capitalism and imperialism than an ethos of tolerance, world citizenship, or multiculturalism.[3]

This view of the period is hard to contest, given the disparaging references to cosmopolitanism that crop up not only in the works of Trollope but also in those of Dickens, Eliot, James, Conrad, and many others. The oft-cited quotations the *OED* employs to demonstrate the nineteenth-century meanings of *cosmopolitan* and *cosmopolitanism* (John Stuart Mill's "capital is becoming more and more cosmopolitan"; Macaulay's "That cosmopolitan indifference to constitutions and religions . . ."; and Carlyle's "A certain attenuated cosmopolitanism had taken the place of the old home feeling") also support Goodlad's assessment.[4]

Yet the two instances of Victorian cosmopolitan discourse I examine in this chapter help to expand our sense of how these words were used and understood. In the Introduction I argued for a dialectical view of cosmopolitanism that sees it both as a championing of globalization and as a critical stance towards it, as well as towards the exclusionary totalities of nation and empire. Correspondingly, this chapter traces the way both these approaches structure responses to the Great Exhibition and the global utopianism of a number of Victorian journals. But I also emphasize the way the language of cosmopolitanism in these cases tends to frame it as a positive project rather than a negative characteristic. These cosmopolitanisms not only complicate current understandings of Victorian thought, but also provide an important context for the affirmative cosmopolitanisms that have re-emerged today.

The Great Exhibition is significant to this study both because it was depicted as the apotheosis of mid-century free trade cosmopolitanism and because it played a significant role in cementing London's reputation as a multi-cultural cosmopolis. The powerful images of global totality that became affixed to the Crystal Palace – the peace congress, the hive, the "family of man," the marketplace of the world – reappear in writings about London until the end of the century. Interpreted both as a display of imperial mastery and as a utopian wish for "peace and understanding between all the nations of the world," the Exhibition was understood in a variety of positive cosmopolitan terms. These cosmopolitanisms did not go uncontested, however. Satirical sketchers such as George Sala and periodicals like *Punch* poked fun at this utopian rhetoric as soon as it began to circulate. Though light-hearted and irreverent, these critiques of cosmopolitanism prefigure those still circulating in our own moment, just as the objects of their critique prefigure today's "new" cosmopolitanisms.

The second part of the chapter examines the way *cosmopolitan* and its derivatives were used to shape periodical culture itself, as well as the various political discourses embedded within it. From the middle of the century to the end, a number of journals employed variations of the word in their titles in order to conjure up a transnational discursive space and to project the ideal of a mobile, sophisticated, and broad-minded readership. I focus in particular on *Cosmopolis* (1896–8), a journal noteworthy for its experiments with cosmopolitan form. Showcasing the wide ideological spectrum over which cosmopolitan ideals ranged, *Cosmopolis* sought to give these ideals life through its multilingualism and international distribution. Its innovative organization, whereby English, French, and German sections were published side by side, allowed contributors to transcend particular cultural and political positions by situating them within a larger imaginary *polis*. *Cosmopolis'* sophisticated endeavor to turn the form of the journal into an intellectual "world-city" illustrates the importance of generic analysis to a fuller understanding of cosmopolitanism's complex history.

The periodicals I examine and the discourse surrounding the Great Exhibition testify to the utopian investments of Victorian cosmopolitanism and show that an engagement with cosmopolitanism often entailed a creative engagement with form as well. Each evoked a different version of the cosmopolis. The Exhibition was a microcosm within a microcosm: a visible version of the global marketplace on display within the larger world of mid-Victorian London. Those who portrayed London and the Great Exhibition as miniature worlds used forms of containment and contraction, determined to capture the London of 1851 in portable images so as to preserve its perceived triumph as a symbol of global modernity. The cosmopolitan journals, on the other hand, each imagined themselves taking part in the *invisible* cosmopolis of an international public sphere. *Cosmopolis* and other periodicals used the dialogic and serial form of the periodical to create an expansive and diffuse vision of cosmopolitanism that might extend indefinitely across space and time. Whether extensive or intensive in their ambitions, progressive or conservative in intent, these examples of Victorian cosmopolitanism set out to manipulate temporal and spatial perceptions in the interest of global visions, testing and defining the boundaries of realism as they did so.

COSMOPOLITANISM AND ITS INTERPRETATIONS

In order to situate my analysis of the Great Exhibition, the periodical, and uses of *cosmopolitan* and *cosmopolitanism* in a wider Victorian context, this section provides a brief overview of how and in what ways these terms entered the vernacular. The different interpretations and values that underlie today's cosmopolitanism debate have been well documented, while a number of critics have provided useful genealogies of cosmopolitanism from antiquity to the contemporary period.[5] Rather than retrace this ground, therefore, I focus on those contexts strictly relevant to Victorian uses of the word. What emerges from this picture is a marked correspondence between the tensions within and between Victorian cosmopolitanisms and those prevalent today: one which suggests that the twentieth century's *fin-de-siècle* contest over cosmopolitanism inherits more than it acknowledges from Victorian debates.

For the purpose of understanding Victorian cosmopolitanisms, Kant's essays "Idea for a Universal History with a Cosmopolitan Purpose" (1784) and "To Perpetual Peace: A Philosophical Sketch" (1795) serve as the most appropriate starting-point, for his equation of cosmopolitanism with the progress of reason and economic globalization was immensely influential on Victorian uses of the word. Kant speculated that rational thought would lead eventually to a federation among nations designed to guarantee the rights of world citizens: "the growth of culture and men's gradual progress toward greater agreement regarding their principles lead to mutual understanding and peace."[6] A transnational public sphere, engaged dialectically with this federation, would ensure that violations of human rights were censured and acted upon by global public opinion.[7]

Kant also noted the importance of economic incentives to perpetual peace: "The spirit of trade cannot coexist with war, and sooner or later this spirit dominates every people. For among all those powers (or means) that belong to a nation, financial power may be the most reliable in forcing nations to pursue the noble cause of peace."[8] This aspect of his argument was particularly influential on Victorian journals that championed rational discourse and cultural exchange and on debates about free trade and international educational ideals. Victorian versions of Kantian cosmopolitanism, however, often missed or ignored the skepticism and hesitancy about the inevitability of human progress that characterizes Kant's essays. Kant was concerned in particular about "the inhospitable actions of the civilized and especially of the commercial states of our part of the world. The injustice which they show to lands and peoples they visit (which is equivalent to conquering them) is carried by them to terrifying lengths."[9] While individual versions of Victorian cosmopolitanism were often more naively idealistic than Kant's, his reservations about the concept reverberated through the nineteenth century as the word amassed a range of positive and negative connotations.

If Kant expressed his doubts about the progressive potential of cosmopolitanism elliptically, the use of the word by Marx and Engels half a century later took the shape of a full-blown critique. As I mention in the Preface, Marx and Engels associate the word *cosmopolitan* with the bourgeois "exploitation of the world-market." But, as Martin Puchner points out, Marx also imagined the *Manifesto* itself as a catalyst for turning the worlding of literature to the ends of international socialism: "the *Manifesto* wants to be the last and most successful example of Weltliteratur, and it also wants to be the first example of a different form of international literature . . . Written from the point of view of the international, countryless proletariat, the *Manifesto* hopes to create its addressee through its own international, literary practice."[10] In its effort to de-center the idea of an original language or culture, the form of the *Manifesto*, as we shall see, is related to the project of Victorian cosmopolitan periodicals. Though Marx's association of cosmopolitanism with bourgeois capitalism has helped to damn the term in the contemporary period and may have influenced its many pejorative uses in the Victorian period, Puchner notes that "Marx's cosmopolitanism, like his experience of exile, is not simply negative; both are categories that the *Manifesto* uses as its point of departure to create a new form of internationalism."[11] Marx's dialectical account of cosmopolitanism, and his performance of it via the *Manifesto*, helped to make it a constitutively ambivalent term in the nineteenth century and beyond.[12]

In the broader context of Victorian print culture, *cosmopolitan* and its variants appeared in a startling array of texts and contexts. The word appeared, for example, in the title of Urban Dubois' book of international recipes *Cosmopolitan Cookery* (1870), which went through three reprintings and was published in both English and French: here it signaled worldliness and the crossing of national boundaries. From it was also derived a popular pseudonym. Articles and pamphlets advocating free trade or narrating adventures abroad in England used the sign-off "a cosmopolite"; in colonial India, the term was used as a pseudonym in English-language texts arguing for religious tolerance. In these contexts, cosmopolitanism signifies, alternately, anti-protectionist politics, elite mobility, and an appeal to a rational and equalizing public sphere – one which, in the colonial context (where Indian journalists were not seen as equals to the British), had more radical connotations than it would have had back home.

While these uses were all positive, many Victorians, as Goodlad notes, understood industrialization and the "cosmopolitan character of production and consumption" described by the *Manifesto* to be a threat to national and moral integrity. The middle of the century saw the efflorescence of pro-cosmopolitan statements in response to the Great Exhibition, and while many critical and radical forms of cosmopolitanism emerged at the end of it, references to cosmopolitanism between these two periods were often less than sanguine. Negative uses such as those by Mill, Carlyle, and Macaulay (cited in the *OED* and above) demonstrate how the concept mobilized two related anxieties: (1) the fear of dispersal – of the loss of national character that many associated with international trade, emigration to the colonies and immigration from them – and (2) the fear of hybridity, "vagrancy," or border-crossing. Thus the label *cosmopolitan* was readily affixed to individuals or groups who appeared to challenge the social, economic, or political integrity of the nation, such as homosexuals, political radicals, artists, Jews, and other "unassimilated" immigrants.[13]

Many of the problems with which cosmopolitanism had become associated by the second half of the nineteenth century are synthesized in Dickens' caricatures of cosmopolitan individuals in *Bleak House*. His satire of Mrs. Jellyby's "telescopic philanthropy" has been much cited in this regard, and Amanda Anderson points also to the cosmopolitan villains in *Little Dorrit* – Rigaud, Gowan, and Miss Wade.[14] But Dickens' fascinating indictment of Skimpole's cosmopolitanism is equally pertinent to his views on the subject. At one point, Skimpole declares to Esther:

I believe I am truly cosmopolitan ... I lie in a shady place like this and think of adventurous spirits going to the North Pole or penetrating to the heart of the Torrid Zone with admiration ... Take an extreme case. Take the case of the slaves on American plantations. I dare say they are worked hard, I dare say they don't altogether like it. I dare say theirs is an unpleasant experience on the whole; but they people the landscape for me, they give it a poetry for me, and perhaps that is one of the pleasanter objects of their existence ... [15]

This gleefully amoral statement economically encapsulates the novel's anxieties about national degeneration. The cosmopolite contemplates different parts of the world but reduces them to abstractions; his interest is aesthetic rather than political; and his ideology is imperialist and exploitative. Skimpole's solipsism places him at the center of the world, where he is content to lie back while slaves toil away for his pleasure at a safe remove. Hovering around the Jarndyce home in order to drain it of its resources, Dickens' most effete and mercenary character is the ultimate "rootless cosmopolitan," devoid of attachments and loyalties.

Despite the fact that Dickens seems to focus only on the negative meanings of cosmopolitanism, though, the passage lends itself to an alternative reading because of the ambiguities built into the concept. If we read Skimpole's belief that he is *truly* cosmopolitan as the object of satire rather than cosmopolitanism *per se* – which we are arguably encouraged to do by the pomposity of Skimpole's declaration and by his equally specious claim that he is "a child" – then the passage conjures up a progressive cosmopolitanism that is the reverse of Skimpole's humbug version: one where the vision of slavery would inspire action, rather than inaction, and would destabilize one's own subject-position rather than reinforce it. In this case, we can imagine that Dickens might have been thinking of the abolitionist movement, or his own outraged response to slavery in *American Notes*, as more virtuous cosmopolitanisms.

While the satire of cosmopolitanism here and in Dickens' other writing is evident, and was a prevalent feature of responses to the discourse in the period, it is worth noting that satire, particularly in Dickens' hands, ridicules in order to reform. Those who criticized cosmopolitanism, in other words, were rightfully suspicious of its exclusions and hypocrisies. In drawing attention to its failures, however, they displayed an investment in the idea of cosmopolitanism itself which, even if negative, suggested the possibility of a better, more robust version.

"THE WORLD'S METROPOLIS": LONDON, THE GREAT EXHIBITION, AND THE GLOBAL IMAGINATION

The commentary that surrounded the Great Exhibition of 1851 also illuminates complexities within the discourse of cosmopolitanism as it emerged at mid-century. Commentators writing about the Exhibition experimented with a range of ways of imagining totality: ones that lent themselves to diverse political positions and new ways of conceiving community. A tangible symbol of *e pluribus unum*, the Exhibition was greeted by utopian celebrations of international and inter-class harmony. It also prompted a range of contemporary responses that explored and critiqued its encyclopedic mission.

The Great Exhibition was hailed by its manager, Henry Cole, as the "first cosmopolitan Exhibition of Industry by the most cosmopolitan nation in the world."[16] Designed to underwrite both the optimistic cosmopolitanism of Cole's claim and its bombastic nationalism, the fair was envisioned as an "Exhibition of the Industry of all the civilized Nations of the World," but one that showcased Britain's industrial and economic primacy, with the lion's share of the space of the Exhibition devoted to British products.[17] Championed by Albert, the Prince Consort, who believed earnestly in its internationalism, the Exhibition was considered a tremendous success by its organizers and the media alike. Twenty-eight countries participated and, over the course of its run from May 1 to October 15, 1851, six million visitors attended. Joseph Paxton's strikingly modern glass-and-iron Crystal Palace in which it was housed, played a major role in its success, as did the exhibits themselves. Alongside numerous machinery and textile exhibits, there were such crowd-pleasers as Hiram Power's provocative nude statue, "The Greek Slave," and the Koh-i-noor diamond.

There have been many insightful analyses of the Exhibition's contents and layout and of Paxton's architecture, ranging from Jeffrey Auerbach's landmark study to works such as Andrew Miller's *Novels behind Glass*, that connect it to a larger fascination with commodification and spectacle in the period. Recent anthologies such as *Victorian Prism* and Louise Purbrick's collection on the Exhibition focus in particular on the way the vision the Crystal Palace presented was rife with contradiction: its multiple significations torn between the view from above and that from below, between national and international arenas, between science and art and between entertainment and education.[18]

What interests me here, however, is the way that these contradictions took shape within a discourse that was both implicitly and explicitly about cosmopolitanism and the cosmopolis. Set up as a miniature city unto itself, the fair helped to define the language and the formal techniques whereby *cosmos* and *polis* would be mapped on to each other. Paul Young calls the Exhibition "a decisive moment in the formation of a world picture that became durably embedded in Victorian society," while critics Kylie Message and Ewan Johnston point out that "Not only did the 'world' appear encapsulated within the city, but it offered and legitimated a diversity of experience and new ways of talking about class that contributed to the reconfiguration of London and its social spaces in explicitly exotic and racialized terms."[19]

In conceptualizing the global scale of the Exhibition, however, many observers described it as a salutary portrait of human diversity and a democratic embrace of humanity. This view rested not only upon the fair's international scope but upon the fact that it was open to the working classes. Though in practice it was only affordable to working people on "shilling days," the idea of the Palace as a model of class and international harmony was a prevalent one.[20] Karen Chase and Michael Levenson note that "from the beginning the discourse of 'all' and 'every' became the consensual language of the exhibition."[21] Shortly after plans for the Exhibition were revealed, *The Times* ebulliently connected the fair's exemplary diversity with London's:

> Nothing can be so proper to London as an exhibition which shall represent the genius and invite the attendance of *all* nations. This peaceful metropolis is the asylum of the outcast and unfortunate. *All* parties find refuge here; the Absolutist here meets his Republican foe, and the Imperialist the rebel to whom he is indebted for his own exile. We have recently opened our ports to the produce and ships of *all* nations. What place so appropriate for the mutual aids and intercourse of peace as this free and open metropolis?[22] (emphasis added)

The repetition of the word "all" accentuates the newspaper's claim that London is a perfect location for the Exhibition because both represent the world as a whole. As well as conveying totality, "all" signals the city's inclusivity and democracy: its function as a sanctuary for outcasts, unfortunates, imperialists, and rebels alike. In *The Times'* portrait, both London and the coming Exhibition are welcoming, peaceful, and profitable spaces that promote "mutual aids and intercourse" between different nations and peoples.

The Exhibition provided an occasion to celebrate not only London's cosmopolitanism but that of the nation. In a speech "On the International Results of the Exhibition of 1851," Henry Cole made use of the simultaneously democratic and imperialistic resonances of the word "all": "What more natural than that the first Exhibition of the Works of Industry of *all* Nations should take place among a people which beyond every other in the world is composed of *all* nations?"[23] While Britain's multi-cultural population and liberalism were emphasized by celebratory declarations such as this, the self-congratulatory terms used to applaud the Exhibition relied upon transparent assumptions about Britain's superiority to other nations. Its cosmopolitanism was figured as a sign not only of its diversity but also of its advanced stage of economic and political development. In a trenchant analysis of the Exhibition's investment in "free trade cosmopolitanism," Paul Young argues that free trade was depicted by champions of the fair as the refinement of the "species."[24] According to Cole, then, "an event like this Exhibition could not have taken place at any earlier period, and perhaps not among any other people than ourselves."[25] Britain's ethnically mixed population made it, paradoxically, representative of "all nations" and *exceptional* in its modernity: the only place in the world fit to serve as an image of the global future. Yet, as Young notes, the free trade principle was seen as universal. It therefore challenged "polygenetic accounts of racial difference" that imagined a different trajectory for different peoples of the world by generating "a global perspective that opened up to humankind the opportunity for providentially inspired interdependency. The "cosmopolitan-philanthropic-commercial hymns of peace" – a phrase Marx used to characterize to Engels the discourse of the Exhibition – sought to bring the rest of mankind into the panoramic purview of the Crystal Palace as equals in the Exhibition's utopian terms but as junior partners in reality: ones who might eventually catch up with Britain in the future nirvana of perpetual peace.[26] This tension between exclusivity and inclusivity characterized much of the rhetoric with which the Exhibition was greeted.

It is perhaps for this reason that George Cruikshank's famous illustration "All the World Going to See the Great Exhibition of 1851" (Figure 1.1), which first appeared in Henry Mayhew's account of the exhibit, *1851: or, The adventures of Mr. and Mrs. Sandboys and family, who came up to London to "enjoy themselves" and to see the Great Exhibition,* pokes fun at the utopianism implicit in the ubiquitous use of the word "all" in relation to the fair. Drawn from the perspective of space, the illustration shows the world in its entirety, with the city positioned at its apex. Represented by the Crystal Palace, London is the center of steamship and train lines, with massive vehicles converging on it from east and west. The Palace takes up a significant portion of the globe and seems eminently capable of encompassing the swarming international multitudes drawn irresistibly towards it. Cruikshank uses a wide array of national costumes and modes of transportation (wagons, elephants, horses, and camels, among others) to literalize, and hence satirize, the bombastic idea that London will serve as host to "all the world." Yet the illustration's vitality and its intricate details – which depict London as gleaming, modern, and populous and the outer reaches of the globe as atavistic and barren – also convey an investment in the vision of British primacy that the Palace often stood for.

This kind of vision explains why so many critics of exhibition culture have read the totality represented by the Great Exhibition and other nineteenth-century world fairs in Foucauldian terms, as part of a discourse of power. In his influential article, "The World as Exhibition," for instance, Timothy Mitchell argues that the exhibition age was dominated

Figure 1.1 George Cruikshank, "All the World Going to See the Great Exhibition of 1851"

by the "conception of the world as an enframed totality, something that forms a structure or a system."[27] He positions the Great Exhibition, "the first of the great world exhibitions," as part of a new world order dominated by visual paradigms: "the age of the exhibition was necessarily the colonial age, the age of world economy and global power in which we live, since what was to be made available on exhibit was reality – the world itself." The world-as-exhibition was one in which "everything seems ordered and organized, calculated and rendered unambiguous" and where "the predominant characteristic of the world is its political decidedness."[28] Similarly, Peter Hoffenberg's *An Empire on Display* argues that organizers of the Great Exhibition intended it

to create its own sense of hierarchy, enabling social intercourse and the shared consumption of culture among the various constituent parts of the diverse Victorian and Edwardian British Empire. This was part of the process by which vision was diffused, shaped and finally established as a dynamic of social control and integration within and between polities.[29]

These analyses help to explain the predominance of totalizing images in mid-Victorian accounts of the Great Exhibition. What they do not explain, however, is the range of different ways of conceptualizing totality that characterizes the accounts – a phenomenon that rendered the meaning of the event more rather than less ambiguous. An analysis of the way that the Exhibition's space was imaginatively reconstructed in visual and written accounts by those observing it (or anticipating its opening), I argue, reveals both the potency of the Exhibition's symbolism and its political complexity. Rather than add to the many insightful analyses of the Exhibition's layout and the Palace's architecture that currently exist, then, I focus on the journalistic and literary discourse surrounding the Exhibition to trace the rich utopian vocabulary it created.

Prince Albert's speech to "her Majesty's Ministers, Foreign Ambassadors, Royal Commissioners of the Exhibition of 1851, and the Mayors of One Hundred and Eighty Towns," for instance, shows how the idea of "free trade cosmopolitanism" built upon Kant's notion of perpetual peace, though it stressed the economic imperative for cooperation over Kant's emphasis on the progress of reason:

We are living in a period of most wonderful transition, which tends rapidly to accomplish that great end, to which, indeed, all history points – *the realization of the unity of mankind* . . . The products of all quarters of the globe are placed at our disposal, and we have only to choose which is the best and the cheapest for our purposes, and the powers of production are intrusted to the stimulus of competition and capital . . . I confidently hope that the first impression which the view of this vast collection will produce upon the spectator will be that of deep thankfulness to the Almighty for the blessings which He has bestowed upon us . . . they can only be realized in proportion to the help which we are prepared to render each other . . . not only between individuals, but between the nations of the earth.[30]

Albert's speech suggests that the "unity of man" is a historical imperative driven by "competition and capital" but also claims that the Exhibition's bounty will function as evidence of God's goodness and the universal resonance of Christian ideals. In his terms, then, the idea of a global marketplace is one way of conceptualizing world unity; the notion of a Christian brotherhood of man is another. Together these different cosmopolitanisms reflect his desire to reconcile capitalism with morality, and British imperialism with free trade (though, as the narrative of cosmopolitan realism will show, this particular nexus of cosmopolitan ideas was not inevitable. Socialist William Morris would later use a Christian framework differently to forge an explicitly anti-capitalist and anti-imperialist cosmopolitanism [see Chapter 4]).

The language of kinship – through which the Exhibition was portrayed as a "brotherhood" or "family of man" – was one way in which the totalizing discourse used to describe the Exhibition attempted to reconcile the notion of British vanguardism with the ideal of equality in which it was also, at least discursively, invested. Most often, these phrases, as in Albert's case, drew upon a Christian vocabulary. Thackeray's "May-Day Ode" to the Exhibition, for instance, referenced the cathedral-like appearance of the Palace, depicting it as a heavenly space around which "the brotherhood of nations met":

> From Mississippi and from Nile –
> From Baltic, Ganges, Bosphorus,
> In England's ark assembled thus
>   Are friend and guest.
>
> Look down the mighty sunlit aisle,
> And see the sumptuous banquet set,
> The brotherhood of nations met
>   Around the feast!
>
> Swell, organ, swell your trumpet blast,
> March, Queen and Royal pageant, march
> By splendid aisle and springing arch
>   Of this fair Hall:
>
> And see! above the fabric vast,
> God's boundless heaven is bending blue,
> God's peaceful sunlight beaming through,
>   And shines o'er all.[31]

Thackeray's poem is full of pomp. Three regimentally regular four-beat lines are succeeded in each stanza by a weighty, three-beat flourish. The meter is appropriate to the subject; the poem brings together the image of a peace conference with royal pageantry and Christian benediction so that Paxton's building becomes simultaneously a meeting-hall, a palace, and a church. The space of the Hall itself is conveyed in vertical and horizontal dimensions, with reference both to the arch and the "heaven" above it and to the royal parade stretching down the aisle. This emphasis on height and depth helps to make concrete, and physically all-encompassing, the image of the Crystal Palace as the New Jerusalem incarnate, with God's light shining over all.

Another celebratory "hymn" to the Exhibition, by popular poet Martin Tupper (cited in Davis, *The Great Exhibition* 204), also portrayed it as the heavenly city:

> Yes, – for all on earth are brothers
> High and low, and far and near.
> And the more we see of others

All the more we hold them dear! . . .
For it is a glorious teaching,

Albert, thou hast taught mankind, –
Greatly to perfection reaching,
And enlarging heart and mind;
Stirring us, and stirring others
Thus to do the best we can
And with all the zeal of brothers
    Help the Family of Man!

While the force of Thackeray's poem rests upon the grandeur of its religious imagery, Tupper mobilizes a more tepid and sentimental multi-culturalism by suggesting that closer contact between cultures necessarily leads to greater understanding. Notably, though, Tupper's poem displays the same inclination as Thackeray's to create a sense of global space by invoking both the vertical and the horizontal in each of the stanzas that ends the poem. In the first stanza cited here, the dimensions of "high and low" and "far and near" suggest the erasure of class and race barriers respectively, while in the second Tupper asks his audience to emulate Albert in reaching upwards (vertically) to heavenly perfection and outwards (horizontally), enlarging heart and mind to take in "the Family of Man."

The kinship metaphor used by both Thackeray and Tupper implies a moral, egalitarian way of viewing the Exhibition's internationalism – one that might elevate it from its materialist agenda of promoting trade and industry. But the connotations of the metaphor varied widely. Tupper's suggestion that a missionary-like "zeal" is necessary to "Help the Family of Man," for instance, borrows heavy-handedly from the language and ideology of colonial paternalism.

If the Exhibition was used to represent the triumph of empire, ethnic diversity, the coming of Kant's perpetual peace, the culmination of Western civilization, and the Christian brotherhood of man, it also served as a foil for visions of international working-class solidarity. Critiques of the Exhibition in the working-class journal *Friend of the People* called for a celebration of "those principles which could unite all nations in one common bond of brotherhood, each contributing to the welfare of all."[32] In this usage, the notion of brotherhood serves as a corrective to the necessary hierarchies and inequalities of an Exhibition that championed capitalist ideals. Peter Gurney draws attention to another socialist version of the Exhibition conjured up by the Owenite periodical the *Northern Star.*

We can imagine a similar World's Show gathered together for very different purposes, but composed of precisely the same materials, to which Labour would flock gladly, as to a high Carnival, and the inauguration of a better era. If instead of avowing that this marvellous collection of skill and industry was made for the purpose of stimulating competition, it had been to ascertain what were the actual means at the command of the world, for producing wealth of all kinds, and for promoting a regulated system of distribution, which would ensure to all nations the full and fair participation of the aggregate wealth so produced, the case would have been very different.[33]

Here the editor is clear about the Great Exhibition's failings, but nonetheless uses its totalizing form to create the image of a world united around the ideals of socialist internationalism. As is often the case with the works of cosmopolitan realism explored later, the versions of cosmopolitanism endorsed by the *Northern Star* and *Friend of the People* are not ones that they see in practice: instead, they are utopian versions that use the shortcomings of reality as departure points for more idealistic visions.

The texts analyzed so far reveal ideological contradictions within individual representations of the Exhibition and ideological conflicts between them. But they also evince a recurrent emphasis on totality: the idea that the Exhibition created the spectacle of the world as a bounded and interconnected space. This emphasis posed an epistemological problem alongside the ideological ones that often beset representations of the Exhibition. If many of those seeking to use the Exhibition as an image of global community had to figure out how to promote equality between nations and people and celebrate British economic and imperial hegemony at the same time, they also had to solve the dilemma of how to imagine totality while paying homage to the Exhibition's unprecedented spectacle of diversity.

The Cambridge philosopher William Whewell's account of the Exhibition addresses these quandaries through the counterfactual notion of a camera that can produce a flat image across the contours of the globe:

We may compare the result to that which would be produced, if we could suppose some one of the skilful photographers whose subtle apparatus we have exhibited there, could bring within his field of view the surface of the globe, with all its workshops and markets, and produce instantaneously a permanent picture, in which the whole were seen side by side ... By annihilating the space which separates different nations, we produce a spectacle in which is also annihilated the time which separates one stage of a nation's progress from another.[34]

Whewell's image of the Fair cleverly allows for simultaneously unified and differentiated views. While he produces a vivid internationalist version of what Benedict Anderson has called "horizontal comradeship," with different nations lined up side by side as equals, he also reminds us of the vertical hierarchy of industrial modernity wherein Britain, presumably, assumes the topmost position.[35]

A similar attempt to integrate vertical hierarchy with horizontal democracy can be detected in the recurring notion of the Crystal Palace as a hive, home to the various "working bees of the world."[36] An illustration entitled "The Opening of the Great Hive of the World" (Figure 1.2), for instance, appeared as a fold-out feature in Mayhew and Cruikshank's serialized novel, *The Adventures of Mr. and Mrs. Sandboys*. In Cruikshank's vision, the unifying image of the hive allows for the notion of equality between workers from different countries but also glorifies Victoria as the "queen bee" presiding over the Exhibition. Unlike the chaos, caricature, and movement that characterize his more famous illustration, "All the World Going to See the Great Exhibition," the drawing of the hive emphasizes harmony, order, and stasis. The members of the royal family, depicted at the opening of the Exhibition, serve as the focal point of the image with the crowds organized neatly and symmetrically around them. While the various flags lined up horizontally on top of the Palace position the nations they symbolize as equals, the illustration's focus on the royal family makes them appear to pay tribute to the far more potent symbol of Britain – the Queen herself.

In producing these various conceptions of the Exhibition – the hive, the international marketplace, the Christian brotherhood of man – writers and illustrators contributed to the global imagination by supplying it with a portable set of images. But the fact that these images were part of a new utopian cosmopolitanism was not lost on satirists, who were quick to critique its hypocrisies and contradictions through images of their own. John Tenniel's cartoon in *Punch*, "The Happy Family in Hyde Park" (Figure 1.3), for instance, takes issue with the metaphor of the "family of man." As Jeffrey Auerbach points out, the illustration stresses national and racial hierarchy over unity: "those in the foreground are Europeans, while those in the background, separated behind the glass windows of the Crystal Palace, are exotic foreigners ... They are alien 'others,' on display as in a museum case or a circus cage, engaged in a bizarre and perhaps primitive dance."[37] Like Mitchell's critique of "the-world-as-exhibition," Tenniel's cartoon highlights the reifying function and orientalizing thrust of global spectatorship.

In similar fashion, George Sala's panoramic sketch-books on the topic of the fair anticipate many current critiques of cosmopolitanism. The form in which the sketches were published paid homage to the

Figure 1.2 George Cruikshank, "The Great Hive of the World"

THE HAPPY FAMILY IN HYDE PARK.

Figure 1.3 John Tenniel, "The Happy Family in Hyde Park"

Exhibition's totalizing impulses. Sala's drawings appeared in small, collectible books that opened out, accordion-style, into long panoramic images containing detailed sketches of notable aspects of the fair. In combining sketch and panorama, Sala alluded to the global scale of the panoramic tradition (see Chapter 2). Yet on the micro-level, a number of his sketches satirize the cosmopolitan ideals with which the Exhibition was associated. Three of the sketches in his panorama entitled *The House that Paxton Built* (1851) draw out different problems with these ideals.

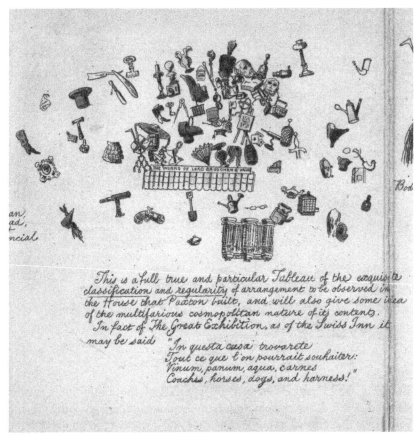

Figure 1.4 George Sala, "This is a full, true and particular Tableau of the exquisite classification and regularity of arrangement to be observed in the House that Paxton built"

The first of these, a sketch of a random collection of objects, untidily floating together in space, makes fun of the Exhibition's encyclopedism – its aspirations to represent, consolidate, and unify the world (Figure 1.4). The picture's caption reads:

This is a full, true and particular Tableau of the exquisite <u>classification</u> and <u>regularity</u> of arrangement to be observed in the House that Paxton built, and will also give some idea of the multifarious cosmopolitan nature of its contents. In fact of the Great Exhibition, as of the Swiss Inn, it may be said

> "In questa casa trovarete
> Tout ce que l'on pourrait souhaiter:

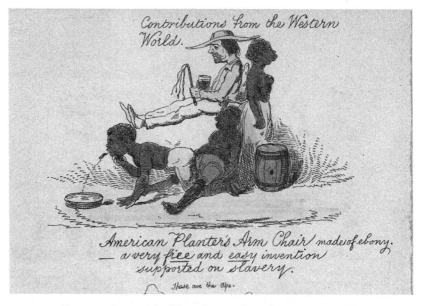

Contributions from the Western World.

American Planter's Arm Chair made of ebony. — a very free and easy invention supported on slavery.

Figure 1.5 George Sala, "Contributions from the Western World"

> Vinum, panum, aqua, carnes
> Coaches, horses, dogs, and harness!"

Both the sketch and the text, with its satire of the Exhibition's much-debated classification system and its multi-lingual doggerel, lampoon the very idea that global totality might be adequately represented by the Palace. Through the tawdry assemblage of objects and the reference to "coaches, horses, dogs, and harness," Sala also deflates the idealism of the Exhibition by pointing to its mundane materialism. Another dig at cosmopolitan ideals takes the form of a sketch of a white planter using three slaves as furniture, accompanied by the caption "Contributions from the Western World" (Figure 1.5). The American contribution to the fair, the image suggests, literally rests on the debasement of black bodies: a fact which gives the lie to the much vaunted idea of the Exhibition as evidence of the "unity of man." Yet this sketch also partakes in a more general condescension towards America evident in the press at the time of the Fair that helped underscore its emphasis on British supremacy; here America's much criticized agricultural contributions to the Fair (rather than the artistic refinements associated with France or the industrial innovations in which Britain took pride) are connected to its moral

Figure 1.6 George Sala, "Civilised World Esq."

backwardness, while Britain, which had abolished slavery throughout the Empire in 1833, seems progressive by comparison.

The final sketch in Sala's panorama – an anthropomorphized globe in gentleman's clothing – drives home its critique of liberal cosmopolitanism with the slogan: "Civilized World Esq. very much elated at the great good social, and otherwise to be derived from the Great Exhibition" (Figure 1.6). With this drawing and slogan, Sala personifies the cosmopolitan discourse that accompanied the Exhibition as a smug Whig, taking pride in his supposedly inclusive outlook while oblivious to his own privilege and the flimsiness of his idealism.

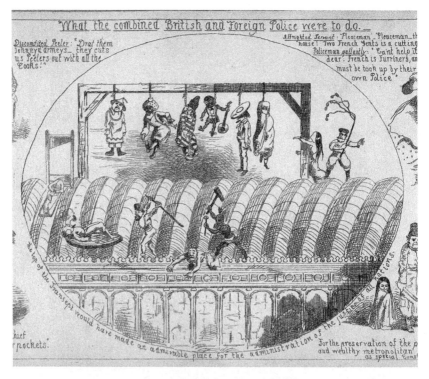

Figure 1.7 George Sala, "The Justice of All Nations"

Like many who critique cosmopolitanism today, Sala notes the elitism of the discourse, along with its inability to account for those excluded from the category of "civilization" or "humanity" (such as slaves), and its aspirations to totality – its impossibly vexed universalism. As was the case with Dickens' satire of Skimpole, though, it is hard to tell whether Sala dismisses cosmopolitanism as an ideal altogether, or whether he is merely suspicious of certain versions of it. A cartoon in another Sala panorama about the Great Exhibition entitled *The great glass house opend, or, The exhibition wot is!!* suggests a cynical outlook. The drawing depicts a number of figures in different national costumes hanging from a scaffold on the roof of the Crystal Palace (Figure 1.7). Next to the scaffold, a man in exotic military dress sadistically lashes a helpless maiden, while elsewhere a nearly naked black figure attempts to nail a white man to the roof with an oversized peg and hammer. The caption reads "The top of the Transept would have made an admirable place for the administration of the justice of all nations." While mocking the over-used phrase "all nations," Sala also implies that the idea of a unified forum for international justice is farcical in light of what he depicts as the barbaric disciplinary practices of other countries. The racist and nationalistic logic of this particular sketch, then, suggests that Sala is critical not only of hypocritical versions of cosmopolitanism generated by the Exhibition but of the concept in general, deemed impossible by his differentiated view of culture. Furthermore, while his individual sketches appear light-hearted in their spoof of cosmopolitanism, as a group Sala's drawings betray a desire to debunk it definitively, thus serving as evidence of its rhetorical force at the time of the Exhibition.

Sala's sketches engage with questions of race because they cut to the heart of cosmopolitanism's purported universalism, exposing the degree to which humanist articulations of the ideal ignored the diminished status of people of other races (as well as ethnicities and classes) within the "Family of Man." Yet those who were earnestly and explicitly engaged with questions of race, such as members of the Anglo-American abolitionist movement, also used the Exhibition as a platform for a Christian and anti-slavery version of cosmopolitanism.[38] *The Anti-Slavery Reporter*, for instance, which addressed both "British and Foreign" abolitionist societies, published a letter on its front page calling for protests directed against American visitors to the fair:

The approaching Exhibition of the Industry and Arts of Nations, in this great metropolis, will, among others, bring, it is expected, a large number of Americans as visitors . . . and will afford you an excellent opportunity of bearing your protest against American slavery, in forms which must be deeply felt, and which cannot fail to prove highly salutary and beneficial.[39]

Whether or not he was following *The Anti-Slavery Reporter*'s mandate, William Wells Brown's account of the Exhibition in his travel narrative *An American Fugitive in Europe: Sketches of People and Places Abroad* (1855) uses it to make an anti-slavery statement directed at Americans. Brown, an escaped slave who became a prominent abolitionist and traveled to Europe to attend anti-slavery conferences, positions the spectacle of diversity at the Palace as a foil to racial segregation in America:

The queen and the day laborer, the prince and the merchant, the peer and the pauper, the Celt and the Saxon, the Greek and the Frank, the Hebrew and the Russ, all meet here upon terms of perfect equality. This amalgamation of rank, this kindly blending of interests, and forgetfulness of the cold formalities of ranks and grades, cannot but be attended with the very best results. I was pleased to see such a goodly sprinkling of my own countrymen in the Exhibition – I mean colored men and women – well-dressed, and moving about with their fairer brethren. This, some of our pro-slavery Americans did not seem to relish very well. There was no help for it.[40]

Perhaps willfully naive in its utopian view of class and race "amalgamation" at the Palace, Brown's description adapts the universalist and democratic language with which the Exhibition was so frequently depicted to the ends of abolitionism. Within the larger trajectory of his narrative the Exhibition is one of many symbols of European progress that position America, rather than non-Western countries, at the margins of civilization. Brown thus puts the dominant discourse surrounding the Exhibition to his own uses by changing its internal hierarchies and ideological effects. For example, he gives specific instances of the "mixing" of class and race that flesh out the abstraction and homogenization often embedded in the rhetoric of totality that attended the Exhibition. His version of community puts "pro-slavery Americans" rather than black Americans outside of the fold, excluded not arbitrarily by country, rank, or caste but by their own ideology, which the spectacle of "perfect equality" that confronts them radically undermines.

To some extent, Brown's description of the Exhibition fits into the form of cosmopolitanism that Elisa Tamarkin describes under the heading "Black Anglophilia." Tamarkin notes that a number of nineteenth-century black abolitionists pit American barbarism against English sophistication: "Abolition trades on a discourse of intellectualism and cultural advancement that is teleologically Anglophilic, that says that Great Britain is simply further along in ways America has yet to manage for itself."[41] This discourse, she argues, associates intellectualism with cosmopolitanism, which the ex-slave identifies with because of his or her "attenuated affiliations – [Frederick] Douglass's 'Aliens are we in our native land.'"[42] As a transnational movement, a human rights stance, and a political position necessarily pitted against the (American) nation, abolitionism becomes a powerful form of cosmopolitanism: one that relies partially on "a kind of snobbery towards racism. These black writers are all but goading white Americans to say, 'O slavery, how provincial!'"[43] Yet Brown's cosmopolitanism is more than simply Anglophilic; while he celebrates London and the Exhibition uncritically, his vision of the Palace is one in which all forms of social differentiation, including national ones, have been upended. Indeed Brown pointedly changes the connotations of "country-men" to mean "colored men and women," thereby evoking an America to which white pro-slavery individuals do not belong.

Mitchell's argument about "the-world-as-exhibition" calls for us to see phenomena like the Exhibition and other forms of metropolitan spectacle as attempts to order the world in the image of European power and, indeed, some representations – like Whewell's, or even Sala's – work to that effect. But others use the same terms and imagery (the idea of brotherhood, for example) to critique the exclusions sanctioned by the

Exhibition or, in Brown's case, to call attention more specifically to the exclusions sanctioned by American nationalism. At the very moment that the world as a whole first assumed the tangible glass and iron shape of the Crystal Palace, it also assumed life as an imaginative form, eminently susceptible to reinvention.

COSMOPOLITANISM IN VICTORIAN PERIODICALS

The presence and significance of a positive discourse of cosmopolitanism in Victorian periodicals has gone largely unnoticed partly because of the genre's ongoing association with political and national partisanship. Yet the ways in which Victorian journals understood the word *cosmopolitan* are significant because they helped to give it currency at the moment it first began to appear with frequency in literary and political writing. In the highly competitive market of mid- to late nineteenth-century journals, these evocations of cosmopolitanism contributed to the elitist resonances the word still has today. The periodical titles connoted urbanity and commercial savviness, and addressed themselves to the well-heeled and well-traveled. The word was also used by some journals to conjure up the kind of international public sphere that Kant imagined might curb the excesses of national self-interest.

Because they adopted cosmopolitanism both as a discursive ideal and as a kind of space that could be inhabited by their audiences, these journals offer a unique historical perspective on the concept and its Victorian incarnations. Periodicals, I suggest, are crucial to an understanding of cosmopolitanism because they were the form in which the term circulated most widely and influentially. Moreover, through the act of buying journals called *The Cosmopolitan* or *Cosmopolis*, readers were helping to identify themselves with concepts that named both their lifestyles and reading practices.

In *The World Republic of Letters*, Pascale Casanova calls for a new "spatialized history" of literary texts, in which literary works are understood in relation to each other, as part of a "world of letters" in which different national traditions engaged in "incessant struggle and competition over the very nature of literature itself."[44] By invoking cosmopolitanism in their titles, journals were self-consciously investigating and defining the increasingly global field of their circulation and the terms of discussion and information transfer therein. If, as Sharon Marcus argues, "even in its heyday, print culture was international and the nation was a relative, hybrid, comparative category," nineteenth-century British journals that

addressed themselves directly to these conditions offer a unique opportunity to interrogate the ways in which that internationalism was understood in its own moment.[45]

By tracing the use of the word in the title of periodicals, I show that a
key split in the concept was exacerbated, and formalized, by these publications. One set of the periodicals that I investigate prioritized the notion
of "neutrality" and of the "cosmopolitan critic" – a figure who practiced
detached reflection and an openness to different national traditions. These
journals saw themselves as neutral zones in which contributors might set
aside their native prejudices, exercise disinterested reason, and acquire
wide-ranging knowledge. Another set of periodicals, however, advertised
their *lack* of disinterest and mobilized the more elitist connotations of
cosmopolitanism. These figured their readership as a network of mobile
individuals connected to the metropolitan center: worldly and privileged
English-speaking readers who sought to accumulate information about
different countries for purposes of business, travel, or colonial administration. Because they were targeted partly at expatriate audiences, the
"network" periodicals created imagined communities that were simultaneously British and transnational in scope, unified via the circulation of
metropolitan knowledge.

This section focuses in particular on the journalistic experiments of
Cosmopolis, an illustrious but short-lived periodical of the 1890s. *Cosmopolis* is significant because it engaged both versions of cosmopolitan community discussed above and generated a new model as well: that of the
public sphere as a global city with a multi-cultural, multi-lingual populace. Published in three different languages in a number of European
capitals, the journal attempted to strike a balance between particular and
universal subject-matter and objective and subjective perspective through
its very format and distribution strategy. Unlike the "neutral" periodicals,
Cosmopolis embraced and made manifest its specific cultural locations;
unlike the "network" ones, it associated cosmopolitanism predominantly
with critical dialogue rather than with the international circulation of
information and finance.

Cosmopolis was only one of a number of Victorian periodicals that
affiliated themselves with cosmopolitanism by using the words *cosmopolite*, *cosmopolitan*, and *cosmopolis* in their titles. While many other British
journals, from *The Westminster Review* to *The Savoy*, engaged explicitly
with the literature and political opinions of those abroad, reporting on
French and German literature, for instance, or inviting contributions
from Continental critics and writers, I focus here on those journals that

Table 1.1. *Cosmopolitan periodicals of the nineteenth century*

Periodical title	Dates of circulation	Site of distribution	Frequency	Circulation figures
Philogene's Cosmopolitan Political and Statistical Review	1839–60	London	Weekly	N/A
The Cosmopolitan Review	1861	London	Monthly	N/A
The Cosmopolitan	1865–76	London New York Paris	Weekly	50,000/wk
The Cosmopolitan Critic and Controversialist	1876–7	London	Monthly (1876) Quarterly (1877)	N/A
The Cosmopolitan	1887–9	London	Monthly	N/A
Cosmopolis	1896–8	London New York Paris, Vienna Amsterdam St. Petersburg	Monthly	24,000 (Jan. 1896)

use the word in their titles, so as to trace both the influence of the concept on periodicals and the influence of periodicals on the concept. The table above enumerates the most significant journals that identified themselves with cosmopolitanism and provides comparative information about where, when, and how frequently they circulated. As is the case with many Victorian periodicals, comprehensive circulation figures and a sense of the reading audience for these journals remain elusive. The few statistics that do exist, though, imply that at least a couple of them (*The Cosmopolitan* and *Cosmopolis*) saw a certain degree of commercial success.[46]

If the concept of cosmopolitanism served as a draw for the readers of these periodicals, what exactly did it mean to them? Apart from *Cosmopolis*, which I will discuss at greater length below, the journals listed in Table 1.1 fall into two broad categories. The first type understands cosmopolitanism in predominantly idealistic terms, as a critical norm constituted through a disinterested stance and multi-faceted dialogue. These journals positioned themselves as the foundation of a neutral public sphere in which writers met on equal terms, freed from the biases of culture and nation. The second type of journal offered a more materialistic interpretation of cosmopolitanism. For this group, cosmopolitanism names a mode of consumption and a disparate set of expatriate lifestyles held together by a dense network of imperialist and capitalist forces. Rather than focusing on ideals of journalistic neutrality, these publications position themselves as nodes of power that focalize the knowledge and information their readers need to succeed in a competitive, differentiated landscape.

As discussed earlier, cosmopolitanism could be used to name an ideal of perpetual peace or the global circulation of capital and these meanings were often entangled within the word's use in the Victorian period, as well as in Kant's eighteenth-century writings. I argue, however, that the disjuncture between these meanings, and therefore the split within the concept itself, is formalized by the way in which the journals build an implied readership around each version of the concept. Favoring one or the other of these two dominant meanings, and positioning themselves as either neutral or networked spaces accordingly, cosmopolitan journals produced different inflections of cosmopolitanism and encouraged varied cosmopolitan practices.

Periodicals used their editorials and content to stake out their chosen version of cosmopolitanism. *The Cosmopolitan Review* of 1861, for instance, falls into the first category: that of the "neutral" journal. It demonstrates its commitment to the utopian promise of international dialogue in its opening article, which declares cosmopolitanism the solution to the growing threat of European conflict. Arguing (like many critics today) that the term must not be identified with a "universal indifference," the editorial identifies it instead with a commitment to world citizenship:

Patriotism was the watchword of despotism; liberty will adopt another, and that will be cosmopolitanism. Cosmopolitanism is a patriotism which knows of no boundaries and no enemies – a patriotism which can withstand the searching look of justice ... We call for the help of those who, whatever may be their name, country, or colour, will be willing to seek with us the best means to bring concord and justice among men.[47]

Articles in the journal – such as an anti-colonial article on New Zealand, another celebrating the worldwide spread of abolitionism, and a piece praising Garibaldi for his cosmopolitan spirit – underscore the *Review*'s Kantian notion that conversations in the public sphere might serve the cause of international justice. Despite the lack of information about the nature and extent of the readership of these periodicals, the fact that this particular journal was reaching at least a portion of its targeted audience is evidenced by the appearance of a supportive letter in one of its issues from Garibaldi himself. While *The Cosmopolitan Review* promotes the ideal of art as a vehicle for understanding other cultures, scientific and industrial progress also serves as evidence, as it did for Kant, of the historical inevitability of a united world. All manner of novelties, such as the decimal system, the international classification of weights, coins, and measures, the Crystal Palace exhibition, and larger structural systems such as railways, telegraphs, steamers, commerce, and printing, are upheld as signs of an irresistible drive towards global harmony.

The Cosmopolitan Critic and Controversialist of 1876 also evokes the progressive teleology of Enlightenment cosmopolitanism in its opening statements. In an address "Dedicated to the Citizens of the World," the journal declares its "Impartiality and toleration to all men, whatsoever party, school, or nationality they may belong." By generating a wide-ranging interchange of ideas, the editors state, they hope to produce "some few sparks of light and truth" that might serve the greater good. *The Cosmopolitan Critic* thus mobilizes a faith in the ethics of disinterest and promotes the idea – associated in the nineteenth century with Matthew Arnold and John Stuart Mill – that a plurality of viewpoints confronting each other in a neutral arena will allow for the triumph of the best ideas. Addressed to a potentially global audience, *The Cosmopolitan Review* and *The Cosmopolitan Critic* figure themselves as transnational and inclusive spaces. Both also leverage the miscellaneous form of the Victorian periodical to showcase a wide range of opinions and topics, thereby substantiating their stated investment in the ameliorative function of diverse points of view.

Philogene's Cosmopolitan Political and Statistical Review fits into the second category of periodicals, which saw its readership as a "network" rather than as "neutral." Both in form and content, the *Review* – a long-lived weekly periodical – represents cosmopolitanism as part of the consolidation rather than the exchange of knowledge. Using tiny fonts and dense tables of statistics to compress masses of information on to each of its pages, the newspaper's layout enacts the act of consolidation and assimilation that it argues is essential to the mastery of modern life. Its editorials speak of the need to understand other countries in order to guard against the territorial or revolutionary threats they posed. At the same time, however, the review pays lip-service to the humanitarian benefits of such knowledge: "only by carefully studying the state of foreign nations, the interests, the views, the measures of their governments [can we] seize every opportunity that may be turned, not to our advantage

only, but to the benefit of mankind at large."[48] By attempting to balance
the aggressive language of "seizing opportunities" to "turn them to
advantage" with appeals to the benefits of mankind, universally construed,
Philogene's Review showcases the way in which cosmopolitan knowledge
was conceived, paradoxically, as a British prerogative that might spread
outwards through imperialist influence.

Another journal called *The Cosmopolitan* used the term in a specifically
imperialist context. Circulating from 1887 to 1889, it provided information to scattered colonial soldiers and supplied its readers with an illusion
of imperial unity via its focus on a nostalgic English past: its individual
issues are filled with articles bearing titles such as "Left Behind" and
"Homes of the British"[49] (Figure 1.8). It also includes anthropological
and sociological information about the colonies, complete with full-color
maps of different colonial spaces. Interestingly, periodicals in English-
speaking settler colonies evoked cosmopolitanism too, even when their
focus and circulation were chiefly national. *Cosmopole*, an 1892 South
African periodical published in English and Dutch, transmitted local
news, while *Cosmos*, an Australian literary magazine published from
1894 to 1889 urges its readers to create their own national literature derived
from their unique experience of farmland and bush.[50] Presumably the
evocation of worldliness in the titles of these periodicals served as a way to
characterize the newly hybrid identities of white settlers and to allay their
sense of isolation and geographical marginality by suggesting a familial
connection to the center.

The *Cosmopolitan* was also the title of a different review: one that
circulated from 1865 to 1876 and was distributed in New York, Paris, and
London. This periodical imagines itself not so much as the central node
in a global network but as a type of network in itself, bringing together
three major metropolises and the different kinds of financial and geopolitical power that they represent. It cheerfully celebrates the association
of cosmopolitanism with the circulation of global capital and advertises
itself as an "international newspaper" that circulates "chiefly among the
highest classes." Avowing its interest in making money, and flatly
denying that it has any political or idealistic goals, the journal states
that it does not "propose either to reform the world or revolutionise
society." Featuring ads for expensive hotels, high-end furnishing companies, and champagne, *The Cosmopolitan* plays unabashedly on the
elitist resonances of cosmopolitanism in order to appeal to the aspirations of its audience.

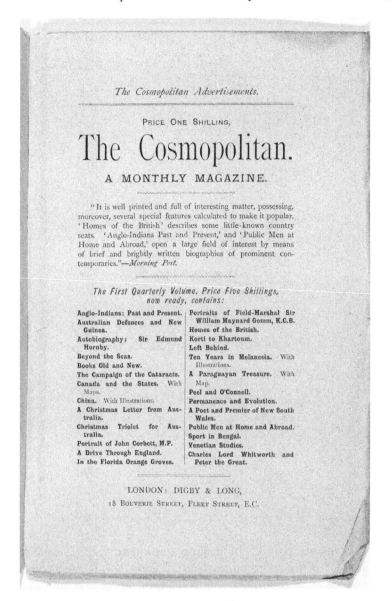

Figure 1.8 Advertisement for *The Cosmopolitan*

Even relatively straightforward evocations of the term such as those in *The Cosmopolitan*, however, contain contradictory messages. The champagne advertisement featured in its pages claims that the wine depicted is

Figure 1.9 Champagne advertisement, "The Cosmopolite Brand"

"the cosmopolite brand." In making this claim, the ad exploits two connotations of the word concurrently (Figure 1.9). Most obviously, it draws on the snob appeal of cosmopolitanism, associating the exclusivity of champagne with the privileged mobility of the bourgeois *flâneur* and the aesthete. But the list of places where the wine is distributed includes British Columbia, which was more an outpost of empire than a cosmopolitan capital. In order to underscore their commercial success, then, the advertisers not only use elitism but also boast of their access to the remote markets provided by British colonialism. British Columbia adds to the wine's cosmopolitanism if the ad also mobilizes the more literal meaning of *cosmopolitan* cited in the *OED*: "belonging to all parts of the world." The ambiguous use of cosmopolitanism in the ad therefore illuminates a contradiction in capitalism, wherein the cultural capital intended to drive purchasing decisions is potentially undermined by the desire for market saturation.

The ease with which Victorian cosmopolitanism, in its periodical form, lent itself to such contradictions made it usefully capacious but also potentially problematic as a platform on which to construct an elite reading public. On the one hand, both types of journals I have discussed could profit from the term's slipperiness. Audiences invested in cosmopolitanism-as-dialogue might also be drawn to the idea of themselves as privileged, mobile consumers; similarly, audiences attracted by the term's association with global finance might also buy into the Kantian notion that the circulation of wealth would lead eventually to the "unity of man." On the other hand, the term's liability to slip from one side to the other of the idealist–materialist binary – to be contaminated itself, just as it often served as a sign of contamination – must have made it a difficult commercial draw: a possible explanation for the short-livedness of many of these journals.

Nonetheless, the abiding differences between its usages in periodicals and the varied forms of the public sphere that were produced as a result are significant. By asking their readers to identify themselves as cosmopolitans through the act of reading and to take on specific relationships to the concept, periodicals had a particular and powerful purchase on the term. In creating an artificial rift between cosmopolitanism's two principal meanings they played a role in undermining the more fully dialectical understanding of the term evidenced by Marx's *Manifesto*.

Cosmopolis (1896–8), however, saw the difficulty of the term as a representational challenge, conceiving of cosmopolitanism as a problem of form from the outset. While the other periodicals set themselves up as spaces that would either erase or transcend the cultural and national differences between their readers, *Cosmopolis* – by mediating between national cultures and international ideals – sought simultaneously to acknowledge those differences and overcome them. Taking into account the limited perspectives and biases of its contributors, the journal enacted an early version of what Bruce Robbins calls "situated cosmopolitanism": a practice that self-consciously acknowledges its own embeddedness in language, culture, and nation while nonetheless exhibiting a "genuine striving toward common norms and mutual translatability."[51] If the journals I have discussed so far envisioned the imaginary space in which the conversations they set up took place as either "neutral" or "networked," *Cosmopolis*, as its name suggests, used both the idea of the ancient Greek city-state (*polis*) and that of global expansiveness (*cosmos*) to construct a utopian site of cosmopolitan civic engagement.

Even though it only lasted for two years, it was evidently the most culturally prestigious of the journals listed in the table above.[52] The eminence of the authors, journalists, and political and social commentators who appeared in *Cosmopolis* over the short course of its run is striking. Among many other illustrious figures, contributors included R. L. Stevenson, Ivan Turgenev, Olive Schreiner, Somerset Maugham, Henry James, Stéphane Mallarmé, W. B. Yeats, George Gissing, Joseph Conrad, Rudyard Kipling, Anatole France, J. M. Barrie, Max Nordau, George Bernard Shaw, Edmund Gosse, and Friedrich Nietzsche.

Cosmopolis was also distinctive in its dedication to generating an undeniably transnational dialogue – one that remained largely phantasmatic in the other publications. While most of the Victorian cosmopolitan journals had predominantly national audiences and contributors despite their internationalist aspirations, *Cosmopolis* was far more ambitious in scope. At first glance, the journal's claims to cosmopolitan stature via a stance of impartiality seem to echo those of its predecessors. *Cosmopolis'* first issue announces that it hopes "by its independence and impartiality, by its moderation and urbanity of tone ... [to] bring about a sense of closer fellowship between the nations – a larger sympathy making, slowly, no doubt, but effectually, for the far-off goal of perfect culture: peace and concord."[53] The journal's objectivity, however, is far less naive than that of the "neutral" periodicals, which rely on mere assertion of editorial independence and breadth of subject-matter to produce the sense of a view from nowhere.[54] *Cosmopolis*, by contrast, used signed contributions exclusively, turning its back definitively on the practice of anonymous publication that predominated earlier. Instead of presenting a consolidated or ostensibly balanced editorial vision, as anonymous periodicals sought to do, *Cosmopolis* based its claims to impartiality on the dialogue it set up between different political, national, and cultural points of view: it had three sections – English, French, and German, as well as a Russian supplement – which were published in the original languages and focused on both national and international concerns.

While the majority of the other cosmopolitan journals were based in London and imagined it as the center of the world, *Cosmopolis* practiced a more decentralized cosmopolitanism; it was printed and distributed, with local versions of the cover and advertisements, in Paris, London, Berlin, and St. Petersburg and planned an even broader distribution over time. It also circulated in America, where the *New York Times* followed its progress closely and reviewed many of its essays, stories, and book extracts.[55]

The form of *Cosmopolis*, then, signaled the cultural affiliation of each contribution and allowed for local context, even as writers from each section commented on each other's cultures, as well as on countries not represented in the journal and on broadly international topics. While aspiring to a detachment from local affiliations, *Cosmopolis'* writers were clearly identified with their respective cultural enclaves in a formal acknowledgment of the impossibility of the kind of perfect objectivity aspired to by other publications of the period. In its self-conscious signaling of the affiliations and biases of its contributors, *Cosmopolis* sought to achieve the delicate balance between universalism and particularism that current proponents of cosmopolitanism see as vital to its integrity as an ideal.[56] Its table of contents page was designed to help readers visualize this balance (Figure 1.10). The layout established clear borders between the different nations represented but, through the equal space and importance allocated to each, also sets them in harmonious interrelation as part of a larger whole.

The journal's commitment to transcending national preoccupations while literally maintaining national boundaries (through its three distinct sections) could also be seen in its negotiation of subject-matter in each of the sections. It was typical, for example, for an article on the state of "Current French Literature" by Edmund Gosse in the English section to appear in the same issue as one by Paul Leroy-Beaulieu on the English writer Richard Cobden in the French portion.[57] Furthermore, recurring articles on cultural phenomena in each section allowed for a comparative perspective: an article on "The Theatre in London" in the English section would be implicitly in dialogue with one on theater in Berlin in the German section and one on the theater in Paris in the French. There were also international symposia on single topics. In a notable forum on the death of Gladstone, "Justin McCarthy in English, Francis de Pressensé in French and Theodor Barth in German eulogize the statesman whose life influenced all of Europe (9: 29–43, 114–35, 205–330)."[58] *Cosmopolis* also published pieces that emphasized the intersection between different European cultures and the irreducibility of certain intellectual exchanges to the space of the nation, such as the letters of J. S. Mill to Gustave d'Eichthal. In multiple and intersecting ways, the

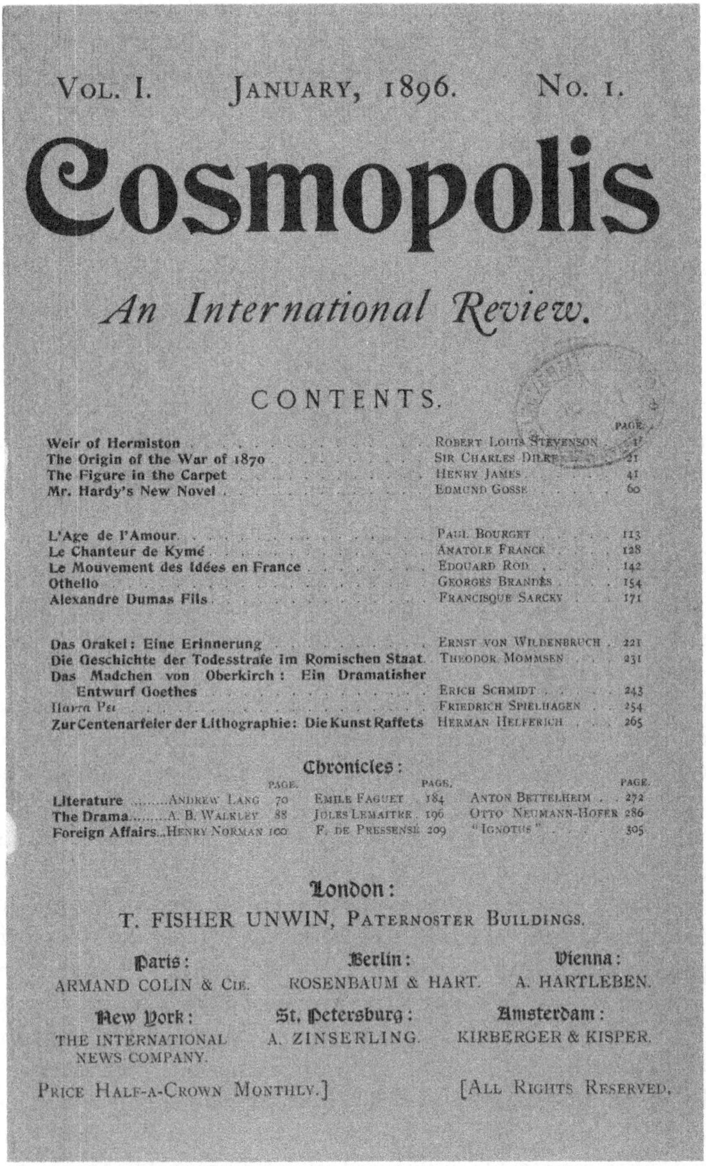

VOL. I.   JANUARY, 1896.   No. 1.

Cosmopolis

An International Review.

CONTENTS.

Chronicles:

London:

T. FISHER UNWIN, PATERNOSTER BUILDINGS.

Paris: **Berlin:**   **Vienna:**
ARMAND COLIN & CIE.   ROSENBAUM & HART.   A. HARTLEBEN.

New York: **St. Petersburg:**   **Amsterdam:**
THE INTERNATIONAL   A. ZINSERLING.   KIRBERGER & KISPER.
NEWS COMPANY.

PRICE HALF-A-CROWN MONTHLY.]   [ALL RIGHTS RESERVED.

Figure 1.10 *Cosmopolis*, Table of Contents.

journal simultaneously set itself up as a model of the kind of transnational public sphere envisioned by Kant *and* acknowledged the importance, even the primacy, of local affiliations.

In the spirit of Kant's perpetual peace, *Cosmopolis* imagined itself fanning gradually outwards over the globe. An article by Frederic Harrison on "The True Cosmopolis" proclaimed that "An ideal *Cosmopolis* should from time to time have space for the five chief languages of Western Europe and for contributions from some eight or ten national centres in Europe, and two or three others in North and South America."[59] In addition to its Russian supplement, the journal planned to introduce others in Holland, Scandinavia, Italy, and Greece. To demonstrate its cosmopolitan idealism in the interim, it regularly published articles or literature on international topics, including contemporary Greek literature, Dutch colonialism in Java, ancient Arabic poetry, and the press in China and Japan. The explicit goal of many of these articles was to transcend cultural bias. For instance, condescending title notwithstanding, a recurrent column by the linguist Friedrich Max Müller on "My Indian Friends" attempted to engage contemporary European stereotypes about Indian culture by arguing for the formative influence of Indian civilization on European ideas about mathematics and music.[60] As well as being innovative in form, *Cosmopolis* was pioneering and plural-minded in content: articles by radical feminist Olive Schreiner, the French anarchist "Gyp," and notable socialists George Bernard Shaw and Henry Hyndman appeared alongside the works of more mainstream thinkers, such as the conservative MP Sir Richard Temple.

Yet despite its utopianism, *Cosmopolis* was unable to circumvent the ideological problems raised by the "network" and "neutral" periodicals. While it ostensibly shared the Enlightenment ideal of the "republic of letters" valorized by the "neutral" periodicals, its innovative, tripartite form shared with the "network" periodicals a marked investment in place. The "neutral" periodicals were largely published in London, but their emphasis on transparent communication generated a fiction of placelessness. *Cosmopolis*, by contrast, embedded itself firmly in culture, but in doing so drew attention to a central axis of European power. Just as *Cosmopolis'* table of contents page evokes the idea of transnational debate, it also vividly demonstrates the hierarchies implicit in its purportedly impartial address – the English section was always listed first, as the language with the widest reach, while the distribution centers habitually listed at bottom of the page read like a map of geopolitical power.

Non-European countries, meanwhile, were visible on the table of contents as objects, rather than producers, of knowledge (as Müller's piece, "My Indian Friends," demonstrates).

Cosmopolis' idealist hope that rational dialogue would impel nations towards cooperation was undermined not only by its fallacious universalism but also by its own doubts about the viability of universal values: a strong countercurrent of Romantic nationalism was represented in its pages as cosmopolitanism's ugly but irrepressible doppelgänger. Whereas cosmopolitanism was identified with objectivity in the majority of the journals under discussion, nationalism was associated with passionate, irrational subjectivity. Though less desirable, its appeal was imagined to be far more irrefutable. A preoccupation with the ineluctable draw of nationalism regularly crept into the journal's political analyses, prompted by all-too-prescient concerns about the escalating scale of war among the European powers: "*Cosmopolis*'s mission to promote social sympathies by encouraging genuine debate [often] seemed threatened, as the Anglo-French relationship in particular degenerated into querulous squabbling over the Egyptian situation."[61] The specter of war and of the atavistic power of nationalism underlay other aspects of the publication as well. Harrison's "The True Cosmopolis" called for a renewed "sympathy with foreign thought," but also focused on the modern-day "increase of national pride, jealousy, and self-assertion fanned by patriotic dreams of empire, Victory, and Leadership of the World."[62] Against Kantian views of the progressive tendency of globalizing forces, Harrison argues that world fairs, free trade, and the compression of the world through "railways, telegraphs, excursion tours, and postal facilities" had all done little to bring about international understanding because "Mankind are governed more by their passions, sentiments, traditions, than by their interests and even their well-being."[63]

Elsewhere in the article, Harrison claims that it "behooves all those who ... devote their lives to the moral sciences etc. to clear ... their own minds from the narrow prejudices of national chauvinism" in the interest of reaching the Arnoldian ideal of "the best that has ever been [which] never is, never can be, in a narrow sense, national."[64] Yet his conviction that mankind is irredeemably irrational, and his reflexive assertion of his own unimpeachable patriotism speaks to the period's deep-seated anxiety about nationalism's overpowering draw. An article by Frederick Greenwood on "The Safeguards of Peace" also questions the conventional wisdom about trade and commerce leading to world harmony, arguing that, in reality, trade competition between nations underlay the majority of recent conflicts, most notably the Scramble for Africa.[65]

A similarly precarious balance between cosmopolitanism and nationalism is discernible in an article by critic and historian Edward Dicey, "Why England is Unpopular," in which Dicey attempts to do justice to the journal's mission of impartiality by stepping outside his position as Englishman to answer the question posed by his title. The piece is rife with contradiction, and demonstrates the ways in which the two different versions of cosmopolitanism, along with the two different kinds of periodical space they invoked ("neutral" versus "network"), contended for primacy in the work of writers grappling with the concept. Though Dicey finds Britain's moral insularity partly to blame for its unpopularity, he also suggests that other countries are merely envious of Britain's advantageous position on the world stage. Moreover, England's distinctive moral culture is, for Dicey, the "secret of our national greatness" and should therefore be preserved at all costs:

Englishmen, who become assimilated to the inhabitants of any foreign country in which their lot is thrown, lose the native strength of their race. Grafting is not a process wont to succeed with Englishmen; and if the graft prove successful, it somehow expels the original sap.[66]

In this passage, which uses its grafting metaphor to evoke cultural and biological determination, Dicey suggests that Englishness is at once something essentially native and irreducible *and* precariously vulnerable to erosion by the very cosmopolitanism he presumably subscribes to by writing for *Cosmopolis*. Conscious of being in dialogue with French and German critics, as well as audiences in the other European cities in which the journal circulated, writers like Dicey struggled to adopt an impartial tone in the service of cosmopolitan idealism but also used their claims to objectivity, paradoxically, to render more forceful their arguments about the inviolability of national distinctions. For Dicey, then, to be a cosmopolitan critic is both to be able to set nationalism aside but also to have the strength of character to exercise this impartiality by virtue of being liberal and English.

Cosmopolis tried to overcome tensions between particularism and universalism by separating its writers into national categories to acknowledge their location in specific cultural and linguistic traditions, while also putting them into structured conversations with each other in a shared "polis" that assumed an *overlap* of cultural and political values. Yet articles like Dicey's – and the journal's obsessive preoccupation with nationalism – demonstrate that *Cosmopolis* also showcased the problems with cosmopolitanism as a journalistic and political ideal. Because of its deep commitment to cosmopolitanism and its willingness to enact it on the level of form as well as content, *Cosmopolis*, more than any of the other journals, threw into relief the impossibility of the view from nowhere; the metropolitan bias of Enlightenment idealism; and the relative anemia of cosmopolitanism as the basis of solidarity when measured against the potent authority of nationalism.

While this chapter has focused on specific references to cosmopolitan thought and global totality across a variety of Victorian media, the chapters to come turn to city literature and show how those references might lead us to read urban realism differently, as a series of narratives constituted by global, as well as national, investments. Like those commenting on the Palace, writers fascinated by the city display the desire to see London as a figure for the world. Adapting the totalizing frame of the realist novel to globally conceived visions, urban writers manipulate literary form so as to mask or make evident the inevitable hierarchies and exclusions that were painfully apparent to Victorians – more than a century before the "new" cosmopolitanisms came along.

CHAPTER 2

The sketch and the panorama: Wordsworth, Dickens, and the emergence of cosmopolitan realism

We had seen the Great Metropolis under almost every aspect. We had dived into the holes and corners hidden from the honest and well-to-do portion of the London community ... We had sought out the haunts of beggars and thieves, and passed hours communing with them as to their histories, habits, thoughts, and impulses. We had examined the World of London below the moral surface, as it were; and we had a craving, like the rest of mankind, to contemplate it from above ...

Henry Mayhew, "A Balloon View of London"[1]

In depicting city and world together, urban writers had to navigate between narrow and broad gesture, brief renderings of city types and large narrative arcs, the individual and the crowd. The visual forms of the sketch and the panorama and their adaptations over the course of the century serve as the paradigmatic antithetical modes of cosmopolitan realism. While visual sketches of the city tended to focus in on individual streets, buildings, or people, panoramic paintings – giant 360-degree canvasses that were popular public spectacles from the late eighteenth century through the nineteenth – were designed to provide an all-encompassing overview of the urban landscape. In "The Great World of London," Henry Mayhew draws upon both the sketch and the panorama to map city on to world. His work first appeared in short impressionistic installments in the *Morning Chronicle* and was self-consciously modeled on the city sketches of Joseph Addison and Richard Steele.[2] Yet his scope was more ambitious than theirs, for he imagined his sketches adding up to a panoramic vision of London that would account for all possible kinds of person and institution.

In order to achieve this momentous task, Mayhew leverages the distinct epistemological power of sketch and panorama. The view from the street – the close-up impressionistic observation of social minutiae based on first-hand experience – yields an intricate, cumulative understanding of the system. The panoramic view from above, however, provides a perspective wherein "the diverse details assume the form and order of a perspicuous unity" (7). A combination of the view from above and from below was characteristic of nineteenth-century urban representation.[3] Mayhew's sketches of various aspects of London society take on global resonances, however, via his transposing of class types on to different national and racial ones (described in the Preface). The distanced view, meanwhile, allows the city to blend into the rest of the world or take the form of the world itself. When he describes London as a planetoid, he sees it as its own world "revolving by itself around the sun" (7); he also depicts the view of the city from a balloon, cited above, from where "It was impossible to tell where the monster city began or ended ... the town seemed to blend into the sky, so that there was no distinguishing earth from heaven" (9). Used in tandem, the different views proffered by sketch and panorama conjure up a global whole.

Walter Benjamin's essay on "The Flâneur," like Mayhew's work, succinctly draws attention to the interdependence of sketch and panorama. In a preamble to his famous analysis of street-walking, Benjamin identifies a popular genre of the 1840s made up of intensely detailed physiological portraits of a range of city types and dubs it "a panorama literature."[4] Though drawn as individual sketches, Benjamin justifies his grandiose name for the portraits by emphasizing the cumulative enormity of their sociological vision, similar to that supplied by the giant 360-degree panoramic paintings that were popular in the same period: "[T]he sketches," he states, "reproduce the plastic foreground of the panoramas with their anecdotal form and the extensive background of the panoramas with their store of information" (35).

The physiological sketches are notable for Benjamin because they represent a historical moment when people had to adapt themselves to modern anonymity and its "rather strange situation ... peculiar to big cities" (40) of individuals not knowing their neighbors. Drawing on the empiricism of eighteenth-century physiognomy, the *physiologies* offered readers a reassuring intimacy with the city's myriad inhabitants: "They assured people that everyone was, unencumbered by any factual knowledge, able to make out the profession, the characters, the background, and the life-style of passers-by. In these writings this ability appears as a gift which a good fairy bestows upon an inhabitant of a big city at birth" (39). Here Benjamin echoes Dickens' famous imploration in *Dombey and Son* "for a good spirit who would take the house-tops off" to expose the vices of "our wicked cities."[5] Both Benjamin's "fairy" and Dickens' "spirit" signal the longing for a benevolent clairvoyance: one that might access encyclopedic levels of knowledge at a glance and in doing so re-enchant the city for its disoriented dwellers. Situating the tics, foibles, and skills of strangers within a readable social context, the sketches addressed the need for such a perspective, functioning as "soothing little remedies" for modernity's epistemological ills (40).

Benjamin was not the first to apply the adjective "panoramic" to nineteenth-century writing. Many realist works were self-consciously panoramic and labeled as such in their own moment; the word was affixed to a wide range of texts, including novels, newspapers, and sociological works. Contemporary critics have continued to use the term for city literature, though they identify it more specifically with the omniscient narrative techniques of the mid-century realist novel.[6] The urban sketch, however, has received significantly less critical attention than the panorama as a component of literary realism and little has been said about the relationship between the two.[7]

Benjamin saw the *physiologies* as transitory forms but his brief analysis of them has implications beyond the narrow historical ones he lays claim to.[8] In labeling the sketches a "panorama literature," he shows how the sketch gestures towards the panoramic and how the contending scales of miniature and gigantic, fragment and totality, are part of the same impulse to render the urban comprehensible. My aim in this chapter is to draw out the full implications of Benjamin's observation about the sketch and panorama in order to show the influence of both scales on realist writers as they sought to represent global space.

If realism involves the search for totality, it relies methodologically on the observation of parts. Larger truths are generated not by traditional systems of belief but by the close examination of quotidian details and specific social conditions. In his influential comparison of the novel to the epic, Georg Lukács explains that the realist novel maintains the epic's desire for totality but cannot, in the context of modern secularism, render totality with the epic's certainty and coherence.[9] That impulse is thus realized via the logic of synecdoche, where a part stands for a whole that is impossible to fully conceptualize or represent. According to Lukács' argument, the "particular web" of Middlemarch is a focused instance meant to recall a wider set of relations. But while provincial novels such as Austen's and Eliot's allude to the world outside Britain, they tend to do so obliquely; their careful delineation of local communities causes the rest of the world to recede into the background. Eliot's narrator in *Middlemarch*, for example, mentions the "growing good of the world" to which

Dorothea's individual life contributes only at the novel's end, as the narrative view pulls away from its close-up on the eponymous town.[10] This is not to say that Eliot is unaware of Middlemarch's implication in global networks.[11] But the town of Middlemarch itself is not meant to stand in for the world so much as to connect to it at its margins. In cosmopolitan realist texts, by contrast, London becomes either the world itself or a figure for global modernity – a telling instance of what the world will become – via literary techniques that mediate between different scales and planes of meaning.

Benjamin's sketches and panoramas are visual ones, but each genre had migrated into verbal representation by the start of the century and become a crucial component of urban writing. Recalling their visual counterparts, the literary sketch and panorama stressed the importance of looking to urban citizenship as well as the different levels at which urban observation should operate. The verbal sketches performed the work of differentiation and classification important to the bourgeois comprehension of the city, as well as the detailing of local culture that grounded urban literature in a particular historical and geographical reality. The panoramic mode, on the other hand, allowed for the unification of that differentiated urban space through the overview of the realist narrator, which drew upon the all-encompassing perspective of panoramic paintings.

The sketch and the panorama produced a sense of the invisible alongside the visible. By conjuring up Dickens' "good spirit," Benjamin's essay hints at the ways in which urban genres required both a moral framework to redeem the city's inequities and uncertainties, and scientific knowledge with which to order and rationalize them. The sketch and panorama addressed these different requirements through their potent mix of anthropological and allegorical epistemologies. Though focused on realistic minutiae detailing ethnic, class, and occupational differences among the city's inhabitants, the sketch of the urban type inherited allegorical resonances from one of its visual predecessors, the Cries of London. These were etchings of urban workers, usually street-vendors, with the sales "cries" they uttered transcribed underneath their images, along with legends identifying the type of work depicted. Their allegorical resonances helped writers to depict city types as parables of urban inequity rather than static figures in a social hierarchy. Similarly, the panoramic perspective of the realist narrator evoked both the wide-ranging verisimilitude of the circular paintings and their sublime effects, which emphasized the shaping power of the human imagination and its moral capacities. The combination of the two perspectives allowed urban writers to register the dizzyingly new variations of life and labor that the city put on view, while repurposing the semiotics of allegory and Christian brotherhood to the imagination of a human family: one visualized in global terms for the first time.

In the rest of the chapter I trace the literary sketch and panorama to their sources – the visual–verbal sketch of the city type and the Romantic panorama painting – as the histories of these modes help us to understand how and why they came to serve the purposes of cosmopolitan realism. I then focus on the work of an unlikely but significant practitioner of urban realism, William Wordsworth, to demonstrate how his formal and thematic approaches to the city prefigured the canonical realism of Dickens and later urban writers.

Begun in 1799, revised until 1832, and left unpublished until 1850, Wordsworth's *The Prelude* is more often associated with Romantic idealism than Victorian realism. As Raymond Williams has pointed out, however, Book 7 is "one of the major early records of new ways of seeing the city . . . with the specific character of the city, as an exceptional kind of social organization, dominant."[12] Though better known in generic nomenclature as a Romantic epic, *The Prelude* is the first major text in the period to use the techniques of realism to position the city within a global frame. The sketch-like cataloguing of urban types and the narrative overview more famously associated with steadfast ethnographers such as Mayhew and blockbuster novelists such as Dickens originally came together in his epic poem.

Wordsworth's poem not only prefigures the global vision of Dickens and the more radical cosmopolitanism of *fin-de-siècle* writing but should also be seen as the progenitor of Victorian city literature's utopian strand. Dickens' mid-century novel *Bleak House*, of course, offers a largely negative view of the city, even as it engages in the formal project of cosmopolitan realism as a means to redeem its own pessimism. By the end of the century, however, we see a return to Wordsworth's ecstatic urban reverie in the work of progressive writers such as William Morris, who take the poet's democratic epiphanies to their formal conclusions by depicting the city as a communal heaven on earth.

THE COSMOPOLITANISM OF THE VICTORIAN URBAN SKETCH

The *OED* offers virtually identical definitions for the visual and verbal sketch, suggesting their similar generic functions in each medium. One is described as "a rough drawing or delineation of something, giving the outlines or prominent features without the detail," the other as "a brief account, description, or narrative giving the main or important facts, incidents, etc., and not going into the details."[13] Both definitions emphasize the preliminary nature of the sketch, suggesting that it serves as the precursor to a more finished, embellished work.

At least in its Victorian urban incarnation, though, the sketch was notable not so much for its absence of detail as for its judicious use of it; both visual and verbal sketches used identifying details to embed their subjects in specific ethnic and class categories and geographical and historical locales. The visual and verbal sketch emerged as distinctive mimetic genres in the second half of the eighteenth century. Positioned as the immediate record of sensory impressions, their incompleteness made them appear more truthful and realistic than earlier forms of representation: "writers and artists in the Romantic period exploited the visual and verbal sketch's execution on the spot, hasty delineation, and discontinuity to situate their 'simple' and 'natural' styles against the overly sensuous, excessively elaborate, ornamental, structured and deceptive rhetoric of neoclassical artists and Royal Academicians."[14]

By the Victorian period, visual and verbal sketches had become central components of journalistic and literary representation. Endeavors as disparate as a woodcut engraving in the *Illustrated London News* and a humorous piece of travel writing by William Makepeace Thackeray partook of the sketch tradition. A number of classic works of urban realism, moreover, employed both kinds of sketches. Dickens' *Sketches by Boz* (1833–6) and Mayhew's *London Labour and the London Poor* (1861–2) are prominent examples; Mayhew's urban study was peppered with sketches of workers based on photographs, while Dickens famously used leading caricaturist George Cruikshank to illustrate *Boz* with scenes of urban life. Even within sketches that were predominantly verbal, then, the visual remained an important influence. As Martina Lauster argues in her comprehensive study of the European sketch tradition, even the written sketch is essentially a "visual-verbal genre [that] engages with processes of change happening 'before the eyes' of contemporaries. 'Sketching' implies a present-tense form of writing that depicts and interprets what is seen, thereby joining the act of 'reading' – in the literal sense – to the process of seeing and interpreting enacted on the page."[15] In their use of vivid language and minute, local detail, verbal sketches were meant to evoke empiricism's equation of vision with knowledge.

Like the *physiologies* described by Benjamin, the Victorian literary sketch was a fragmentary description of an urban scene or type, most often a gritty impression of working-class life, written in the voice of a *flâneur*-narrator who presents it as an off-the-cuff imprint of his wanderings around the city. As well as the works of Dickens and Mayhew cited above, famous sketch collections include Blanchard Jerrold and Gustave Doré's *London: A Pilgrimage* (1872) and John Thomson and Adolphe Smith's *Street Life in London* (1877).[16] Notably, even though Jerrold's introduction speaks of the "Great World of London," it elevates the sketch approach to urban representation over the panoramic mode: "It is impossible to put the world in a nutshell. To the best of our judgment we have selected the most striking types, the most completely representative scenes, and the most picturesque features of the greatest city on the face of the globe – given to us to be reduced within the limits of a volume."[17]

Three different epistemological contexts within which sketches operated gave them a cosmopolitan purview: one moral-allegorical, one transnational-comparative, and one artistic-anthropological. While these contexts necessarily overlap and inform each other, I have disaggregated them below in order to identify the specific traditions on which they drew and to analyze the different ways in which they worked to situate sketches within the city as a whole, and the polis within a wider world.

The moral-allegorical context

Much of the impact of the urban sketch's social critique derived from its moral tone, which urged its readers to bear witness to the plight of the poor. How did the sketch solicit this sympathy, though, if it was also producing a sense of the racial otherness of London's working classes? One way in which the genre balanced a universal humanism with its industrious production of difference was by reference to the Cries of London, the earliest forerunners of the Victorian visual and verbal sketch.

Starting in the sixteenth century, these illustrations took stock of the new social hierarchies created by the city by dividing urban life, typologically, into various categories of labor. Though they significantly pre-dated the encyclopedic sociological and anthropological projects undertaken by later urban chroniclers, the Cries – with their meticulous attention to detail and their identification of different workers with the kinds of clothing they wore – were also devoted to producing a sense of the enormous variety of "types" in the city. They thus served as a model for the more scientific attempts of sociologists like Mayhew to account for the vast range of employment and unemployment among London's

Chimney Sweep
Ramonner la Cheminee
Spazza Camino

Maurón delin: *P. Tempest exc:*
                                                                    cum Privilegio

Figure 2.1 Marcellus Laroon, "Chimney Sweep"

working poor.[18] Published as an ensemble of sketches in 1687, and reissued regularly up through 1821, Marcellus Laroon's *The Cryes of the City of London Drawne after the Life* were the most influential, frequently imitated, and widely circulated of these illustrations. Just as Laroon's sketches laid a claim to realism in their very title, so did Victorian sketch-series, such as Dickens' *Sketches by Boz*, which purported to be "Illustrative of Everyday Life and Everyday People" (Figures 2.1 and 2.2).

The London Begger
Le Gueux de Londres
La pouera di Londra

Figure 2.2 Marcellus Laroon, "The London Begger"

But even as they provided a mimetic view of the city, contributed to the development of a realistic artistic tradition influenced by newer scientific modes, and focused on the specificity of different local spaces and peoples, Laroon's sketches also worked allegorically, serving as a sign of God-given social hierarchies. As well as scientific discourses like natural history, the Cries were visually indebted in style to the art of religious iconography and the allegorical illustrations of Renaissance emblem books. Sean Shesgreen notes that: "the presiding figures of early Cries were empowered by the realms of religion and the supernatural."[19] Figures in early Cries, such as the watchman and the bellman, often looked like "medieval guildsmen from a unified and godly city."[20]

The Cries circulated widely in the Victorian period; "Everybody who studies London possesses, among his collection, pictures of the street cries," Walter Besant declared.[21] The Cries were popular among art collectors and urban investigators, while Katie Trumpener has shown that urban picture books used them to teach middle-class children to empathize with the urban poor.[22] Mayhew's work, for instance, was identifiably influenced by the style of the Cries. According to Alexander Welsh, "some features of Mayhew's work may readily be traced to ... books that exhibited the street cries and costumes of London as oddities worth illustrating to the gentry."[23] One such feature is Mayhew's use of props in his sketches. Tim Barringer notes that, as in Laroon's illustrations, the tools of Mayhew's workers symbolize their place in a social hierarchy: "tools take the place of attributes in traditional Western Christian iconography by which individual apostles or saints were identified within a known scheme."[24]

Victorian urban sketches differ from the London Cries, however, in their emphasis on environment. While Laroon's figures are lifted out of their milieu and placed against a white background, Boz's and Mayhew's illustrations tend to situate their urban types within a distinct setting (Figure 2.3). The written sketches that accompany their illustrations embed city-dwellers even more precisely within specific systems and locations in order to stress the toll these environments take on the urban poor. Even less journalistic and more avowedly impressionistic accounts of the city, such as Jerrold and Doré's *London: A Pilgrimage*, which claimed to be "a touch and go chronicle," presented detailed wood-engravings of figures of poverty, such as that of a match-seller (Figure 2.4), that were meant to epitomize the specific locales detailed in the narrative.

In their contemporaneity, Victorian urban sketches built up a secular moral vocabulary that combined a Christian sense of compassion for the poor with a social science language of diagnosis and prognostication. Both of these visions aspired to a Cries-like universalism tempered by a steadfast dedication to local context – a vision that we might think of as "cosmopolitan" in its attempt to deduce from the specifics of urban life a larger human collectivity with which the reader might identify. The vast and "invisible" world of global capitalism, though not named as such,

THE JEW OLD CLOTHES-MAN.

" Clo', Clo', Clo'."

Figure 2.3 Richard Beard, "The Jew Old Clothes-Man"

is often indicted as the larger system of causality uniting mankind. Mayhew's depiction of "The Maimed Irish Crossing-sweeper" in *London Labour and the London Poor*, for instance, traces the sweeper's doleful trajectory from his birth in Ireland to the job of bricklayer in Wales, and finally to

LE MARCHAND D'ALLUMETTES.

Figure 2.4 Gustave Doré, "Le Marchand D'Allumettes" ("The Match-Seller")

his occupation as match-seller and crossing-sweeper in London. Much of the sketch is fleshed out by a series of quotes from the subject in response to an interview question: "Yes, sir, I smoke; it's a comfort, it is. I like any kind I'd get to smoke. I'd like the best if I got it."[25] While these pedestrian statements seem designed to underscore the realism of Mayhew's documentary work, the sweeper's words are overlaid with a metaphorical significance underscored by Mayhew's brief introduction to the character: "He says he is thirty-six, but looks more than fifty; and his face has the ghastly expression of death."[26] Though the middle-class reader is called upon to pity, rather than identify with, the pathetic figure of the maimed sweeper, the parable-like format of the sketch turns the worker from a social outlier into a grim specter of mortality and social inequity, compelling readers to respond with their consciences to the sketch's allegorical resonances.

The fact that this tale is placed alongside a myriad of similar ones also means that the reader must translate a conventional moral response into a far-reaching understanding of the broad social context that has produced so many wretched figures: a context that might move a man from Ireland to Wales to London and "maim" him along the way. While the moral-allegorical context of the urban sketch was borrowed partly from the Cries, it did not have full recourse to the medieval Christian framework to which Laroon alluded. As Richard Maxwell has argued, "the allegorical method appropriate to exploring a divine reality could not be borrowed to make sense of city experiences" – yet it could be adapted to include "new criteria for what it means to know the city."[27] Written sketches of the city aspired to a kind of natural supernaturalism – a "secularized form of devotional experience" – wherein the vexing details of urban life served as evidence of a vast global network of interconnection: one that demanded a capacious and redemptive moral vision.[28]

The transnational-comparative context

Lauster's study of the sketch in European journalism emphasizes its transnational circulation: "visual-verbal sketches as thumbnail social studies thrived and traversed medial and national boundaries with ease."[29] The scope of her study, which examines the sketch in Britain, France, Germany, and Austria and moves between these national contexts, also testifies to the sketch's transnationalism. In some cases, moreover, aspects of the sketch tradition incorporated a process of cross-cultural comparison, whereby individual artists and writers appropriated the sketches and caricatures of their peers in other European countries and used them to satirize or describe their own countries, while implicitly reflecting on the country of origin. *Punch*, for example, borrowed from illustrations in the French *Le Charivari*, as did a *Charivari* collection published in Leipzig;

"This constitutes one of the examples of cross-national sketch production," Lauster argues, "where the image is assimilated to the national context of the respective satirical journal, but thanks to the recognizably Parisian provenance of the image, the text of the sketch also vibrates with cosmopolitan sentiment."[30]

The influential trope of the devil Asmodeus in the sketch tradition also speaks to the sketches' comparative character. A lame demon who first appeared in *El Diablo Cojuelo* by Luis Vélez de Guevara (1641), then in Alain René Lesage's *Le Diable boîteux* (1707), Asmodeus featured in a number of eighteenth-century British texts before resurfacing in Edward Bulwer-Lytton's serial "Asmodeus at Large" (published in the *New Monthly Magazine* from January to June 1832).[31] A satirical figure who could lift off rooftops to expose the vices within, Asmodeus is the transnational progenitor of Dickens' more domesticated good fairy in *Dombey and Son.* He embodied "a supranational spirit of the times ... representing overviewing and penetrating vision and an acute ability to diagnose the state of the contemporary European body."[32]

While particular kinds of sketches like the *Charivari* or the Asmodean ones focused on individual national ills, readers would have been aware of their larger, transnational context because of recurrent characters (like Asmodeus himself) and the recognizable artistic styles that were replicated across national traditions. In *Bleak House,* for instance, Inspector Bucket famously looks out on the city imaginatively from a "high tower in his mind"; it is no doubt because of this Asmodean quality of seeming omniscience that Hortense, the French maid he arrests for Tulkinghorn's murder, repeatedly calls him a "devil."

In a sketch in his "Streets of the World" series, George Sala – whose interest in cosmopolitanism took the form of satire in relation to the Great Exhibition (see Chapter 1) – evokes Asmodeus in berating the "noble lords and rich merchants" responsible for London's tenements: "What spiteful Asmodeus could have whispered evil counsel in their ear, and cozened them into erecting comfortless hovels, in order that he, the lame devil, might more at his leisure unroof them, and expose the crimes, follies, and miseries sweltering within?"[33] The fact that this statement appears in a sketch about Paris rather than London is telling, for Sala's comparison of the two cities is vital to his critique.

The "Streets" sketches, published in *Temple Bar* from 1863 to 1866, take full advantage of the transnational mode. It is not surprising that Sala, originally an artist, was drawn to the visual-verbal form of the sketch; the ambitious "Streets" series gave him ample opportunity to paint the impressionistic "word-pictures" associated with the sketch form. The series charts an impressive range of streets and cities, including La Cannébière in Marseilles, Pall Mall in London, the Puerta del Sol in Madrid, George Street in Sydney, the Balschoï-Morskaïa in St. Petersburg, Broadway in New York, Calle del Obispo in Havana, Calle San Francisco in Mexico, and the street of Bab-Azzoun in Algiers. The introduction to the series stresses both the detail of the sketches – "the microscopic observation and the marvellous word-photography" and their panoramic scope.[34] Sala calls the sketches "my panorama of the Streets of the World" and compares himself at the end of his journey to Odysseus returning to Penelope, simultaneously driving home his cosmopolitan status and the epic expanse of his work.[35]

While Sala's street sketches are meant to function primarily as a form of entertainment, he cannot resist contributing to the discourse of social reform with which the sketch genre had become associated by mid-century. London, the home of his target audience, is the locus of his intermittent calls for reform, but the sketches rely on their panoramic breadth as an international series for the force of their individual critique. Comparing the Passage de Panoramas in Paris favorably to London's major streets, Sala laments the effect of feudal laws and aristocratic property rights on the crowded and dilapidated architecture of British cities: an architecture he associates with "dirt, disease, destitution, profligacy, vice, and crime."[36] Sala's "Streets" series is a unique blend of the urban and travel sketch, but it demonstrates the degree to which sketch writers assumed a familiarity with the Asmodean tradition and its transnational comparative character.

The artistic-anthropological context

As well as being part of a satiric tradition, urban sketches partook of the nineteenth-century nexus of art and anthropology. Though focused on local city scenes, the urban sketch evoked the exoticism and cosmopolitan *flânerie* of art produced on aristocratic journeys to the Continent and colonies, for many eighteenth-century visual sketches were the work of gentlemen-artists on their Grand Tour.[37] Wordsworth's sketches of Europe, for example, "promised to deliver a virtual letter-press Grand Tour."[38] The travel sketch-writing of authors such as Thackeray and Anthony Trollope performed a similar function, delivering the revolutionary cities of Europe and the uncharted expanses of empire to the doorstep of less leisured or adventurous readers. Drawing on their association with travel sketches, urban ones accentuated the home-grown exoticism of the scenes they depicted. Thus, in his description of a disreputable gin-shop, Boz stresses his own intrepidity by noting that "[t]he filthy and miserable appearance of this part of London can hardly be imagined by those (and there are many such) who have not witnessed it."[39]

If the urban written sketch took on the cultural voyeurism and cosmopolitan glamour of the travel sketch, it also adopted the scientism of physiognomy sketches (the type referred to by Benjamin as *physiologies*). In *The Artist as Anthropologist*, Mary Cowling describes the ways in which Victorian artists, particularly those interested in the city, used physiognomy to tell detailed stories about the character and class of the individuals they depicted. Anthropology, she argues, contributed to the methodology and interpretive framework of physiognomy in both visual and verbal sketches.[40] Mayhew, for example, drew explicitly on one of anthropology's foundational texts, James Cowle Prichard's *The Natural History of Man* (1843).[41] Imitating the language of synthetic projects like Prichard's, which sought to prove the unity of man through a massive study of "native" cultures around the world, Mayhew stated that his own project was to construct a "thorough and correct grouping of objects into genera and species, orders and varieties."[42]

The urban sketch's connection to anthropology was one of the ways in which it connected London to other parts of the world. Because of the city's diversity, it was thought by many to contain, in physiognomic terms at least, all possible types of person. As a result, it could supply those who wished to study humanity with a vision of the globe in microcosm; an article in *Household Words* stated that "We have no need to go abroad to study ethnology ... a walk through the streets of London will show us specimens of every human variety known."[43]

As many critics have noted, this anthropological frame often led to the treatment of "uncharted" working-class territories as uncivilized backwaters, there to be discovered by the *flâneur*-narrator and interpreted to the less intrepid. General William Booth notoriously made the connection between imperial and urban exploration explicit in the title of his reformist work, *In Darkest England* (see Chapter 4), while in earlier sketch-writing workers of different ethnicities became stereotypically associated with certain kinds of labor – Jews with trade, for example.[44] Boz depicts both Irish and Jewish city-dwellers unflatteringly, while Mayhew systematically identifies various races as well as classes with different kinds of work and street entertainment, thereby naturalizing the relationship between identity and labor.

If the language of racial exoticism informed urban sketches, the sociological value of the urban sketch as a tool of assimilative knowledge informed imperial writing as well. Abundant sketches, both visual and verbal, were produced by British travelers and administrators in the colonial context to provide those back home with information about newly conquered territories. Sketches thus took part in the process that David Cannadine calls "Ornamentalism," whereby the empire was "the vehicle for the extension of British social structures, and the setting for the project of British social perceptions, to the ends of the world – and back again."[45]

In the face of the seemingly overwhelming proliferation of "types," cataloged both in the urban landscape and across the empire, sketches attempted to capture people and places with scientific accuracy, arresting the seeming chaos of time in the process.[46] But their scientific outlook also reified social hierarchies by depicting them as biologically determined. In "Meditations of Monmouth Street," for instance, Dickens' use of the language of natural history elides the social mobility and shifts in community characteristic of urban polities. Boz observes that:

The inhabitants of Monmouth Street are a distinct class; a peaceable and retiring race, who immure themselves for the most part in deep cellars, or small back parlors, and who seldom come forth into the world, except in the dusk and coolness of evening, when they may be seen seated, in chairs on the pavement, smoking their pipes, or watching the gambols of their engaging children as they revel in the gutter, a happy troop of infantine scavengers.[47]

In some cases, however, the sketch genre used the artistic-anthropological mode to critique the exoticism and condescension often implicit within it. In a 2007 exhibition at the Yale Center for British Art, Gillian Forrester, Tim Barringer, and Barbara Martinez-Ruiz showcased the visual sketches of Jewish Jamaican artist Isaac Mendes Belisario, *Sketches of Character, in Illustration of the Habits, Occupation, and Costume of the Negro Population in the Island of Jamaica* (1837). The curators demonstrated how Belisario, who was born in London, referenced the Cries tradition (Figure 2.5) and argue that his sketches of workers and carnival-goers can be read as an attempt "to bolster a sense among its inhabitants of Jamaica's sophistication, rather than to convey it to a metropolitan constituency, since there is no evidence that he made any effort to distribute the series outside Jamaica."[48] In the preface to his work, Belisario explicitly pitted it against caricature, suggesting that he may have seen it as a corrective to representations of

Figure 2.5 I. M. Belisario, "Water-Jar Sellers"

black people in Britain, many of which appeared in caricature form. By contrast, Belisario's sketches of the formerly enslaved give the sense that "on becoming 'full free,' they will perform their role as citizens in the creation of a new order for Jamaica":

His subjects are neither "images of the outcast," to use Sean Shesgreen's characterization of the "Cries" tradition, nor even necessarily representatives of the "urban poor" ... but apprentices or free blacks, on the threshold of acquiring economic and political autonomy in a new Jamaica.[49]

In London, meanwhile, minority writers used sketches to accentuate the city's diversity and undermine the racial and ethnic caricatures frequently found in mainstream sketch-writing. The Anglo-Jewish writer Amy Levy subtitled her short novel *Reuben Sachs* (1888) "A Sketch," thereby evoking the ethnographic veracity associated with the term. Though heavily inflected by contemporary stereotypes of Jewish life, her detailed portrait of a London Jewish family counters the thinness of the sketches of Jewish street-merchants that proliferated elsewhere, while her embedding of the family in London life and local community challenges the stereotypes that associated Jews exclusively with transience and commerce.[50]

In a different urban context, W. E. B. DuBois employed many of the sketch techniques used by mid-Victorian urban writers in his 1899 socio-logical work, *The Philadelphia Negro*; while he replicated the tendency of these writers to stratify urban society into those who were more or less to blame for their plight, his emphasis on structural obstacles to social advance-ment cut to the core of American discourses of racial inferiority. William Wells Brown's *Sketches of People and Places Abroad*, meanwhile, uses the sketch tradition to accentuate the internationalism of the abolitionist move-ment and to contest stereotypes of black illiteracy and backwardness with the cosmopolitan knowledge of art and travel that his own writing demonstrates (see Chapter 1). While frequently involved in the cataloging and maintenance of class and racial hierarchies, the sketch genre could also produce a more capacious and multi-faceted view of the city's different cultures.

The different cosmopolitan frameworks outlined above – moral-allegorical, transnational-comparative, and artistic-anthropological – were interwoven throughout the Victorian urban sketch tradition. Rather than retrace argu-ments about whether the sketch form consolidates or unsettles the freedoms and privileges associated with the middle-class artists and writers who created them, I have instead drawn attention to how these different contexts contended with the scale of urban modernity and how, in doing so, they took part in both reactive and progressive views of social change.[51] The next section shows how the urban panorama embodied a similarly large-scale yet conflicted stance. As the sketch and panorama became part of the architecture of urban literary realism, so did their ambivalent visions of urban collectivity.

"PAINTING WITHOUT BORDERS": THE CITY PANORAMA

Early nineteenth-century panoramic paintings grew out of the Romantic landscape painting tradition and its association of aesthetic experience with the contemplation of nature. Many panoramic paintings chose as their subject-matter a suitably sublime natural spectacle, such as the *Ascent of Mont Blanc*.[52] Perhaps the most innovative and fashionable subject of panoramas, however, was the city, for the panoramic spectacle was itself an urban phenomenon. In Britain, the spectacle appeared mostly in London, where it was first patented, but it appeared in other large British cities as well, such as Edinburgh and Manchester. As its popularity grew, the panorama increasingly reflected the urban context of its production, specializing in the representation of the British capital and other international cities.[53] Panoramas of London, such as Thomas Girtin's *Eidometropolis* (1802), Henry Aston Barker's *Panorama of London from the Albion Mills* (1792), and Thomas Hornor's *Panorama of London* (1830) in the Colosseum, were the best known and best attended of these.[54] Other city panoramas, such as those of Rome and Constantinople, also drew crowds and were shown as many as three times apiece.[55] (While panoramas were vast static displays, they were usually put up for discrete periods of time; they were then dismantled, so they could be exhibited at different locations around the nation.)

The spectacle was understood to "transport" the viewer in two ways; first, through the intensity of its sublime grandeur and, second, through its extension of the experience of the aristocratic Grand Tour to the middle and working classes. While the panorama drew upon, and exaggerated, the scale of Romantic landscape art in its attempt to produce an affective response in its spectator, it also had a self-consciously pedagogical function, educating its viewers about contemporary events (such as imperial and Napoleanic battles) and different parts of the world. Whether critics focus on the aesthetic appeal of the panorama, with its aspirations to Royal Academy approval, or on its anthropological, educational function as a chronicler of the development of cities and of the living conditions of people around the globe, they remain divided on the question of its ideological valence.[56]

A number of commentators have made much of the simultaneous emergence of the 360-degree painting and Bentham's notorious panoptical tower.[57] Jonathan Crary argues, for instance, that early nineteenth-century visual technologies were central to the "capitalist rationalization of visual attentiveness."[58] Urban spectatorship, as incarnated in such forms as the panorama, participated in the "sovereignty and autonomy of vision and the standardization and regulation of that vision," turning the individual into a "mobile consumer of a ceaseless succession of illusory commodity-like images."[59] Stephan Oettermann, also concerned with panopticism, draws a damning parallel between the panorama and the enclosures of the Romantic period, arguing that the literal appropriation of nature by bourgeois agriculture during the enclosures is mirrored by the visual appropriation of land sponsored by the panoramas' all-encompassing gaze.[60] Bernard Comment, too, emphasizes the convenience of panoramic form to nineteenth-century modes of assimilative knowledge: "It gave individuals the happy feeling that the world was organized around and by them, yet this was a world from which they were also separated and protected, for they were seeing it from a distance. A double dream came true – one of totality and of possession; encyclopaedism on the cheap."[61]

Imperial history and geography were important and pervasive subjects of the panorama in this regard: for the mass public, panoramas served as part of an "imperial archive" (Thomas Richards' term) of knowledge about parts of the world in which British interests lay.[62] Alongside visual depictions of imperial battles, such as the *Storming of Seringapatam*, and landscapes that depicted colonial territories, the panoramas also provided anthropological and geographic information about different countries through the "Descriptions" that accompanied them: booklets which mapped out and provided detailed facts about the spectacle at hand and that were often designed to encourage emigration, financial speculation, or simply bureaucratic-imperial knowledge of the area. A "Description" of a Panorama of Mexico, for example, states that "Mexico offers the greatest advantage to commercial speculation," while one of Calcutta carefully delineates the role of various Indian servants in the landscape; a "Bihishtee ... or water carrier ... supplies houses with water ... they are a very numerous body of Hindoos, and invariably dress in deep red cotton cloth."[63]

Within the rounded space of the panorama, viewers attained what Crary helpfully dubs an "ambulatory ubiquity," able to take in every aspect of the "world" enclosed by the panoramic space and thus to participate in the illusion that foreign lands might be apprehended at a glance.[64] Apart from the wide range of cities and foreign landscapes portrayed, which in itself aided the public's sense that panoramas were a portal to the rest of the world, the fact that they often included fully accurate, to-scale paintings of every visible building in the landscape implied a systematic, cartographical knowledge of their subjects. London's "Great Globe" exhibit, for instance, catered to Victorian desires literally to see the world as "a closely organized whole."[65] A three-dimensional panoramic exhibit on view at the same time as the Great Exhibition, it consisted of a giant hollow globe painted internally with a map of the world. While usually not three-dimensional in form, the more conventional 360-degree city panorama would also have suggested a worldly perspective through its circular and bounded shape, even when it focused on a single city.

Despite the panoptical and imperial valences of the panorama, however, another set of critics argues that the worldly knowledge and experience it offered had egalitarian resonances. William Galperin, in a reading of the form influenced by Benjamin, challenges the idea that it had an inherently disciplinary function and argues that, rather than cultivating an aura, the panorama generated a dependence on the *eye* (as opposed to the highly evolved and educated *mind* of the Romantic poet), making it a democratic and novel experience rather than a conservative one: "the Panorama can be said to appeal to the body seeing, to a body that is anybody's, and therefore any body."[66] Furthermore, its dislocating formal effects prevent it from lending the viewer the "stable and controlling subject-position" often constructed by classical painting perspective.[67]

Correlatively, Richard Altick's historical perspective traces, in the panorama's appeal to a mass audience, and in its wide-ranging subject-matter, a movement towards less elitist forms of art and less rigid and exclusionary ideas about culture. The panoramas' educational quality, he argues, had the salutary effect of decreasing British insularity, however superficially, at a particularly jingoistic moment. He cites one commentator in the *Athenaeum* remarking exuberantly (if also exaggeratedly) on the fact that "Lucknow, New York, Canton, San Francisco, Delhi, Constantinople and St. Petersburgh are all as familiar, even to our children, as Paris or Rome, Brighton or Bath."[68] An important aspect of the panorama's historical function, then, was the fact that it was an influential art form actually accessible to the working and middle classes at a time when museums and galleries rarely offered public exhibits.

Panoramas, like the Crystal Palace, were not always open at times working people could attend them and were commercial enterprises that demanded entry fees. Yet the fact that they were systematically marketed to a mass audience suggests that they expected, and received, such an audience in sizable numbers.[69] Furthermore, the public nature of the viewing experience would necessarily have made it different from the individuated experience of "totality and possession" that Comment and others argue was produced by the panorama's panoptical form. Since virtually anybody who could pay the modest entrance fee could attend the panorama, the visitor would always have been viewing with a varied and excited crowd. Contributing to the experience of a shared and volatile, rather than exclusive, space was the fact that the panorama placed every spectator in the center of the painting at once. The commanding view offered by the panoramas was thus open not only to everyone, but to everyone simultaneously.

Panorama painters themselves exploited the language of democracy and the idea that they were bringing the "Grand Tour" to the public. J. R. Smith's moving panorama, the *Tour of Europe*, for instance, was accompanied by a description that touted his art's educational and enlightening qualities – "A Panorama is a moving lesson, a pictorial guide, a refined and elegant manner of bringing before the mind of the spectator the appearance and characteristics of different countries" – and hence its democratic virtues: "The Telegraph, the Railway, and the Steamboat have been making great changes and doing their utmost to bring about a brotherhood of nations; may not also the pencil of the artist claim its share in this great work?"[70] Smith's suggestion that the panorama performs a complementary function to modern technologies of travel and communication that made the world experientially smaller serves as a powerful claim for the spectacle's modernity and timeliness. Mobilizing contemporary excitement about the progressive potential of a world made smaller, Smith puts the panorama and its representation of world cities at the vanguard of globalizing forces by implying that the artist's delicate and creative "pencil," as opposed to the automaton energy of the telegraph, railway, and steamboat, might be particularly well suited to render visible and accessible the "great work" of international brotherhood.

As this account of panorama criticism makes clear, the 360-degree spectacle, like the verbal and visual sketch, was a deeply ambivalent formation, complex enough to be read as both conservative and progressive; adaptable enough to serve as imperial propaganda-tool or as champion of cosmopolitan democracy. Ever since D. A. Miller famously associated the panopticism of the Victorian novel with the deployment of institutional power delineated by Michel Foucault in *Discipline and Punish*, its totalizing overview – like that of the panoramic painting – has been coupled with the exclusions and strictures of bourgeois ideology. But, like the panoramic painting, literary panoramas had utopian resonances as well. In the early part of the century, before the mid-century realist novel adopted the panoramic perspective associated with Romantic painting, Wordsworth's *The Prelude* used the panorama's sublime horizons, together with references to the sketch tradition, to read London as a metaphor for the "unity of man." Notwithstanding his suspicion of the mimetic ambitions of the panorama, these popular entertainments provide the occasion for Wordsworth's simultaneously reified and destabilized vision of the city, to which I now turn.

THE SKETCH, THE PANORAMA, AND THE URBAN SUBLIME: WORDSWORTH'S UTOPIAN CITYSCAPE

Halfway through his epic fourteen-book poem *The Prelude*, William Wordsworth changes subject from the country to the city, presenting a view of London as a dazzling, bewildering conglomeration of sights and spectacles. Among the visual "entertainments" that come under his scrutiny are panoramic paintings, which he satirizes as "those sights that ape / the absolute presence of reality" (7.232–3).[71] Here and throughout Book 7, Wordsworth's implicit critique of mimesis is connected to his ambivalent attitude towards the city and the alienation and commodification that accompany its pleasures. The panorama is only one in a series of spectacles that contribute to his disoriented experience of London as a "perpetual whirl / Of trivial objects, melted and reduced / To one identity, by differences / That have no law, no meaning and no end" (7.725–8).

Despite Wordsworth's antipathy to the city's capitalist energies, his mildly derogatory view of the panorama seems itself to have been forged in the spirit of competition. The giant, 360-degree spectacle that proliferated across the same period in which Wordsworth was composing and revising his epic poem was, like his work, a large-scale, ambitious, and public attempt to comprehend the city's mind-boggling size and heterogeneity. Though he was evidently suspicious of the panorama, I will argue that Wordsworth's vision and that created by the city panorama are closely connected in their use of a mode best described as a type of urban sublime. In both *The Prelude* and the panorama, this mode serves as a vital conduit between image and imagination, the realist detail and the romantic infinite, the local and the global.

Wordsworth famously describes panoramas as:

> ... those sights that ape
> The absolute presence of reality,
> Expressing, as in mirror, sea and land,
> And what earth is, and what she hath to shew.
> I do not here allude to subtlest craft
> By means refined attaining purest ends
> But imitations fondly made in plain
> Confession of Man's weakness and his loves;

Whether the Painter, whose ambitious skill
Submits to nothing less than taking in
A whole horizon's circuit, do, with power
Like that of angels or commissioned Spirits,
Fix us upon some lofty Pinnacle,
Or in a Ship on Waters, with a World
Of Life, and life-like mockery, beneath
Above, behind, far-stretching, and before. (7.232–47)

Here, Wordsworth's concern that panoramas "ape" reality and that they are "imitations" that betray "Man's weakness" with their "life-like mockery" prefigures Crary's sense that the panorama produces a simulacral experience of "illusory commodity-like images." Both writers, in other words, are concerned about the panorama's alienating effect – its ability to substitute representation for direct experience. Similarly, Wordsworth's description of the Painter's "ambitious skill," in which the artist greedily settles for nothing less than "taking in / A whole horizon," thereby assuming a god-like, "lofty" view of the world ("that of angels or commissioned Spirits"), overlaps with Oettermann's critique of the omniscient realist gaze constructed by the panorama and its complicity with modern structures of power that depend on surveillance and rationalization.

A crucial element of the panorama's effect, however, is its ability to proffer both an abundance of realist detail and an experience of the sublime. While some critics, such as Gillen D'Arcy Wood (and Wordsworth himself, in Wood's account), argue that the panorama is in fact "anti-sublime" because of its "'narrow taste' for life-like detail," its appeal to the imagination of global space at the horizon meant that it necessarily transcended its visual dimensions, encouraging a new kind of interiorization that was, paradoxically, outward-looking rather than solipsistic.[72]

The panorama, through its sheer size, dwarfed the Romantic landscape painting's attempt to convey the sublime. More importantly, though, it deliberately played up its potentially sublime effect, doggedly contesting the relegation to "low art" status that accompanied its commercial character and mass appeal. Robert Barker's panoramas, for example, made use of the "contrast between the darkened platform and intense lighting that fell from a concealed source onto the canvas" in order to suggest infinity, while panoramas' descriptions often employed aesthetic language.[73] The description of a *Panorama of Edinburgh*, for instance, draws the viewer's attention to the fact that the painting is both "beautiful and sublime."[74] Similarly, a souvenir-book that accompanied the panorama in Regent's Park stressed the spectacle's "grandeur and sublimity":

The ocean viewed from the summit of a high cliff – a boundless expanse of country, when seen from the apex of a lofty mountain, are unquestionably objects of grandeur and sublimity; but both are dull and vacant, when compared with the astonishing view of London from the top of St. Paul's . . . The Colosseum as a building, and the panoramic picture it contains, are works of such novelty, magnitude and singularity, that they seem almost to defy the powers of description, and to baffle all attempts at being represented through the medium of language.[75]

What most effectively bolstered these claims to sublimity, though, was the panorama's horizon, which both reinforced and deconstructed its representation of bounded space.[76]

In his essay "The Sublime in Landscape," Wordsworth himself theorizes that the sublime is produced by "whatever suspends the comparing powers of the mind and possesses it with a feeling or image of intense unity without a conscious contemplation of parts," and the sublime effects of *The Prelude* most closely recall this formulation.[77] Nature provides an awe-inspiring spectacle that perplexes the mind but also inspires it to greater heights of imagination and momentary perceptions of totality.

The mind itself is often represented through spatial images in order that the poet can represent the relationship between the landscape that the mind considers and the mind's response to it: "The tendency of these spatializing metaphors . . . is to bestow upon the mind what Descartes had declared to be the essential and distinguishing characteristic of matter alone, namely, extension."[78] Here, as in Wordsworth's view of the city in "Residence in London," the imagination depends on an image – on the mind's reproduction of the visual field in order to view itself viewing nature. In Book 13, when Wordsworth returns to the idea that his love of man originated in nature, he describes the experience of moving from nature to man using the imagery of mental extension ("the horizon of my mind enlarged" [13.51]); in the ascent of Mount Snowdon in Book 14, nature and the human mind become temporarily indistinguishable:

> There I beheld the emblem of a mind
> That feeds upon infinity, that broods
> Over the dark abyss, intent to hear
> Its voices issuing forth to silent light
> In one continuous stream; a mind sustained
> By recognitions of transcendent power,
> In sense conducting to ideal form . . .   (14.70–76)

Wordsworth's view from the summit offers a sense of unity between mind and matter, and between form and infinity.

The panorama is undoubtedly more dependent on the visual than *The Prelude*, but its form, like Wordsworth's, foregrounds an act of imaginative assimilation. Hornor's Colosseum panorama, for example, depicting the view of London from the top of St. Paul's Cathedral attempts to represent the boundlessness of its chosen subject while simultaneously enacting the mind's ability to encompass this "infinity" through the horizon. Visitors to the panorama viewed it from platforms that put the horizon at eye-level. Yet the impossibility of taking in the whole of its 360-degree circumference meant not only that the viewer was destabilized, as Galperin contends, but that she was required to conceptualize the globe suggested by the panorama's shape without being able to look at it all directly. What she would experience, then, was Wordsworth's interiorized "feeling for the whole."

Its size and overwhelming attention to the details of the city's architectural and anthropological life were important aspects of the panorama's attempt to convey the sublimity of the urban. Part of its dizzying nature stemmed from the shift in scale from the foreshortened architectural detail at the front of the painting to the infinite space represented by the sea and sky in the background, but the circular shape of the horizon holds the whole together to provide a sense of unity. In a description of the Colosseum panorama in the *Daily News* of April 22, 1851, the writer claims to be rendered "breathless" by the spectacle, but still describes it in the language of organic form:

... the spectator, by the magic power of machinery, is gently spirited away to a giddy elevation, whence as fine an imaginary view of the 'Modern Babel,' with its vast circulatory system – its great arteries of traffic and the lace-like fretwork of smaller streets, and lanes, and alleys, by which the mighty pulse of busy restlessness is conveyed to and from its most hidden recesses – can be obtained as from the breathless height of St. Paul's gilded cross.

In this account, the unfathomable otherness of the city evoked by the familiar comparison of London to Babel is resolved into a provisional totality by humanizing images relating to the body and to artistic production: "circulatory system," "arteries of traffic," and "fretwork."

The painting is constructed to lend itself to such a reading (Figure 2.6). Offering a view of London from St. Paul's cathedral, a central architectural node of the capital, the perspective is set up so that the "main arteries" of streets, rows of houses, and the river, extend from the viewer's perspective outwards and gradually fade away at the horizon, which holds the whole system together in its enveloping light. As the painting's rendition reminds us, the dome of the Cathedral was, in the moment of the painting, covered

Figure 2.6 "Colosseum Panorama."

with scaffolding for repairs. It was thus conveniently accessible to Horner, the panorama's painter, who assembled most of his sketches for the final painting from that vantage-point. Including the scaffolding in the painting itself was a way of providing realistic immediacy, but also another method by which the panorama brings into view the shaping hand of the artist, stressing the imposition of form on formlessness.

While the horizon helps to give the impression of a totality, knitting the highly differentiated spectacle of the city together, it also opens the painting outwards. Even more than horizons in traditional paintings, the panoramic horizon symbolizes infinity because of its curve, which suggests circularity. The natural light let in from the top of the panorama, reflecting against the lighter colors of the painted sky and the clouds as the eye moves upward, augments the impression of a heavenly radiance around the city, and of the idea of infinity at the point of the horizon. The horizon thus simultaneously imposes form and undoes it through the opposing suggestion of endless regress and plenitude. In the Colosseum panorama, in particular, the buildings continue as far as the eye can see – no pastoral space neatly hems in the city. The painting, then, demands the use of both the eye *and* the imagination. By extending the city outwards into the world, it asks the viewer to contemplate the infinite.

Their use of the horizon provides an explanation for why panoramas were described by contemporaries as "paintings without borders."[79] They were global not only because they depicted a range of cities from around the world but because, in their emphasis on the infinite and all-encompassing extension of the horizon, they situated their landscapes within a global whole. Through the encircling form of the panorama, the city *became* the world. In defiance of the empirical knowledge bestowed by the panorama descriptions (and by the topographical accuracy of the paintings), the horizon conveyed mystery, leaving the world depicted undefined at its borders and idealized by lighting effects meant to evoke a heavenly aura. It trained the eye to see not only the world on the canvas but the other world out there, at the limit of the canvas. The heavenly city, global brotherhood, and the expanse of empire, all alternately associated with the panorama in this period, were contending visions of totality and infinity brought into view through the panorama's sublime effects.

Thus when Wordsworth describes the panorama as taking in a "whole horizon's circuit," its "World of life" is all-encompassing: "Above, behind, far stretching, and before." Despite the poet's disparagement of the "mockery" of the panorama, the meter and sense of this line echo that with which he celebrates the powers of the imagination in Book 6. Just as he redeems the disappointment of the Simplon Pass crossing by re-reading natural sights as "Characters of the great Apocalypse / The types and symbols of Eternity, / Of first, and last, and midst, and without end" (6.638–40), so Wordsworth moves in Book 7 to employ the simulacrum as a visionary instrument.

The importance of Book 7 to the 1850 *Prelude* and its representation of the "growth of a poet's mind" is evidenced by its placement in the structural and symbolic center of the poem. In the literal and metaphorical journey that makes up the poem's trajectory, Wordsworth's visit to London assumes a vital position, presenting a jarring contrast to the harmonious rural setting of the poet's childhood at the poem's beginning and prefiguring, in its tumultuous imagery, the revolutionary upheavals in France that Wordsworth records in Books 9 to 11. "Residence in London" thus contains one of the poem's most vivid crises of the imagination before its restoration in the second half of the poem, beginning partially in Book 8 (which responds directly to the poet's experience of London) and reaching its climax in Book 14, with the ascent of Snowdon. Book 7 is crucial not only to the poem's trajectory as a *Bildungsroman*, but also to its chief rhetorical conceit: the address to Coleridge. As the poem itself emphasizes on more than one occasion, Coleridge, rather than being nurtured in nature like the speaker himself, possesses an imagination "trained / In the great City" (13.364–5).

Just as Wordsworth imagines himself in dialogue with Coleridge throughout the poem, the city, while possessing an inferior and far more troublesome role in the growth of the poet's mind, is always implicitly in dialogue with the country because it is through this exchange that the "Love of Nature," in the logic of the poem's structure, leads to the "Love of Man" so important to the poem's developing moral compass. This argument, which brings together aesthetic and social values, is pivotal not only to Book 8 (where it is first outlined explicitly) but also to Wordsworth's overarching project, his attempt to assume the mantle of a great poet speaking on behalf of his country in favor of democratic ideals. The panoramic image of the world that Wordsworth produces in response to the city in Book 7 thus plays a critical role in this project, paving the way for the culmination of the poet's egalitarian vision of a unified humanity in the second half of the poem.

Because of Wordsworth's self-consciously epic objective, as well as the poem's celebration of British pastoral landscape and rural tradition, *The Prelude* has been more readily associated with Romantic nationalism than with urban cosmopolitanism. However, the shoring-up of national identity elsewhere in *The Prelude* through the immortalization of rural and knowable communities might be seen as a reaction to its dismantling at the heart of the poem in Book 7. While Wordsworth's treatment of the panoramas assumes that they are a less respectable form of art than the "subtlest craft" to which he himself aspires, his treatment of the city in *The Prelude* creates a sublime effect that depends on the urban view represented in the panorama: one central both to his poetic consciousness and to his French Revolution-inspired revolutionary utopianism. As in the panoramic viewing experience, the poet's ability to achieve a sense of aesthetic wholeness in response to his universal "love of man" requires the transforming and destabilizing presence of the city. While Book 8 purports to describe how the love of nature leads to the love of man, Wordsworth's celebrations of democracy in that book take up his imaginary reconstruction of the visual experience of urban space in the preceding section of the poem.

In "Residence in London," Wordsworth describes his experience in the city as an intoxicating yet terrifying encounter with "[t]hat huge fermenting mass of human-kind" (7.621): a phrase that suggests both the city's overwhelming enormity and, through the verb "fermenting," the idea that it embodies tumultuous change. Because of this early association of the city with social diversity and visual chaos, Wordsworth's descriptions in Book 7 are connected implicitly to the first-hand experience of France that he outlines later. In Book 7, for instance, he describes the "thickening hubbub" (211) of the crowd in London; in Paris he sees the "Revolutionary Power" (9.50) of the people as a "hubbub wild" (9.58) – both phrases make reference to the "universal hubbub wild" of Chaos in *Paradise Lost.*[80]

Early in Book 7, Wordsworth welcomes this hubbub and chaos as a "pleasing" indication of London's diversity:

> ... the mighty concourse I surveyed
> With no unthinking mind, well pleased to note
> Among the crowd all specimens of man,
> Through all the colours which the sun bestows,
> And every character of form and face.   (219–23)

Here, the pleasure that he derives from the spectacle of the crowd around him anticipates the idea of the "unity of man" (8.668) that he comes to associate with the city in Book 8, and with the Revolution after that, for in Paris his first encounter with the "hubbub" of revolutionary fervor provokes a similar mental embrace of humanity:

> ... I gradually withdrew
> Into a noisier world, and thus ere long
> Became a patriot, and my heart was all
> Given to the people, and my love was theirs   (9.121–4)

In London, the spectacle of diversity is "pleasing" not only in its suggestion of "the people," with whom he increasingly identifies, but also in its global reach – the idea that "*all* specimens of man" can be found there. Despite being constantly overwhelmed by the numerous forms of representation – sights, spectacles, and entertainments – he perceives in the city, the poet is able, at this juncture, to stand back and "survey" the crowd and, equally importantly, to incorporate it into his imaginative vision. In this act of surveillance, he takes care to note, he is not "unthinking." Rather, he exercises agency over the spectacle, distinguishing among the crowd a variety of specimens, differentiating them by sight according to "colour" and "character," and identifying them by social categories such as race and class.

The sketch tradition is important to this process of differentiation. Wordsworth grappled with the provisional nature of the sketch form explicitly in his early work *Descriptive Sketches* (1793), a narrative poem that prefigures *The Prelude* in recounting the poet's wandering in the Alps. In Book 7 of his later poem, however, Wordsworth turns the touristic gaze of the travel sketch from natural sights on to London, producing a rich catalog of city types that prefigures the work of investigators like Mayhew. (Wordsworth's use of the sketch may in fact have been directly influential on Charles Booth and Henry Mayhew, both of whom seem to riff on Wordsworth's melancholy observation that in London "life and labour seem but one" [7.71] in the titles of their anthropological studies, *Life and Labour of the People in London* and *London Labour and the London Poor* [1861].)

Wordsworth takes note of different social and occupational types – "the Nurse is here, / The Bachelor, that loves to sun himself, / The military Idler, and the Dame" (7.207–9) – and also of different national and ethnic ones:

> The Swede, the Russian; from the genial south
> The Frenchman and the Spaniard; from remote
> America, the Hunter-Indian; Moors,
> Malays, Lascars, the Tartar, the Chinese
> And Negro ladies in white muslin gowns.   (7.224–8)

Wordsworth's cataloging process here points both forward and back within the sketch tradition. On the one hand, he relies on older visual urban sketches like the Cries for the vividness of the city-scene he so rapidly paints in this section, and for his readers' familiarity with the different types he enumerates. His emphasis on both types of labor and ethnic types, however, also points forward to the work of urban sociologists such as Mayhew, who not only attempted to address problems of poverty and social unrest by cataloging and dissecting the "labour" of those in London, but also understood the transformation of urban space in terms of the different ethnicities who had come to occupy it.

Like Mayhew after him, Wordsworth pays particular attention to London's street entertainments and attempts to observe and record as much of the variety on view as possible. In his description of Bartholo- mew Fair, he evokes a Muse to lift him above the crowd in order to take in the spectacle. Rather than the isolated mountain peak of the traditional Romantic prospect, however, he imagines himself transported to "some showman's platform" (7.686), an artificial stage on which he himself is part of the urban spectacle, much as the audience would have been at a panorama viewing. Observing the crowd from this vantage-point, he witnesses:

> The silver-collared Negro with his timbrel,
> Equestrians, tumblers, women, girls, and boys ...
> All moveables of wonder, from all parts,
> Are here – Albinos, painted Indians, Dwarfs,
> The Horse of knowledge, and the learned Pig
> The Stone-eater, the man that swallows fire,
> Giants, Ventriloquists, the Invisible Girl ...   (7.704–10)

This section of the poem occurs much later in Book 7 and evidences the turmoil the speaker has undergone in his attempts to understand the city. Here the careful sketch-like enumeration of urban types gives way to a hallucinatory hodge-podge of beings. Ethnicity, race, occupational status, and ontological status are jumbled together and blurred by designations such as "Albino" and "painted Indian." Animal and human become interchangeable, too, given the horse's knowledge and the pig's learning, while the very status of the visible, and hence of the poet's surveying gaze, is called into question by the "Invisible Girl." By the end of Book 7, then, the beautiful – Wordsworth's pleasure at the diversity of the city and his ability to give it form and function – has given way to sublime disorder.

Nowhere is this more evident than in his famous encounter with the Blind Beggar. Blind beggars were, as Wordsworth points out, a "sight not rare" (7.638) in nineteenth-century London. Both Charles Booth and Mayhew (again, possibly because of Wordsworth's influence) mention them in their reports on the poor. Mayhew, for instance, describes a conversation with one beggar in particular which reveals precisely how he makes and spends his money; he also records rumors of fraudulent blind beggars in his report on the men, as if supplying for his readers the sociological details that Wordsworth chooses not to represent.[81] Mayhew's account, then, accords with his project of charting the lives of the poor and the way they in which they do and do not fit into the existing economic system. In Wordsworth's representation, however, the anthropological mastery of urban space through the activities of looking and recording emphatically breaks down before the unreadability of the Beggar, so that what might appear to be an empirical sketch of another urban type turns instead into an allegory of the city's sublimity.

As many critics have noted, the encounter with the Beggar signals an epistemological crisis of written representation and of sight, forms of knowledge constantly evoked in *The Prelude* as critical to the poetic imagination. Yet the Beggar's sign is grossly insufficient to explain him, while his "steadfast face and sightless eyes" reveal nothing and reflect the speaker's subjectivity back to him as blind and illegible, his sign "an apt type / ... of the utmost we can know, / Both of ourselves and of the universe" (7.644–5). This section not only presents a failure of the imagination but most vividly acknowledges the relation of this kind of poetic crisis to the preponderance of difference in the city: a problem that anthropology sought to resolve through the kind of mapping that Wordsworth pioneers in the poem, but which the poet never fully recuperates after this encounter. Wordsworth conceives of a character who does not have access to the poet's form of agency – sight, the crucial origin and instigator of imagination in the poem – and, in doing so, dramatically and presciently underscores the problematic of otherness in the work of urban spectatorship. As Galperin points out, the moment with the Beggar marks the point at which Wordsworth is no longer *spectator ab extra*, but part of the spectacle, an "other," himself:[82] "the spectacle of the beggar is by turns the spectacle of oneself: the knowledge of a spectator/actor 'amid' the 'moving pageant.'"[83]

After the spectacle of the Beggar, the speaker is reduced to perceiving the city as "one vast mill" (7.719) of difference – a Babel of commodities and meaningless signs:[84]

> Oh, blank confusion! true epitome
> Of what the mighty City is herself
> To thousands upon thousands of her sons,
> Living among the same perpetual whirl
> Of trivial objects, melted and reduced
> To one identity, by differences
> That have no law, no meaning, and no end – .   (7.725–8)

That the problem the Blind Beggar represents is a uniquely urban and modern one is made clear by the fact that Wordsworth's celebration of his country home earlier in the poem rests partly on its legibility. In the rural landscape, the people the poet encounters, familiar both as friends and as types, are easily readable: "The face of every neighbor whom I met / Was like a volume to me" (7.67–8); their traditional occupations, such as "woodman" and "shepherd," make even their interiority transparent to the poet's gaze: "I read, without design, the opinions, thoughts / Of those plain-living people" (4.212–13).

In the city, by contrast, the poet is shocked to find that: "'The face of everyone that passes by me is a mystery!'" (7.628–9). The spoken address to himself here underlines the fragmentation of self-identity that accompanies this realization. In this moment, the sketch's ability to contextualize and unmask the city's mysteries is dramatically reversed.

The lack of intimacy between city-dwellers poses for Wordsworth the paradox of having to imagine a community of strangers, a paradox which becomes the insuperable epistemological dilemma of Book 7:

> . . . Above all, one thought
> Baffled my understanding: how men lived
> Even next-door neighbours, as we say, yet still
> Strangers, nor knowing each the other's name.   (115–18)

This paradox is also important to the poet's larger task of reconciling the "love of nature" and his solitary artistic calling with his "love of man" and his commitment to democracy. To do this, Wordsworth ends Book 7 by reasserting a sense of mastery over the city, using a language of aesthetic unity that dissolves the distinction between country and city. Looking at the city as an artist, he suggests, involves seeing "the parts / As parts, but with a feeling for the whole" (7. 735–6). The poem ultimately argues that the way to resolve the swirl of difference generated by the alienating, commodity-laden city, and to make meaning out of the "one identity" that London produces, is to encircle the world mentally by extending the mind from its stifled, over-stimulated confinement in the city out to the continuous, spreading horizon: to allow "the horizon of his mind" to extend, as it does in Book 8. At this point, Wordsworth departs from the visual sketch – "the picture" that will "weary out the eye" (7.731) – and uses his imagination to project outwards from urban space to an image of endless nature. Thus the poet "reflects" upon (rather than looks directly at) how

> the everlasting streams and woods
> Stretched and still stretching far and wide, exalt
> The roving Indian. On his desert sands
> What grandeur not unfelt, what pregnant show
> Of beauty, meets the sun-burnt Arab's eyes.   (7.745–9)

His "early converse with the works of God" (7.742) has trained his imagination to move from the contemplation of external details to inner ideals so that he can make the mental leap from the city out into the world, and make that world newly meaningful and familiar (despite the fact that it is still peopled by strangers). The Indian he imagines on the desert sands recalls Wordsworth himself as a child running free in the countryside "as if I had been born / On Indian plains ... A naked savage" (1.297–300); the Arab reminds us of the Arab with the stone and shell of his dream in Book 5 (who, like the Indian, is identified with Wordsworth through his role of poet-prophet). Here, then, cultural otherness becomes a tool through which Wordsworth can recognize and name his own earlier moments of dislocation and internal otherness.

Yet in order to perform the seemingly magical feat of turning London from a chaos of difference and dissolution into a spectacle of unity and identification, Wordsworth's aesthetic act refers back to the visual, mirroring the work of the panorama. Moving out from the blur of difference he has experienced at the heart of London, the poet ends Book 7 by fixing his mind's eye upon a vision of a horizon:

> And, as the sea propels, from zone to zone,
> Its currents, magnifies its shoals of life
> Beyond all compass spread, and sends aloft
> Armies of clouds – even so, its powers and aspects
> Shape for mankind, by principles as fixed
> The views and aspirations of the soul
> To majesty.   (750–56)

In these lines, he describes the point where the sea, bringing together the world of Londoners, Arabs, and Indians that he has conjured up, meets the sky, with its "armies of clouds" – the horizon point is vital to his imagination of how the picture might be contained and made meaningful "by principles," despite the fact that it is one of infinity, "Beyond all compass spread." Thus Wordsworth's experience of urban space, no longer differentiated to the point of meaninglessness, is consolidated by a global panoramic vision.

Interestingly, a similar mental gesture also takes place, as Herbert Lindenberger notices, in *Tintern Abbey* at a moment in which Wordsworth describes the mind of man fusing with the sublime aspects of nature:

> A sense sublime
> Of something far more deeply interfused,
> Whose dwelling is the light of setting suns,
> And the round ocean and the living air,
> And the blue sky, and in the mind of man.[85]

Here, too, "the mind of man" mimics the shape of a panorama, extending to the horizon and expanding to become one with the circular form of "the round ocean and the living air." The image of a circle lending form to a spectacle of infinity is also instrumental in a more explicitly "touristic" prospect-view in Wordsworth's writing, in his book on the Lake District, where he envisages himself lifted above the land-scape (as in the Bartholomew Fair scene) and asks the reader to imagine that the lakes and valleys he sees before him are connected "like spokes from the nave of a wheel."[86]

Wordsworth's use of circular form in all these instances, but particu-larly in response to the ruptures of the city, can be seen as a triumphant reassertion of the imagination's ability to contain the world and to master the difference within it – the beauty of the horizon in Book 7 takes the place of the sublime figure of the Beggar. Thus the excited "blank confusion" of the earlier lines describing the encounter with the street entertainments and with the beggar is replaced by a more measured and sedentary meter. By the last line of Book 7, "Composure, and ennobling Harmony" (770), the caesura and restoration of regular meter enact the closure that the words describe.

Despite the common association of Book 7 with Wordsworth's most powerful and engaged urban vision, it is in Book 8, where Wordsworth professes his "love of humanity," that he returns to the image of the city to express his strongest feeling of utopian potential, a "trust / In what we may become" (649–50):

> ... among the multitudes
> Of that huge city, oftentimes was seen
> Affectingly set forth, more than elsewhere
> Is possible, the unity of man
> One spirit over ignorance and vice
> Predominant, in good and evil hearts;
> One sense for moral judgments, as one eye
> For the sun's light. The soul when smitten thus
> By a sublime idea, whencesoe'er
> Vouchsafed for union or communion, feeds
> On the pure bliss, and takes her rest with God.   (8.665–75)

The "sublime idea" that Wordsworth articulates here is that of the "unity of man," one that he returns to over and over again in relation to the sublime in the rest of the poem. After the failures of the Revolution, utopia for him resides chiefly in the ability of the "mind of man" to be "A thousand times more beautiful than the earth" (14.450–51). At the very end of *The Prelude*, too, he has recourse to the image of a global panorama: "Anon I rose / As if on wings, and saw beneath me stretched / Vast prospect of the world" (14.382–4). In this passage from Book 14, the unity he constructs no longer foregrounds England's predominance on the stage of world history ("the vast metropolis ... Fount of my country's destiny and of the world's" [8.592–3]), but moves towards a more explicitly democratic vision, demanding "one sense for moral judgments." While the poet claims, at the end of Book 8, that "Nature has led me on" to the love of man which he continues to reassert despite his horror at the Revolution, it is, as we have seen, the city that is repressed after Book 7, when the poet turns instead to the "sublime idea" of international democracy.

Like his conviction that he is a "patriot of the world" in the early stages of the French Revolution, which then gives way to dismay at the events leading up to and following the Terror, this is an idea whose status in the poem is fundamentally unstable. Whereas early in his development the revolutionary ideals he encounters convince him that democracy can exist – "Not in Utopia ... But in the very world, which is the world / Of all of us" (11.140–44) – his sense that the world is ready for the enactment of the "sublime idea" recedes with his increasing disillusionment with France. The poem's sense of sublimity, in fact, comes to reside in the oscillation between the loss of imaginative potential in the face of absolute difference and urban alienation, and its recovery through the idea of the unity of man, an oscillation which is represented as a mental movement from the swirling center to the horizon, and an imaginative dissolution of center and periphery. It is also depicted, as John Plotz has shown, as a simultaneous perception of part and whole – or of sketch and panorama: "The relationship between the whole and ... heretofore unmanageable part – the crowd of St. Bartholomew's Fair and of London more generally – remains volatile, precisely because the introduction of the whole depends on the parts' being well seen as parts first."[87] As is the case with the city panorama, Wordsworth's attempt to enclose the world through anthropological knowledge, and the sublime liminality of the horizon, results in a poem that reveres form but also retreats from it, thereby anticipating the Victorian novel's loose bagginess.

The Prelude and its unlikely interlocutors, the sketch and the panorama, in their conjoining of the image of the city to the imagination of the world can thus be understood as early and prescient responses to the advent of globalization. While many critics are inclined to see in the connection of nineteenth-century forms to ideas of the global a baleful predominance of center over periphery and of the aesthetic over the political, I have argued that they were crucial to the articulation of cosmopolitan values – the rights of man, the idea of world brotherhood – as well. Allowing the majesty of the ideal of global kinship to co-exist with a dizzying fear of the psychical distances to be overcome, a desire to contain and control difference to live alongside the knowledge that this is impossible, Wordsworth's urban sublime becomes a technology for managing antithetical ideas about a world made whole.

SKIMPOLE'S SKETCHES AND FOGGY PANORAMAS: DICKENS' DYSTOPIAN CITYSPACE

Between Wordsworth's pioneering portrait of London in Book 7 and the end of the century, when writers such as James, Doyle, Morris, and Conrad would take up the theme of the global city, the most significant examples of urban realism are the London novels of Charles Dickens. But Dickens' dark view of the city and its international imbrications departs from the utopian tone of the cosmopolitan visions I have thus far traced through periodicals, portrayals of the Great Exhibition, and Wordsworth's panorama in Book 7. As *Bleak House*'s famous satire of "telescopic philanthropy" suggests, Dickens sought to elevate domestic and national communities over the broad spheres of influence conceived by his unlikable philanthropists, Mrs. Pardiggle and Mrs. Jellyby. Yet his indelible vision of London and his development of realism's totalizing forms made his writing deeply influential on cosmopolitan realism at the *fin de siècle* and beyond. In this concluding section, I examine Dickens' critical engagement with the sketch and panorama in *Bleak House* to show how he enabled the cosmopolitan visions of later realists, even as he struggled to resist the global dimensions of London that they would embrace.

Dickens' national focus is typical of much realist fiction at mid-century. Condition-of-England novels such as *Sybil, or the Two Nations* (1845), *Mary Barton* (1848), *Alton Locke* (1850), *North and South* (1854), alongside Dickens' *Bleak House* and *Hard Times* (1854), render divisions within a localized landscape in order to plead for cross-class community and social reform. This is not to say, of course, that the space depicted in these works was exclusively British. Edward Said's influential *Culture and Imperialism* demonstrates that "imperial concerns [are] constitutively significant to the culture of the modern West and that the empire is constantly if marginally present in Victorian fiction."[88] The end of *Mary Barton*, for example, relies on the colonies as a space of moral and economic renewal, a counterpoint to the novel's mainly industrial terrain.

As James Buzard persuasively argues in *Disorienting Fiction*, however, the growing global consciousness produced by empire incited novelists to pay even closer attention to the state of the nation by engaging in a process he labels "metropolitan autoethnography." This complex narrative movement between outside and inside perspectives sought to provide a consolidated national vision for a country divided on the one hand by class conflict and on the other by the dispersions of empire. Novels like *Bleak House*, in Buzard's account, use realist devices such as the panorama to delimit a national terrain: "Rehearsing a deliberate, though conflicted, turning away from the boundariless world in which England's fortunes were so much embroiled, *Bleak House* offers its iconic spaces as an analogue for the space of culture that might unify and demarcate the nation."[89]

The particular engagements with the sketch and the panorama that I note here, nevertheless, highlight Dickens' lack of confidence that the forms he used could depict a "space of culture" adequately impermeable to the entropic energies of that "boundariless world." A master of both the sketch form and the narrative overview, Dickens employs each genre to great effect in *Bleak House*. The novel is chock-full of the urban types associated with sketches and famously draws attention to the panoramic overview of the omniscient narrator by contrasting it intermittently with Esther Summerson's first-person narrative. But Dickens also indicts each form by associating it with his negative view of cosmopolitanism. As a result, his most explicitly anti-cosmopolitan novel draws attention, in spite of itself, to the formal impossibility of representing a purely national space.

The sketch form comes under attack in the novel's portrayal of Skimpole. Dickens' journalistic and literary writings, as the first part of this chapter indicates, make ample use of the sketch, especially in their caricatures of urban types. Dickens' rendering of Skimpole, however – itself a kind of sketch caricature – contains an oblique but significant critique of the genre. As we saw in Chapter 1, Skimpole claims he is a cosmopolitan and is associated with many of the negative definitions of the term.[90] He is disloyal to family and friends and uses the nonsensical claim that he is merely a child to refuse the moral and financial responsibilities of adulthood and citizenship. His disregard for community ties is one significant way in which Skimpole is associated with cosmopolitanism; his idle artistry is another. Esther characterizes his main activities as follows: "Mr. Skimpole ... betook himself to beginning some sketch in the park which he never finished, or to playing fragments of airs on the piano, or to singing scraps of songs, or to lying down on his back under a tree, and looking at the sky."[91] His fragmentary songs on the piano, his unfinished drawings, and his casual insistence that natives in Africa or slaves in plantations possess meaning only as subjects of his aesthetic contemplation, help to identify Skimpole as one of the novel's most sinister characters.

It is the incompleteness of Skimpole's sketchy artistic works, however, that most succinctly demonstrates his lack of commitment to any project or person beyond himself and his voyeuristic, solipsistic relation to the subjects of his regard. Through his portrayal of Skimpole, Dickens skewers what I have called the artistic-anthropological context of the sketch tradition by highlighting its connection with idle privilege, imperialistic exploitation, and self-indulgent entertainment. In doing so, he necessarily calls into question his own use of the genre, particularly in works such as *Sketches by Boz*, where the sketch is presented as a standalone fragment by a *flâneur*-narrator who observes the working classes with a Skimpole-like disinterest.

If Skimpole's association with the sketch's cosmopolitanism makes the genre morally suspect, the opening of *Bleak House* casts suspicion on the panorama as well, undermining its association with legibility and community. In its magisterial overview of London, the first scene in *Bleak House* is evocative of 360-degree paintings such as Hornor's Colosseum panorama. But Dickens' narrator offers a literally dim view of the city landscape. The scene is unified not by images of an infinite sky, echoing the grandeur of the "mind of man," as in *The Prelude*, but by a malignant and foreboding fog. The omniscient narrator sees everything from the Lord Chancellor in Lincoln's Inn Hall to the river, the "Essex Marshes," the "Kentish heights," and dogs and horses in the mire, but connects these details, paradoxically, by means of the obfuscating miasmas that play a fatal role in the novel. As in many famous London panoramas, the city pictured opens outwards through the image of the river, but here, too, is fog, "hovering in the rigging of great ships" and "drooping on the gunwales of barges and small boats." The clarifying balloon-view of the city championed by Mayhew in "The Great World of London" has no purchase in this context, the narrator indicates, for "people on the bridges peep[ed] over the parapets into a nether sky of fog, with fog all around them, as if they were up in a balloon, and hanging in the misty clouds" (49).

Even as *Bleak House* seeks to privilege English over global space, that space remains present for most of the novel as a problem that cannot be wished away. The opening panorama, though obfuscated, reminds us of Britain's naval connections to the rest of the world and foreshadows the destructive pull of that wider world on the novel's tightly interwoven cast of characters; *Bleak House*'s plot suggests that London's global dimensions are only ever part and parcel of its problems, rather than signs of man's sublime and democratic capacities (as they are in *The Prelude*).[92] The lawyers of the Chancery court travel around the world neglecting their duties, while Jellyby's misplaced missionary attentions to Africa turn her abandoned children into "savages." The manifold interconnections between people and places high and low, near and far, that make for the panoramic integrity of the novel are equally problematic; Skimpole's "cosmopolite" indulgences underlie the downfall of Charley's working-class family and a French maid brings murder to the doorstep of an English estate. Ultimately, the novel's insistence on the virtue of smaller rather than larger circles of influence is reflected in the narrative's trajectory from the miasmic impersonal panorama of the first chapter to the cozy first-person domesticity of its ending.

Dickens' antipathy to the global imbrications of urban space is partially responsible for *Bleak House*'s crisis of representation, wherein language and law fail to give access to truth and justice.[93] How to imagine urban community if sketches project only idealized versions of Others (as Skimpole's use of them suggests); if the only human connections that panoramic overviews reveal are of disease and of commerce (as the opening scene of the novel implies)? Elsewhere in his writing, Dickens saw the utopian possibilities of the panorama as a means of conceptualizing collectivity. His early use of a panoramic prospect in his sketch-story collection, *Master Humphrey's Clock* (1840–41), follows Wordsworth in turning a baffled reaction at the city's size and diversity into a spectacle of imaginary cohesion. In one of Master Humphrey's stories, the narrator recounts his visit to that popular panoramic vantage-point, the dome of St. Paul's. At first, the narrator is overwhelmed by despair at the disparities he imagines in the city below. London is depicted as a series of "clustering housetops" – an agglomeration of physical divisions that prevents individuals from acknowledging each other's suffering. The cathedral's clock, which the narrator dubs "the Heart of London," only accentuates the mechanical relentlessness of city life and its ongoing threat to human community. "Does not this Heart of London, that nothing moves, nor stops, nor quickens – that goes on the same let what will be done – does it not express the City's character well?" the narrator asks mournfully.[94] By the end of his anecdote, however, the clock chimes have been claimed for a revivified humanism:

Heart of London, there is a moral in thy every stroke! As I look on at thy indomitable working ... I seem to hear a voice within thee which sinks into my ear, bidding me, as I elbow my way among the crowd, have some thought for the meanest wretch that passes, and, being a man, to turn away with scorn and pride from none that bear the human shape.[95]

In a dilated moment of looking and imagining, the narrator transforms the previously oppressive chimes into the still, small voice of Christian conscience, and the clock into the vital central organ of a London that can now be seen as a social totality of "human shape."

Some of this enthusiasm for the unifying potential of the panorama reappears in Dickens' journalism. As well as reporting on the opening fête of Hornor's Colosseum panorama, he wrote admiringly in *The Examiner* in 1848 of a panorama of the Mississippi: "To see this painting is to have a thorough understanding of what the great American river is ... and to acquire a new power of testing the descriptive accuracy of its best describers."[96] Most famously, his piece *Some Account of an Extraordinary Traveller* describes the worldwide travels of Mr. Booley by way of panorama. Despite the piece's mockery of the vulgar cosmopolitanism afforded by the popular spectacles, Booley's idealistic exclamations at the end of his "travels" seem meant to be taken in earnest: "Some of the best results of actual travel are suggested by such means to those whose lot is to stay at home. New worlds open out to them, beyond their little worlds, and widen their range of reflection, information, sympathy and interest. The more man knows of man, the better for the common brotherhood of us all!"[97]

Notwithstanding this earlier enthusiasm, the opening panorama of *Bleak House* is informative only insofar as it tells us that the city is beyond redemption. A space in which ties of kinship, friendship, and religion have been replaced by those of commerce and bureaucracy, London fails dismally as a symbol of national community. Yet, in his search for an alternative vision of collectivity in the novel, Dickens doesn't entirely abandon the panorama. Instead of a revealing overview, the novel provides a kind of time-elapsed panorama wherein the connections between individuals, and an expanded sense of community, emerge from the accumulated knowledge provided by its various parts. Inspector Bucket exemplifies the new kind of skill required by the city when he mounts "a high tower in his mind and [looks] out far and wide" (824) to seek the knowledge that binds the different characters together. In similar fashion, the reader is called upon to map the fateful connections that link *Bleak House*'s myriad of characters. The answer to the novel's famous question – "What connexion can there be, between the place in Lincolnshire, the house in town, the Mercury in powder, and the whereabout of Jo the outlaw with the broom, who had that distant ray of light upon him when he swept the churchyard-step?" (272) – clearly resides beyond the visual, in the imaginative and metaphysical realms (an implication ponderously underscored by the allegorical ray of light).

Rather than rely solely on the autoethnographic articulation of culture as a source of fellow-feeling, then, the novel also insists that the sympathetic imagination, like Wordsworth's sublime panorama, must extend beyond the details of city life to embrace a universalist conception of humanity. Thus the narrator's second formulation of the "What connexion" sentence transforms it from a question to a statement and from the present tense to the past: "What connexion can there have been between many people in the innumerable histories of this world, who, from opposite sides of great gulfs, have, nevertheless, been very curiously brought together!" (272). In this iteration, the panorama of humanity is "curiously brought together," the sentence suggests, by the cumulative effect of the writer's art and the reader's dedication to piecing the narrative together. But its universalism is not the abstract kind that Dickens abhors, and satirizes in figures like Jellyby and Pardiggle, because the reader must develop intimacy with the novel's characters in order to earn the sense of connectedness the novel produces over time.[98]

Locating agency in the reader's engagement with his work, Dickens' humanist cosmopolitan ideal co-exists, however uneasily, with the novel's sober sense of the reified divisions of capitalism and urgent demand for national consolidation. (Interestingly, a similar vision of the writer's work as cosmopolitan in scope and ethos is articulated by Wordsworth in the Preface to *Lyrical Ballads* and is enacted in poetic form, as we have seen, by his experiments in *The Prelude*: "In spite of difference of soil or climate, of language and manners, of laws and customs, in spite of things silently gone out of mind and things violently destroyed, the Poet binds together by passion and knowledge the vast empire of human society, as it is spread over the whole earth, and over all time."[99]) The panoramic plot of *Bleak House* ultimately seeks to prove that the sketch – indeed representation itself – isn't idle, meaningless, or exploitative (like Skimpole's pastimes) if it functions as part of an integrated whole pieced together over time, like Wordsworth's redemptive vision of London, rather than perceived instantaneously. In his combination of the sketch and panorama, and of equally antithetical narrative techniques, Dickens dares to hope that London's visible details and individual storylines are part of a larger canvas in which everything might connect meaningfully.

Nonetheless, Dickens' profound unease with the uncontainable form of the city prevails at the end of the novel, explaining why it must end in Jarndyce's country house rather than the original Bleak House. Because of the problems visited upon it by the Chancery suit, the London-based Bleak House, for which the novel is named, metonymically telescopes out, like Jellyby's philanthropy, to stand in for the city, the nation, and the wider world on to which the city spills in the opening passage. By situating the estate of the last chapter in the country, the novel reverses this telescope, training it on the renovated domestic sphere presided over by Esther. Through this ingenious compression of narrative space, the novel briefly exorcizes the terrifying implications of its initial vision. Because of its safe distance from the city, Jarndyce's second Bleak House no longer threatens a metonymic resonance with the world and can comfortably stand in for an idealized version of the nation instead.

Bleak House is worth noting in the context of cosmopolitan realism in spite of Dickens' antipathy towards Britain's global imbrications, because of both its self-conscious use of the antithetical scales that I have identified as crucial to the Victorian global imagination, and its insistence that those scales be used together in the service of a transcendent humanist vision. The *fin-de-siècle* visions of London as an international realm are unthinkable without the vivid imagination of invisible connections between city-dwellers that Dickens so memorably rendered, even if he himself attempted to constrain the reach of those connections.

In tracing the sketch and the panorama from their uses in artistic traditions to their juxtaposition in realist views of the city, I have stressed both their interdependence and their significance for writers who sought to move from local to global scales and from the visual to the visionary. The two forms allowed literature to take stock of the city's diverse populace and note the differences therein, but also to posit a unified space in which those differences might be transcended.

In Part Two, I will argue that the totalizing forms of realism used at mid-century were adapted to explicitly global visions by the century's end. The opposite scales of these genres reappeared in writing of this period, but the city's by then incontrovertibly international landscape demanded exaggerated versions of the sketch and panoramic forms used at mid-century. Thus James and Doyle amplify the disconnect between romance tropes and realist detail in their stories of international conspiracy, while Morris and Booth make the ethnographic and allegorical elements of the sketch and panoramic perspectives far more explicit than writers like Wordsworth and Dickens.

Negative views of the city such as that memorialized in *Bleak House* were more rather than less entrenched by the *fin de siècle*, yet this period also inspired some of the most radically utopian depictions of the city. While London's cosmopolitanism was no less a source of anxiety than it had been earlier, its vitality and connections to the wider world were also seen as a possible source of regeneration. In representing a more intimate relationship between metropolitan and global space at the end of the century, writers continued to make use of the contrasting dimensions epitomized by the sketch and the panorama, but adapted these forms in ways that would test the limits of realism and the boundaries between city and world.

PART TWO

Cosmopolitan Realism at the Fin de Siècle *and Beyond*

The realist spectator and the romance plot: James, Doyle, and the aesthetics of fin-de-siècle *cosmopolitanism*

I can imagine no spectacle more touching, more thrilling and even dramatic, than to see this great precarious, artificial empire, on behalf of which, nevertheless, so much of the strongest and finest stuff of the greatest race (for such they are) has been expended, struggling with forces which perhaps, in the long run, will prove too many for it.

Henry James, from "Letter to Grace Norton" (1885)[1]

Writing from London to his friend Grace Norton, Henry James envisages the demise of the British empire as a moving spectacle and a tragic epic narrative (he evokes the past of empire, on which "the strongest and finest stuff ... has been expended," in heroic terms and anticipates a ruinous future: "forces which perhaps, in the long run, will prove too many for it"). Casting his political perceptions in the terms of aesthetic appreciation ("I can imagine no spectacle more touching ... ") and of literary form (the epic), James also draws attention to empire as a kind of art by calling it "artificial." This chapter moves the story of cosmopolitan realism to the *fin de siècle* to examine works in which the effort to imagine the world through the city intersected with the formal self-consciousness of British aestheticism. While not necessarily anti-imperialist, *The Princess Casamassima* and *A Study in Scarlet* cast doubt on the project of empire, and other totalizing moral and political projects, by stressing their fictionality rather than historical inevitability.

By the end of the century, cosmopolitan thought was a notable feature of intellectual life. Journals such as *Cosmopolis* (1896–8), Arthur Symons' and Aubrey Beardsley's *The Savoy* (1896), and W. T. Stead's *The Review of Reviews* (1890–1936) practiced various forms of it. *Cosmopolis*, as we have seen, arranged its structure and content so as to create a transnational conversation. *The Savoy* made Decadence, rather than Britishness, its organizing principle and published a number of literary works in translation. *The Review of Reviews*, meanwhile, showcased an imperialist cosmopolitanism. Reprinting reviews in English from all over the world, it hoped to create a global union of "English-speaking folk," that might help to "save the English empire." In literary circles, feminist writers such as Olive Schreiner and Vernon Lee, and queer writers such as Oscar Wilde and Edward Carpenter implicitly connected cosmopolitan philosophies and lifestyles with freedom from traditional gender roles, while those advocating for workers' rights, such as William Morris, imagined socialism in internationalist terms. Leela Gandhi's fascinating account of radicalism at the *fin de siècle* argues that a range of oppositional stances – from sexual dissidence and aestheticism to animal rights and spiritualism – shared an anti-imperialist, internationalist politics and credits the socialist revival of the 1880s with the rise of this internationalism.[2]

Aestheticism and socialism, then, were two prominent *fin-de-siècle* movements in which international ideals and frames of reference played a central role. This section of the book uses the concept of cosmopolitan realism to re-evaluate both movements. While aestheticism has often been associated with an apolitical elitist stance and socialism with the rejection of aesthetic values, Chapters 3 and 4 make the case that aesthetic and political ideas become indispensable to each other within later works of cosmopolitan realism, once the task of imagining global community increasingly seems, to borrow James' language, both "artificial" and "precarious."

If internationalist ideals were more prevalent in political thought by the end of the century, the idea of London's cosmopolitan character was more pervasive in literature. An array of late Gothic novels, such as *The Picture of Dorian Gray* (1890), *The Sign of Four* (1890), *Dracula* (1897), *The Beetle* (1897), and *Heart of Darkness* (1902), suggests that routes of financial exploitation and moral contamination serve as pernicious links between London and other parts of the world, while shadowy international conspiracies fuel the urban narratives of Robert Louis Stevenson and Fanny van de Grift Stevenson (*The Dynamiter*, 1885), Joseph Conrad (*The Secret Agent*, 1907), G. K. Chesterton (*The Man Who Was Thursday*, 1908), as well as the novels I examine in this chapter, *The Princess Casamassima* (1886) and *A Study in Scarlet* (1887). These two texts have more in common than the international anarchists and London mysteries of their plots, however. Henry James and Arthur Conan Doyle, who lived and wrote in London during the same period, also share a fascination with aesthetic perception and its relation to global perspectives and urban experience.

James' and Doyle's indebtedness to the British Aesthetic Movement is visible not only in their characterization of their protagonists as refined aesthetes, but also in their desire to give form to the city as subject, despite their sense of its infinite complexity. By the second half of the nineteenth century, the Aesthetic Movement was most often associated with such literary figures as Wilde, Ruskin, Swinburne, and Morris. Most famously, aestheticism's concept of form as an artificial and transitory, but creative and necessary, human imposition on direct sensory experience is connected with Walter Pater and his "Conclusion" to *The Renaissance*. The "Conclusion" famously invokes the form-giving capacity of the mind through the memorable images of a "design in a web" and a "hard, gem-like flame": metaphors that enact the paradox of form and flux that Pater considered central to aesthetic perception. In positioning aesthetic perception as a central component of urban living, *The Princess Casamassima* and *A Study in Scarlet* commit themselves to related literary paradoxes, but ones that function on the level of plot rather than image.

In his debut appearance in *A Study in Scarlet* (1888), Sherlock Holmes solves the mystery in question by demonstrating that a murder in the British capital is connected to political and religious oppression in Utah. In order to reach this unlikely insight, Holmes undergoes an eccentric and intuitive detection process that involves not only the observation of factual clues but also the ability to see London as part of a blood-tinged "study in scarlet": an enormous web in which the city is only one intricate component of a global totality. Hyacinth, the protagonist of Henry James' *The Princess Casamassima* (1889), also strains to see London in formal terms – to perceive it, in other words, aesthetically. He understands the mysteries and paradoxes of London, its juxtaposition of wealthy and poor, as inextricable from its artistic riches and the larger fabric of world history: the suffering of London's working class as inevitably related to the capitalist and imperialist formulations upon which the city's grandeur is based.

As we have seen, earlier realist texts such as Book VII of *The Prelude* used the urban sketch and panorama to present visions of the city as a microcosm of humanity. By the century's end, writers were more aware than ever of the city's international imbrications, but this heightened awareness of the necessarily global scale of urban plot made the carefully delineated social vision of realist narrative (George Eliot's "particular web") harder to reproduce. Rather than seeming to enclose the world, London appears to spill out on to it, no longer subject to the unifying gaze of the omniscient narrator. In their vocations as urban aesthetes, the novels' protagonists, Hyacinth and Holmes, look closely at the city and see details that make sense only in a global context. In order to bring together the hybrid spaces that their novels delineate, both James and Doyle use a peculiar, often jarring, blend of realist and romance modes, drawing attention to the artifice of their narratives at key moments in the unfolding of their plots. Their pronounced consciousness of the discontinuities of urban space – but their will to present different unified visions anyway – is emblematic of the intersecting projects of aestheticism and cosmopolitanism in the period.

Both *A Study in Scarlet* and *The Princess Casamassima* address the representational question of how to bring the unfathomability of urban space into focus as spectacle, if only as a vexed and unstable one. Through the mystery plots they weave – in which the protagonists must attain a holistic view of London in order to see through its web of connections to the various "truths" that they seek – Doyle and James engage with this problem self-consciously. If the impossible task of assimilating the city's disparate elements within a single vision is the central formal problem of each work, this task also underwrites the novels' cosmopolitan perspective.

Because contemporary critics of cosmopolitanism are understandably concerned about the concept's association with Enlightenment universalism, the "new" cosmopolitanisms have been reconceptualized as a negotiation between local and global perspectives: a complex attempt to imagine affiliations and human rights across national, ethnic, and racial boundaries while attending to the historical embeddedness of one's own position in doing so.[3] Like aesthetic perception, these cosmopolitanisms, according to the theorists who propose them, require an awareness of the inadequacy of the totalizing vision even while that ideal is being asserted. A critical cosmopolitanism, in other words, like aestheticism, might be said to demand attention to form through self-consciousness about the medium and means through which any kind of unification is represented. Yet James and Doyle, I argue, display the very kind of caution and self-consciousness in formulating their cosmopolitan visions that contemporary writers see as "new."

This is not to claim that the novels solve problems of cosmopolitan representation with which we are still grappling today, or that they share the political progressivism of the new cosmopolitanisms. Indeed, in their representation of political conspiracies – the oppressive interventions of the Mormon church in private life in *A Study in Scarlet* and the revolutionary plottings of international socialist groups from the Continent in

The Princess Casamassima – both James and Doyle pointedly ignore the historical reality of Irish nationalism and other anti-imperial movements as the basis for contemporary fears and fascinations with conspiracy. They evince a deep unease, moreover, about the global imbrications that they uncover, and neither achieves a consistent vision of the city as heterogeneous spectacle. Both novels, however, owe their generic complexity to their alternate evasion and engagement with the political implications of their aestheticism.

THE WEB AND THE CITY: MORAL VISIONS IN "A STUDY IN SCARLET"

A Study in Scarlet, the first Sherlock Holmes novel, is presented as part memoir, part medical casebook, authored by Dr. Watson.[4] Returning to London after serving in the imperial army in Afghanistan, the doctor ends up rooming with a stranger, Holmes, whose eccentric career as private investigator immediately intrigues him. The two take on a murder case that appears to be the work of international political conspirators: the German word "*Rache*" (revenge) has been written spectacularly in blood over the murdered body. As the incompetent police are led astray by their literal readings of the crime scene (one assumes that "Rache" is an unfinished "Rachel"), Holmes dramatically solves the crime and catches the villain.

The second half of the novel supplies the "history" of the events documented in the first half. Entitled "The Country of the Saints," this section is strikingly different in tone: an omniscient melodramatic narrator replaces the pedantic Watson. The pioneer John Ferrier and his daughter Lucy are rescued by Mormons from starvation on the plains of Utah on the condition that they join the Mormon community. They coexist with the Mormons without incident until the day Lucy comes of age and the Mormons expect her to marry one of their wealthiest members. When her father refuses to hand her over, he is murdered and she is abducted. Shortly after being forced to marry, Lucy dies of shame and grief. Jefferson Hope, a fellow pioneer and non-Mormon who became Lucy's true love, dedicates the remainder of his life to tracking down and killing the two Mormons who had competed for Lucy's hand and whom he blames for her death. Pursuing them around the world, he eventually finds and kills them in London, where he is stopped in his tracks by Holmes. The novel ends with Holmes triumphantly recounting the empirical method by which he was able to deduce the facts behind the romance-narrative set in Utah.

In his work on urban imperialist narratives, Joseph McLaughlin argues that the Sherlock Holmes novels mark a shift from racist representations of "us against them" to "us as them," due to growing anxieties about national degeneration and "the savage within." Watson's exhaustion and "irretrievably ruined health" on his return from the colonies, for instance, are legible signs of his degradation from imperial exposure.[5] Holmes can guess that Watson has been in Afghanistan without any prior knowledge of his history because of the doctor's tanned skin and fragile demeanor – both signs (one related to race, the other to masculine vigor) that Watson's identity has been diluted by his sojourn abroad. The national identity of London itself is similarly called into question when Watson describes the capital as a "great cesspool into which all loungers and idlers of the Empire are irresistibly drained" (6).

As well as marking a shift in imperialist narrative, the representational strategy of "us as them" enables Doyle to engage in a totalizing form of cosmopolitan thinking. One of the most pervasive Victorian understandings of culture, articulated most influentially in E. B. Tylor's *Primitive Culture* (1871), brought the world together under an all-encompassing definition of the term. According to Tylor's developmental schema, culture was singular rather than plural: "primitive" culture related to British culture by virtue of representing it at an earlier stage. The savage ancestor, popularized versions of the idea suggested, was still visible in primitive cultures around the empire and, more alarmingly, traceable within the European individual, leaving the latter continually wary of the appearance of atavistic characteristics.[6]

An important component of understanding culture as developmentally continuous is to understand it as subject to pattern and form. The "primitive," according to Tylor's narrative, is what we all have in common, and for Doyle, as for writers like Sir James Frazer or Freud, it resides in the deep structures of stories that cultures recurrently tell themselves. Because Holmes' approach to his investigations is insistently scientific, stressing empirical observation and the accumulation of factual evidence, the tales in which he is featured tend to be more commonly associated with realism than romance. In Holmes' close readings of crime scenes, the elaborate forensic investigations of modern detective work are represented for the first time. Furthermore, his solutions to mysteries always end up providing a "realistic" explanation for what seem to be otherworldly, uncanny, or inexplicable phenomena, while gritty evocations of contemporary London lend the tales historicity and immediacy.

However, Doyle is indebted to romance as well as to realism in *A Study in Scarlet*, and in his second Sherlock Holmes novel, *The Sign of Four*, he self-consciously notes the tension between the two forms. *The Sign of Four* begins with Holmes reproaching Watson for his representation of the case the doctor has by now labeled *A Study in Scarlet*: "'You have attempted to tinge it with romanticism, which produces much the same effect as if you worked a love-story or an elopement into the fifth proposition of Euclid.'" Watson's response cleverly turns the idea of romance on its head: "'But the romance was there,' [he] remonstrated. 'I could not tamper with the facts.'"[7] Here Doyle acknowledges his use of romance but lets Watson disclaim the tale's fictional contours by reasserting its basis in positivistic knowledge.

Despite Watson's protestation, romance is typically defined in antithesis to the world of facts. Providing a cosmology with a coherent moral framework, the genre creates an idealized, ahistorical fictional space, freed of the experience and ambivalences of everyday life. Underscoring imperial romance's mobilization of religious epistemologies, for instance, John McClure points to its origin in "chivalric romance and spiritual romance (tales of saints, martyrs, apostles and missionaries) [which] are set in the religious cosmos, celebrate religious styles of being, and promote religious programs of salvation."[8] Another feature of romance is that it "depends considerably upon a certain set distance in the relationship between audience and subject-matter."[9] It is not surprising, then, that most of *A Study in Scarlet*'s romance features appear in the Utah half of the novel – a section both geographically and stylistically distant from the more familiar terrain, to Victorian readers, of contemporary London. The romance tropes identifiable in this sequence include idealized characters (the vengeful questing hero, Jefferson, the virtuous, wronged maiden, Lucy); a location represented as both exotic and primitive (the "Wild" West); a sequence of uncanny events (the Mormons taunt Lucy's father by leaving threatening messages in his house at times when they could not have gained access); and a Manichean structure of good and evil that gleefully shuns the tentative relativism of the late Victorian novel (the Ferriers are innocents, the Mormons unrepentantly villainous).

Thus when the characters from the Utah scene intrude on the more realistic part of the novel – the domain of Holmes – Holmes puts them back into the realm of ahistoricity through an "aesthetic" reading of them as types out of a romance, performing scripted roles. Because Holmes cannot know the political context of the Mormons' persecution of Hope and the Ferrier family, he uses storybook conventions to read the crime scene instead. Deducing that the murder committed by Hope was motivated by a lost love via the clue of the wedding ring left on the victim's body, Holmes further extrapolates that Hope's victims were rivals for his fiancée's hand. In the larger context the novel creates, Hope could be read as a political vigilante, a figure closer to the international terrorist implied by the word "*Rache.*" He is, after all, an enraged victim of the Mormons' cultural intolerance and the imperialistic methods of coercion (rape, murder) by which they enforce their "brotherhood."

Yet Holmes' retrospective reconstruction of the story ends up removing Hope from this context, reifying both his identity and his motivations into those of a romantic hero on a quest to satisfy his lost honor. In doing so it erases the disturbing history of the Mormon empire that the murders recall, as well as that of the other empires that it evokes (but which Doyle conveniently elides) – America's larger nascent empire and Britain's existing one.[10] The way in which the idea of "narrative" gets used in *A Study in Scarlet*, then, is central to the novel's form and to how its cosmopolitan idealism is articulated. Doyle's novel participates in an emerging structuralism that implicitly, but nervously, places its faith in the recognition of a kinship between the "primitive" world of Mormon tribalism and the equally arcane "street Arab" nomadism attributed to London's seedy underclass: a strategy which might now be seen as a fearful wish to read an increasingly differentiated and unassimilable world as one recognizable whole.[11]

The characterization of Holmes himself relies on a kind of typology. That Doyle is both drawing upon and contributing to contemporary stereotypes of the aesthete in his creation of Holmes is evident;[12] a bachelor given to intense contemplation, affected postures, brilliant perceptions, and spontaneous overflows of tortured violin-playing, Holmes also uses the language of aesthetic experience to describe the process of his detective work. His investigative method, which relies upon "observation" and seeing with one's "own eyes," deliberately evokes the radical empiricism of the nineteenth-century Aesthetic Movement. A later Sherlock Holmes story, "The Adventure of the Engineer's Thumb" (1891), makes a point of demonstrating Holmes' aestheticism to the reader by playing with the distinction between the stereotyped aesthete that he at first evokes and the true aesthete that the reader is meant to come to recognize beneath the deceptive surface. Watson describes Holmes' gaze at a crime victim as "the weary, heavy-lidded expression that veiled his keen and eager nature."[13] Though his "heavy-lidded" weariness is reminiscent of the dissipated physicality of the stereotypical degenerate decadent, Holmes' essential, but carefully "veiled" nature is more inclined to the kind of "keen" aesthetic perception prescribed by Pater than the opiate-enhanced lethargy to which the detective is also prone.

Holmes' scientific outlook, then, is importantly allied with artistic experience – his tortured appreciation of the violin and his "immense" knowledge of sensational literature (16) prepare him for his crime-solving as well as, if not better than, his knowledge of either chemistry or the law. From his understanding of the ways of street urchins to his knowledge of German, Holmes creates for himself a richness and diversity of experience that, the plot's logic tells us, his shaping artistic mind will later be able to put to use.[14] When Watson says that Holmes works mostly "for the love of his art," then, he means that the detective's work *is* literally art.[15]

However, as many critics have noted, his detective novels seem more interested in shutting down than in opening up the instability of know-ledge that late-Victorian aestheticism invoked. While Holmes might resemble an aesthete, his aestheticism is actually more Coleridgean than Paterian, relying ultimately on the assumption of certain absolute (in Holmes' case, cultural) truths.[16] While he is interested in empirical observation, he ultimately deduces rigid general principles from the details he observes: truths that enable a cosmopolitan vision and cosmo-politan knowledge in their ability to transcend national boundaries, but that also evince a Kantian, or Arnoldian, universalism which obliterates cultural particularity. In his most optimistic moments, Arnold imagined cosmopolitan knowledge as an "empire of facts"[17] that would eventually unite the world (or at least Europe) in "one great confederation, bound to a joint action and working to a common result."[18] Likewise, Holmes boasts to Watson that he can solve most of his crimes from his armchair because of his ability to intuit the truth from the *narratives* of his clients and to treat the world as one great confederation of stories. Solving a crime, he points out, involves not only first-hand experience but also the ability to read generically, to move from the particular to the universal by seeing a clue as part of a larger pattern of predictable human behavior.

Though Holmes' "Book of Life," from which Watson first gleans the detective's philosophy, suggests that the truth is accessible by mere obser-vation and that Holmes can "by a momentary expression, a twitch of muscle or a glance of an eye ... fathom a man's innermost thoughts" (18), it also states that a knowledge of the "history of crime" will reveal the deep-seated patterns underlying human behavior (20). Holmes can solve certain crimes from his armchair if only people will tell him stories because, he proclaims, there is a "family resemblance" about misdeeds that allows him to deduce what plots will be followed.

The "family resemblance" among crimes that Holmes detects thus relies on Victorian cultural anthropology's notion of a "family of man." Both rest upon a developmental notion of culture that allows Holmes to insert the evidence he assembles into a hierarchical model in which everything, at least to the knowledgeable, cosmopolitan individual, is connected and comprehensible. Understanding the diversity of the city inside out, from the number of people who reside in it ("five million") to the world of cabdrivers to the netherworld of homeless "street Arabs" who track down the culprit for him, Holmes shows himself to be the master of an "empire of facts" both empirical and cultural. Describing his impressions of Holmes' visitors, Watson states:

> There was one little sallow, rat-faced, dark-eyed fellow, who was introduced to me as Mr Lestrade ... One morning a young girl called, fashionably dressed, and stayed for half an hour or more. The same afternoon brought a grey-headed, seedy visitor, looking like a Jew pedlar, who appeared to me to be much excited, and who was closely followed by a slip-shod elderly woman. On another occasion an old white-haired gentleman had an interview with my companion; and on another, a railway porter in his velveteen uniform. (17)

The characters in Holmes' waiting room, representing both different classes and different racial and occupational "types" (the excitable Jew, the man in uniform), demonstrate his range of experience and constitute a "family of man" that is readily legible to the well-trained eye.

As other critics have noted, the similarity of Holmes' name to "home" is no accident.[19] Holmes is, at least in some ways, the consummate cosmopolitan, imaginatively at home anywhere in the world. The plural implied by his name is thus appropriate as well, for his "home" extends beyond the domestic sphere (the place where we are most likely to encounter him) to wherever he happens to find himself. As a result, he is never discomfited by his surroundings or at a loss to understand them. In *The Sign of Four*, for example, he is able to recite the names of streets as he passes them in a cab, despite the fact that his companion, Watson, declares himself to be utterly disoriented.[20] Thus one of the most egregious gaps in the detective's knowledge – the fact that he is not aware that the earth revolves around the sun – ends up working to his benefit, allowing him to hold on to a traditional humanist cosmology with himself, rather than humanity in general, at the center of the world. Being able to take advantage of all his senses, a skill that his aesthetic sensibility has helped to cultivate, means that he is always perceptually, if not physically, at the focal point of the action. Hence his attachment to London, which represents for Holmes an intensity of experience and a kind of centrality upon which his aesthetic identity depends.

In "The Adventure of the Cardboard Box," Watson testifies to Holmes' love of the city, saying that:

> [N]either the country nor the sea presented the slightest attraction to him. He loved to lie in the very centre of five millions of people, with his filaments stretching out and running through them, responsive to every little rumour or suspicion of unsolved crime.[21]

Envisioning Holmes as a spider in the web, this image lends a "homely" and naturalistic quality to the peculiarly modern and destabilized subjectivity of the "networked" individual. Holmes' "filaments" are his connections with the street Arabs, the diverse set of contacts he has with the "different classes" that come to his office, and his transatlantic telegraphs – all of these connections made possible by the new diversity and technological sophistication of urban life.

Doyle's use of web imagery here picks up on its earlier use by a range of Victorian writers, including Carlyle, Eliot, Darwin, and Pater. Recurrently in the nineteenth century, web images functioned as a way to visualize the aesthetic problem of how to apprehend an infinity of connections (especially between people) while retaining a clear sense of any specific part of the whole. Eliot famously refers to Middlemarch as "this particular web," thereby indicating both the myriad of connections discernible in the town's community and the fact that there is a larger, more "general" web to which it belongs and for which she does not (or cannot) account.[22] James, too, addressed this conundrum: "Really, universally, relations stop nowhere, and the exquisite problem of the artist is eternally but to draw, by a geometry of his own, the circle within which they happily appear to do so."[23] Pater's use of the web in his "Conclusion" also reflects upon James' "exquisite problem." His is a radically destabilizing image, placing the subject at the periphery of the perceptual world, rather than at its center: "That clear perpetual outline of face and limb is but an image of ours, under which we group them – a design in a web, the actual threads of which pass out beyond it."[24] In Pater's view of the aesthetic act, we put ourselves artificially at the center of the world by creating "images" and seeing "designs" in the web. In actuality, though, there is no center – only a multiplicity of relations that extends out into the world. Doyle joins Pater in equating the act of perception with the aesthetic pleasure of producing an outline within a web of knowledge, but Holmes' web is ultimately quite different. Rather than passing out before him, the threads of Holmes' web lead, conveniently, directly to him. His "outline" therefore seems to encompass all webs, instead of any "particular" ones. Able to see all connections (all "five million" in the case of London) by virtue of being at their center, he is then able to trace each thread of knowledge outward to the various truths that he seeks.

In the speech to Watson that gives the novel its title, Holmes' grim aesthetic pleasure in the face of murder is made explicit:

> I might not have gone but for you, and so have missed the finest study I ever came across: a study in scarlet, eh? Why shouldn't we use a little art jargon? There's the scarlet thread of murder running through the colorless skein of life, and our duty is to unravel it, and isolate it, and expose every inch of it. (40)

Through this graphic image, Holmes self-consciously equates his detective work with art: the act of interpreting murder is a "study" at once scientific and artistic. What makes Holmes able to solve crimes is not only his ability to read details ("every inch" of thread) but also to perceive and to "unravel" the form as a whole. It is not just the objective contemplation of facts but also the assumption of a unified cultural sphere – and hence the readability of stories across cultures and nations – that enables Holmes to read backwards from the clues at the crime scene to the romance-adventure in Utah. The objective fact – a wedding ring found on the body – immediately makes the murder narrative recognizable to Holmes as a romance: "'Clearly,'" he asserts with unswerving confidence, "'the murderer had used it to remind his victim of some dead or absent woman'" (125). Holmes' cosmopolitan stance, and his ability to solve crimes across national boundaries, thus resides in his being able to observe, through the lens of the city, universal correspondences. Because the stories have a common "thread," Holmes can assert a transcendent vision of history, reading both across time (by connecting Hope's story to that of any man avenging a wronged woman) and across space (by tracing Hope's history back to his adventures in Utah).

Paradoxically, the tale's real mystery or "magic" rests not so much in the whodunit tale as in the details of its solution. We marvel not at the revelation of the criminal or his capture but at Holmes' logic in action. Contrary to popular conceptions of the detective novel, the protagonist's deductions are not, in fact, marvelous because of their scientific brilliance. Instead they are marvelous – magical even – because they involve a *leap* of logic. In the case of *A Study in Scarlet*, this leap takes place when Holmes deduces that a ring on a dead man's body means that the killer must have been angry about his fiancée's death. While he mocks the police for assuming that the word "Rache" is an abbreviation of Rachel, he too sees the world through romance-tinted lenses. With his "intuitive" leap of logic, Holmes' empirical gaze becomes imperial, providing access to truth so completely that the whole world, from Afghanistan to Utah, is unified and rendered intelligible.

This gaze, however, is not only that of the all-seeing "imperial eye" but also that of the active looking of a selective, artistic process. Resembling a Romantic poet as much as a Victorian detective, Holmes has faith that the hidden patterns of the world will reveal themselves to him over time and that, correspondingly, meaning will be revealed to others through the activities of his shaping intellect. While these patterns for Holmes are largely secular ones (a ring signifying a lost love, for instance), the novel imbues these patterns of behavior with spiritual significance. Holmes' book, with its Biblical title, *The Book of Life*, offers a secular epistemology of detection that, the novel's ending demonstrates, coincides conveniently with the moral epistemology of religion. As the romance form of the Utah section meets the realist form of the London section, events begin to take on an allegorical aura. London, by the end of the novel, is not only the imperial city that opens out on to the wider world, but is also the still center that draws the world back in. There, the Mormons, Drebber and Strangerson, meet with what the novel implies is the fate they deserve, even as Holmes catches and convicts their murderer.

Playing a strange version of Russian roulette with each of his victims, in which he forces them to eat one of two pills (one of which is poisoned) while he eats the other, Hope, associated by his name with one of the faithful in Bunyan's *Pilgrim's Progress*, states of Lucy's murderer that "'Providence would never have allowed his guilty hand to pick out anything but the poison'" (120). Hope also conveniently dies of a heart attack before he can be submitted to the judicial process, another indication that a "higher" justice than that of the courts has prevailed. London may be the City of Damnation (the "cesspool" and "great wilderness" Watson describes early on in the novel), but it is also, by the end, the Heavenly City, the place where Hope finds peace. Hope, in negotiating the city, is navigating his way to justice, as is Holmes. Both know it intimately: Holmes through his diverse "contacts" with residents of the city and Hope by impersonating an inhabitant and navigating it, literally, in the role of cabdriver. Drebber and Strangerson, however, like the unfaithful pilgrims they represent, stumble drunkenly around the city and wander into Hope's vengeful clutches, betraying their own profound lack of cosmopolitan judgment.

The novel seems to imply that in hijacking a Christian God for their imperialist aspirations (Drebber says to Hope that the Lord will gather him and "all the nations" into "the true fold ... in His own good time" [92]), the Mormons demonstrate their gross misreading of cosmic purpose. Presuming to know God's purpose at all times, they neglect to look for evidence of its functioning in the empirical. Holmes' superior "natural supernaturalism" links interiority with exteriority. *The Book of Life* that outlines his secular religion states that "a momentary expression, a twitch of a muscle or glance of an eye" can allow one to "fathom a man's inmost thoughts." Particulars are thus linked to universal cultural and behavioral patterns. As Holmes says, "there is nothing new under the sun, it has all been done before" (29). A crime is interpretable through its signs because of its typicality – a typicality which Holmes understands as infinitely generalizable: "all life is a great chain, the nature of which is known whenever we are shown a single link of it" (18–19). Here, Holmes unites the language of cosmology (especially through his evocation of the Great Chain of Being) and positivism to argue that individual clues will inevitably reveal a larger pattern. Doyle's use of the web metaphor, which makes the world, and the connections therein, transparent to Holmes, similarly forces together romance and empiricism, allowing the novel to make the argument that observing the world intensely and carefully will allow for the unraveling of its mysteries *and* provide a basis for judgment and justice.

To us now, the infallibility of Holmes' reading seems a magical exercise of control over an increasingly unknowable city and world. In the contradictions between the romance tropes and the facts of observable evidence to which Holmes gives allegiance, the novel ends up exposing the gaps in meaning it is trying desperately to close, and expunging the question of the political repercussions of having foreigners on English soil. Holmes' declamation about the murder: "It must have been a private wrong, and not a political one, which called for such a methodical revenge" (125) thus appears spectacularly arbitrary, especially in light of the fact that real-life terrorism in London was being methodically practiced by Fenians at the time Doyle was writing.[25] Despite its investment in the web of connections, the novel expends its formal energy reducing the political to the personal, and making the empirical a signpost for the spiritual.

Herein lies a possible explanation for Doyle's turn to the occult, which began during this period and eventually became his chief intellectual passion.[26] Involved in seances, spirit photography, automatic writing, as well as the notorious fairy photograph scandal,[27] he became what might be called an occult imperialist, "increasingly interested," as Patrick Brantlinger describes it, "in the spiritualist rebuilding of nothing less than world civilization" with England at its center.[28] If radical empiricism, in the face of an increasingly cosmopolitan and unassimilable world, inevitably exposes a gap between facts and the modes by which they can be judged, fiction, Doyle suggests, offers means by which to close it. Hence the policeman writing down Hope's confession puts "finishing touches" to it (121); the artistic imagination must, Holmes' story tells us, round off the ragged edges that scientific observation leaves behind. Though Holmes' mixed epistemology initially suggests to us that art will make us better readers of the world, by the end of the novel, art (in the form of the romance-allegory that Hope's story becomes) must be superimposed on the world, not so much a world apart as a spirit-world hovering uncertainly above.

"PUT TOGETHER OF SUCH QUEER PIECES": HAUNTINGS AND HYBRIDITY IN "THE PRINCESS CASAMASSIMA"

The Princess Casamassima is as ambitious in its geographical range of reference as *A Study in Scarlet*.[29] Just as Doyle draws seemingly impossible connections between Mormon pioneers in Utah, secret societies on the Continent, and private relationships in England, James' London is a place where Italian, American, German, and French, as well as English characters conspire together. Like Holmes, Hyacinth Robinson, James' protagonist, is an aesthete and a cosmopolite who must cultivate a distanced, yet worldly outlook on the city in order to understand the international implications of his day-to-day experiences and to unlock the mysteries that surround him. Though the mysteries of Hyacinth's world turn out to be unsolvable (an important difference from *A Study in Scarlet*), they share with Holmes' a new sense of geopolitical scale. The *frisson* that accompanies the mysteries of both novels, in other words, is generated in part by an awe at the imbrication of the individual in world politics, even if, by the end of the novels, this imbrication has been partially, if not wholly, disavowed by their protagonists.

Despite the fact that he briefly adopted the "objective" stance of urban investigator and visited Millbank prison in order to create a "realistic" description of Hyacinth's mother's incarceration, James describes the process of writing *The Princess Casamassima* in his preface to the novel as a largely subjective imaginative experience:

I recall pulling no wires, knocking at no closed doors, applying for no "authentic" information ... To haunt the great city and by this habit to penetrate it, imaginatively, in as many places as possible – *that* was to be informed, *that* was to pull at wires, *that* was to open doors, *that* positively was to groan at times under the weight of one's accumulations. (48)

Unlike other documenters of the city's grittiness, such as Henry Mayhew and General William Booth, James shuns the objective stance of the urban investigator in this description, adopting the role of "haunter" instead. Though, like Holmes, he professes a faith in empirical method – "the fruit of direct experience" (47) – he is more interested in autoethnography (the study of his own cultural experience) than ethnography (the study of others). He thus imagines himself as a repository of urban knowledge, "groaning" at the richness of his first-hand encounter with city life. This idea of novel-writing also reflects the methods he recommends in "The Art of Fiction" (1888): "A novel is in its broadest definition a personal, a direct impression of life: that, to begin with, constitutes its value which is greater or less according to the intensity of the impression."[30] In his rapturous celebration of London as a city productive of this very kind of intensity, James is reacting to the discovery of a new aesthetic subject: it is significant, in light of this, that his contemplation of "the hard modern twinkle of the roof of the Crystal Palace"[31] evokes Pater's "hard, gem-like flame."

Jonathan Freedman's *Professions of Taste* offers a definitive study of James' close relationship to the British Aesthetic Movement.[32] Yet the novelist's connection of aesthetic experience with the experience of the cosmopolitan city demands closer attention if one is to see the conjunction between aestheticism and cosmopolitanism as productive of something more than an affected elitism – particularly since James is often upheld as the paradigmatic example of the privileged *flâneur* whose cosmopolitanism is implicated in imperial arrogance. Judith Walkowitz, describing James' attitude towards London, argues that his voyeuristic flâneurship "presupposed a privileged male subject whose identity was stable, coherent, autonomous; who was, moreover, capable through reason and its 'science' of establishing a reliable and universal knowledge of 'man' and his world." She also points to a contradictory feature of the Jamesian *flâneur* – the fact that alongside his rational view of the cityscape, he nourished a fantastical view of it, transforming it into "a landscape of strangers and secrets." Within this mysterious landscape, the *flâneur* thrives on the exploitation and suffering around him, transforming it into a "vivid individual psychological experience."[33] While Sherlock Holmes corresponds closely to the kind of Victorian *flâneur* Walkowitz describes, James is a more ambiguous figure. That he inhabits a privileged position is undeniable, but the transformation of the city into a landscape of strangers and secrets in his work on London can be seen as emblematic of his deliberate undoing of a "stable, coherent, autonomous" position and his formation of a resolutely *un*stable perspective in its place: one from which one's perception of the city's treasures is inseparable from a simultaneous view of the suffering upon which its plentitude often depends.

James' interest in the British capital was at its height when he wrote *The Princess Casamassima*, for 1888 was also the year of his essay "London." While the city, for him, represented the "epitome of the round world," it also represented a chance to prove his credentials on a wider scale than ever before:

I aspire to write in such a way that it would be impossible to an outsider to say whether I am, at any given moment, an American writing about England or an Englishman writing about America ... and so far from being ashamed of such an ambiguity, I would be exceedingly proud of it, for it would be highly civilized.[34]

In London, James came to define his literary goal in explicitly cosmopolitan terms; interestingly, he associates creativity and achievement, indeed the very act of being "civilized," with the loss of national identity. As Alexander Zwerdling argues, James had always attempted in his novels, famous for their parade of different national characters, a cosmopolitan fusion of types and behaviors.[35] Yet here he clearly wants to embody this fusion himself, much as Hyacinth does in *The Princess Casamassima*. London seemed the ideal place in which to achieve this formidable goal because it offered "the biggest aggregation of human life – the most complete compendium of the world."[36] Along with, and because of, its diversity, London also offered an unparalleled intensity of experience: "[T]he British capital is the particular spot in the world which communicates the greatest sense of life."[37]

Here the conjunction between aestheticism and cosmopolitanism in James' investments becomes clear. The series of sensations, or Pater's "quickened sense of life," is achieved for James through the experience of the city because the diversity of cultures there, and the profusion of sights that accompany them, provide the most intense of all possible experiences. Yet the urban experience is also linked to cosmopolitanism for James because together with his recognition of the city's capacity for producing *sensation* went a belief in its promulgation of *sensitivity*. As London is "the property and even the home of the human race," James argued, "one's appreciation of it is really a large sympathy, a comprehensive love of humanity."[38] James' description of the experience of city living is therefore simultaneously aesthetic – an "appreciation" – and cosmopolitan – with its "comprehensive love of humanity." The two qualities are related by their interchangeability: the "appreciation" is "really a large sympathy."

In his preface to *The Princess Casamassima*, James revisits this theme. "This fiction," he writes, "proceeded quite directly, during the first year of a long residence in London, from the habit and the interest of walking the streets," and functioned as a response to "the urgent appeal, on the part of everything, to be interpreted and, so far as may be, reproduced" (33). In his emphasis on the "many impressions" produced by "the great city upon an imagination quick to react" (33), James echoes Pater's description of the "quickened" sensation of the aesthetic experience. By lending the sights of London subjectivity, the ability to "urgent[ly] appeal" to the observer, he also formulates the relationship between city and *flâneur* as the mutual shaping of object and subject. This unstable formulation not only reproduces the indeterminacy of aesthetic theory but also posits a way of thinking about the city experience as a cosmopolitan willingness to be radically reshaped by the encounter with difference inevitably demanded by urban experience.

Though London is too vast to grasp as a whole, the spectator derives pleasure both from the act of imagination that provisionally assimilates it, and from the self-consciousness of seeing himself as part of the whole:

Practically, of course, one lives in a quarter, in a plot, but in imagination and by a conscious mental act of reference the accommodated haunter enjoys the whole ... He fancies himself, as they say, for being a particle in so unequalled an aggregation.[39]

In this passage, James delineates an almost auto-erotic enjoyment (he "fancies himself") of the effacement of the self against the background of the enormous city. This vision of the relationship between spectator and city emphasizes not the spectator's centrality – the view from above that allows him to see the whole (as Walkowitz's argument about James might lead one to expect), or Holmes' nodal position as the cunning spider in the middle of the web of "five millions of people" – but instead his insignificance. Rather than performing an act of assimilation, as Holmes does, the spectator's imagination dissolves his subjectivity into that of a ghost ("haunter"), or particle.

The image of the disintegration of the self against the background of the urban spectacle, while certainly productive of pleasure, is only in part the pleasure of panoptical power; pleasure also simultaneously derives from the *loss* of male bourgeois voyeuristic authority as the spectator is absorbed into the spectacle and displaced by it. The aesthetic experience of the city that James describes, then, is akin to the pleasure and pain of the sublime, for the limits of the subject himself are as much a part of the act of perception as the city is. Power and powerlessness exist side by side; the spectator is always aware of his position as such in his "enjoyment of the whole," but is never able to transcend the spectacle and assimilate it as something apart from himself. This inability, the lack of god-like perspective, is part of the vexed pleasure of the experience, of James' self-fancying.

James' focus on the ineffability of London, through images such as that of the "accommodated haunter" in the quote above, and his repeated insistence in his essays, letters, and *The Princess Casamassima* on London's "magnificent mystifications," suggest a kind of mystery writing different from, though related to, Doyle's. The fact that both James' and Doyle's writings employ mystery plots and gothic tropes is not coincidental. The unknowability of the city, because of its size and the range of cultural difference that it offers, demands, for these novels, the language of the uncanny, while their preoccupation with conspiracy and murder reflects the thinly veiled anxieties that this exciting but terrifyingly vast space produces in its observers. While Doyle's Sherlock Holmes novels and stories often lend closure to the specific mysteries they represent, containing the anxieties they mobilize, larger existential mysteries are occasionally hinted at, as in Holmes' unanswered question to Watson in "The Adventure of the Cardboard Box": "'What is the meaning of it, Watson? ... What object is served by this circle of misery and violence and fear?'"[40] James' novel, however, makes it clear that the specific mysteries laid out by its plot (whether Hyacinth's mother killed his father; who Hyacinth is to kill, and why) are necessarily less important than the mystery and sublimity of the city itself, and it shuns closure for this reason.

The class tension central to the plot of *The Princess Casamassima* is epitomized by the conflicted heritage of Hyacinth Robinson, whose working-class French mother has been jailed for killing the English nobleman she believes to be his father. Brought up in London by a seamstress, Miss Pynsent, Hyacinth is divided between loyalty to the working class (represented by his wronged mother) and a sense of superiority to it because of his allegedly aristocratic roots. He works as a bookbinder, a trade with artistic ambitions, and falls in with a motley group whose radical ideas appeal to his sense of alienation. These include an English working-class character, Paul Muniment, and the Princess Casamassima, an Italian cosmopolite who seeks to escape her husband and aristocratic life by joining the revolutionary struggle – a movement that remains shadowy and unnamed throughout the novel. A mysterious German, Hoffendahl, is one of its leaders, and Hyacinth is momentarily inspired by him to perform a dramatic gesture of self-renunciation, agreeing to sacrifice his life for the revolution if called upon to do so. Ironically, however, the Princess's growing interest in Hyacinth as a revolutionary member of the working class exposes him to a world of luxury and privilege that appeals to him more than revolution. Shortly after proclaiming that the accumulated artistic achievement of tradition is the justification for upholding it, Hyacinth is called upon to assassinate a duke in the name of the revolutionary cause. Distanced from the Princess, who now finds Paul a more "authentic" member of the working class than himself, and unwilling either to break his oath or to repeat history by reproducing the crime of his mother (killing an aristocrat), Hyacinth kills himself instead. The dramatic tableau he creates in death, with his white face, bloody chest, and outstretched arm, is reminiscent of another aestheticized rendering of a bourgeois revolutionary, David's *Death of Marat*.

Due to the novel's tragic outcome, it is often read as positing an impassable divide between aesthetics and politics.[41] Hyacinth's acquisition of taste under the guidance of the Princess seems to lead inevitably to his rejection of revolution. Moreover, it is hinted that his ability to cultivate taste is innate (inherited from his nobleman father), and thus needs only the right environment in order to surface. He is destined, as a consequence, to be led away from the revolutionaries by his superior sensibility. The seeming disjunction between aesthetics and politics, however, is not as pat as the over-determining role of class in the outcome of the novel might suggest. James also represents Hyacinth's relation to the city very much as he does his own: as an ongoing aesthetic experience that, in allowing a perception of the self as inseparable from a larger whole, has political repercussions.

Hyacinth, like James, conducts "interminable, restless, melancholy, moody, yet all-observant strolls through London" (102). As he does so, he demonstrates a kind of split flâneurian vision, in which he becomes simultaneously conscious of his own direct experience of the city and able to extrapolate from that experience to what lies outside it:

he was perpetually, almost morbidly, conscious that the circle in which he lived was an infinitesimally small, shallow eddy in the roaring vortex of London, and his imagination plunged again and again into the waves that whirled past it and round it, in the hope of being carried to some brighter, happier vision – the vision of societies in which, in splendid rooms, with smiles and soft voices, distinguished men, with women who were both proud and gentle, talked about art, literature and history. (145)

While this famous passage depicts Hyacinth hallucinating himself into a higher social order – a not particularly egalitarian mental exercise – it anticipates future moments in the novel where this kind of split vision allows for the simultaneous perspective of different class positions. Here, as a member of the lower middle class, he imagines himself as an aristocrat; later in the novel, when he is "raised" from his class position by his association with the Princess, he empathizes with "the immeasurable misery of the people" (446). The narrative produces no stable viewpoint from which Hyacinth can seek refuge from history.

Mixedness, then, is the novel's constant theme. The fact that Hyacinth can imaginatively juxtapose two worlds is reflective of his identity throughout the novel. Due to the hopelessly mixed nature of his heritage, and hence of his perceptions, Hyacinth wavers constantly between identification with, and objectification of, other classes, nationalities, and sexes. In moments of kinship inspired by revolutionary fervor, he describes the crowd he walks through as his "brothers and sisters" (106), but he is equally likely to feel alienated by them, and to perceive his working-class girlfriend Millicent and her set as vulgar and childlike:

for our hero she was magnificently plebian, in the sense that implied a kind of loud recklessness of danger ... She summed up the sociable, humorous, ignorant chatter of the masses, their capacity for offensive and defensive passion ... their ideal of something smug and prosperous. (161)

Reducing both Millicent, and the class she represents for him, to promulgators of "bad taste," Hyacinth here uses a limited definition of the aesthetic to disidentify himself from the class with which he is most familiar.

His sexual identity is as fickle as that of his class. Alternately courted by Paul Muniment and the Princess Casamassima for his value as a political ally, his feelings for both are represented in romantic language. Paul's approval of him gives him a "strange, inexpressible heartache," while the Princess becomes his romantic ideal, described as "a radiant angel" (407) whose every action is "rare and fine" (431). Hyacinth is described as "put together of such queer pieces" (170), and Medley, the name of the Princess Casamassima's home (where Hyacinth refines his aesthetic sensibilities), suggests the mixed blessing that is the Princess's life, the mixed nature of the myriad of aesthetic objects that it contains, and the mixed perception that aesthetic appreciation demands.

Mixedness is also brought to the reader's attention on the level of form in the novel. Indeed, in its self-consciousness about the impurity of the forms that it employs, *The Princess Casamassima* presents a marked departure from some of James' earlier work. For instance, James addresses the reader at various points in the novel, drawing attention to the narrative "I," and breaking the illusion of fiction that he so rigorously prescribes in "The Art of Fiction": "Certain accomplished novelists have a habit of giving themselves away which must often bring tears to the eyes of people who take their fiction seriously." Arguing that the novel must "insist on the fact that the picture is reality, so the novel is history," James insists on a "direct impression of life" rather than a mediated one.[42] *The Princess Casamassima*, however, perversely persists in bringing the reader's attention to the surface of the text, reminding us of its artifice.

Its deployment of romance is a source of this artificial effect. If *A Study in Scarlet* asks to be read as a romance, as I have argued, so, to some degree, does *The Princess Casamassima*. In his review of the novel, Lionel Trilling, for example, does not hesitate to treat it in this way, despite its explicit character as "social problem" novel. He says of Hyacinth that "[h]is situation is as chancy as that of any questing knight of medieval romance," and maintains that "through the massed social fact there runs the thread of legendary romance, even of downright magic."[43] He cites Rebecca West to support his reading, pointing out that she thought it "one of the big jokes in literature that it was James, who so prided himself on his lack of *naïveté*, who should have brought back to fiction the high implausibility of the old novels which relied for their effects on dark and stormy nights, Hindu servants, mysterious strangers, and bloody swords wiped on richly embroidered handkerchiefs."[44] While these critiques put their fingers on the heavy-handedness of James' use of romance (hard to ignore in a novel with both an orphan and a princess), they obscure the intention behind his theatricality. In this novel, much more than in his earlier ones, James is profoundly skeptical about the ability of stories to draw upon universal types and their ability to tell us anything "direct" about the nature of reality.

Romance tropes, therefore, are heavily ironized in *The Princess Casamassima*, most obviously in the representation of Hyacinth. Ross Posnock argues that "Hyacinth is a hero unable to escape an obsession with the 'romantic innuendoes' of his origins because he constructs the self by internalizing the mythic romances of the popular press to which he was addicted as a child."[45] Hyacinth also reads his friends – Paul Muniment, the Princess, and Millicent – through the lens of romance, seeing them as either heros, saints, or martyrs, much as Holmes reads the clues at the crime scene as evidence of a romance plot. Unlike Holmes' romantic attitude, however, Hyacinth's is satirized by the narrator, who draws our attention to his conflation of history and the fictive iconography that accompanies it:

Having the history of the French Revolution at his fingers' ends, Hyacinth could easily see [Millicent] (if there should ever be barricades in the streets of London), with a red cap of liberty on her head and her white throat bared so that she should be able to shout the louder the Marseillaise of the hour. (161)

While we are told elsewhere that Millicent is both apolitical and notably unsympathetic to the brand of organizing that Hyacinth becomes involved in, here Hyacinth "easily" gives her a heroic central role in his fantasy of future revolution, demonstrating that his view of her, because of her class and gender, is based more on fictional typing than on fact. Rather than inserting his characters into romance narratives in this novel (as he does in earlier ones, such as *The American*, whose very title suggests that the characters within function as national and behavioral types), James instead shows how characters insert each other into roles which they, in turn, refuse to live up to: roles always glaringly out of synch with the mixed nature of experience.

The tension between determinism and essentialism in the novel also complicates the question of how to read character. Hyacinth's "aristocracy," noted by all who meet him, is a case in point. Is he aristocratic because his father was an aristocrat (the identity of his father, however, is never finally determined in the novel), because he was spoiled by Pynsent who believed his father was an aristocrat, or merely because he possesses "refinement," a somewhat undefined and random quality in the novel? By leaving all these questions frustratingly unanswered, James makes an argument about the inadequacy of fiction to reflect reality and the general inscrutability of people to each other – an inscrutability brought glaringly to light by the intensity of the urban experience.

The Princess Casamassima's undermining of typicality is related to its redefinition of authenticity as well. Hyacinth is authentic and sincere paradoxically because he never chooses a position and is always in a state of flux, moving restlessly from one identification to the next. The Princess, on the other hand, is inauthentic and insincere precisely because she chooses positions. When she tells Hyacinth that she wants an "authentic" experience of the city (201), we know she will never be able to have it because her language indicates her alienation from it. Hyacinth himself does not escape contingency (he must see the consequences through of the revolutionary oath he has taken, for instance) but he steadfastly refuses to move from a liminal identity to a fixed one by committing any act (such as the Princess' renouncement of wealth) that will identify him firmly with one group or another.

True perception – aesthetic perception – in *The Princess Casamassima*, then, is identified most consistently with a palimpsest-like vision. While the Princess and her amoral sidekick Sholto are ostensibly aesthetes and cosmopolitans, their boredom is an inevitable result of the relative stability of their identities. Hyacinth's constant moral and political equivocation, on the other hand, is represented as an intensely pleasurable response to the plenitude of the city:

He suspended, as it were, his small sensibility in the midst of it, and it quivered there with joy and hope and ambition, as well as with the effort of renunciation. (480)

Like James in his role as the "accommodated haunter," Hyacinth wants at once to observe the city and become one with it, to remove himself from contingency and identity but also to perceive this removal, the "effort of renunciation." Hyacinth is the novel's most sympathetic character, not because he is "worldly" in the sense that the well-traveled Princess and Sholto are but because he is simultaneously open to being changed by the world and willing to try to change it himself (if only, in the end, by removing himself from it). As Posnock argues in his analysis of James' dialectical understanding of consciousness: "James emphasizes ... the production of difference generated by the dissolving of identity. Difference is what makes for a 'richer saturation' of an ongoing process that avoids closure."[46]

Hyacinth's hybridized view of the world is thus equated with a transcendent vision that is valorized over the "healthy singleness of vision" possessed by the dogged revolutionary stance of Paul Muniment (445). When Muniment states "[t]he way I've used my eyes in this abominable metropolis has led to my seeing that present arrangements won't do" (445),

Hyacinth produces in response an interior vision that is at once imperial in its vision of the aristocratic splendor of the world-city and notably compassionate in its inability to turn away from the spectacle of suffering:

He saw the immeasurable misery of the people, and yet he saw all that had been, as it were, rescued from it: the treasures, the felicities, the splendours, the successes of the world. All this took the form, sometimes, to his imagination, of a vast, vague, dazzling presence, an irradiation of light from objects undefined … He presently added a hundred things Muniment had told him about the foul horrors of the worst districts of London, pictures of incredible shame and suffering that he had put before him, came back to him now, with the memory of the passion they had kindled at the time. (446)

If culture – the "successes" of the world – is upheld here as a transnational (and implicitly Western) principle, as it is in *A Study in Scarlet*, it is also shown to be radically contingent, both on the "shame and suffering" that underlie it and on the perspective of the viewer. Unlike *The Prelude*'s narrator, Hyacinth responds to the city's complexity with a split rather than unified vision. Within his montage-like portrait of urban space, realistic details, from "treasures" and "felicities" to the "foul horrors of the worst districts of London" refuse to disappear in a moment of sublime integration but remain suspended together in irreconcilable tension.

The city as microcosm of the world, and the historical condition of mixedness that it provides, thus play the same role as the work of art in the novel. A "quickened" aesthetic consciousness and political conscience, the novel argues, produce, and are produced by, urban space and it is precisely the vertiginous pleasures of hybridity detectable in Hyacinth's mixed vision which allow for an openness to the future, even if that future is sometimes unimaginable (as Hyacinth's death demonstrates) and alarming.

Just as Doyle's novel extends the realist novel's "knowable community" on to the world through the forms of romance, James' novel moves beyond realism as well, even more dramatically. His omniscient narrator, for instance, is tellingly flawed; the reader is left without a clear view of the revolutionary leader Hoffendahl, who has been surrounded by mystery from the start (like Kurtz in *Heart of Darkness*); we are barred from the sequence of thoughts that lead Hyacinth to kill himself (the perspective in the last chapter shifts to that of the Princess and a fellow conspirator, who are equally in the dark about his decision); and we never understand the actions of the Princess or Paul, who appear alternately mercenary or hypocritical. The narrator adds to this obfuscation by drawing attention to his occasional lapse in omniscience. When Hyacinth meets the

Princess' husband, for example, the narrator leaves his thoughts ambiguous, saying: "[i]t is needless to go into the question of what Hyacinth ... may have had on his conscience" (516). Arbitrary and inconsistent as these restrictions to the narrator's omniscience are, they serve all the more to remind us of the "limited circle" of the writer's art to which James refers in *Roderick Hudson*. Leaving characters only partially understood, communities shadowy and fragmented, and "mysteries abysmal" unnamed, James abandons the omniscient, "worldly" perspective of the realist narrator to acknowledge the mystery of the Other.

If there is any universalist conception of humanity in *The Princess Casamassima*, then, it consists of this shared mystery, or unknowability. James' use of romance and realism works to remind us of the conventionality of both and their insufficiency for adequately representing the sublime experience of the city. Thus when he writes in his preface that "there are London mysteries (dense categories of dark arcana) for every spectator" (35) he signals the inevitable proximity of the known and the unknown in urban space. We may, like Henry Mayhew, categorize the urban arcane, but it is ultimately our effort to do this impossible thing that is what is aesthetic about both city-living and novel-writing.

Anticipating accusations of sketchiness in his novel, James' preface offers this defense: "the value I wished most to render and the effect I wished most to produce were precisely those of our not knowing, of society's not knowing, but only guessing and suspecting and trying to ignore, what 'goes on' irreconcilably, subversively beneath the vast smug surface" (48). Collapsing the city and the individual together through the personifying adjective "smug," he testifies to the mysteries of both and, unlike Doyle, who insists on unraveling the secrets he sets up, refuses the comforts of a merely artistic solution to any of the thoroughly political questions he raises.

Holmes' aesthetic vision is that of a culturally homogeneous world that assumes the fictional contours of romance narrative and displaces issues of British imperialism on to the brutal and seemingly antediluvian territory of Utah. London's own cultural conflicts pale in comparison with the violent assimilationism of the Mormons, and it becomes a redemptive center into which all the characters are drawn, and where spiritual justice and liberal tolerance can coincide, with Holmes presiding over their dispensation. Hyacinth's aesthetic vision is an image of the city's size and variety as sublime and mystifying: an image that confounds, rather than confirms, his knowledge of the world and ability to act in it.

Both novels thus demonstrate the relationship between aestheticism and cosmopolitanism and the ways in which they become intimately and meaningfully related in the Victorian *fin de siècle*. The literary representation of a world brought together under a universal conception of human community entails the imaginative assimilation of humanity through the lens of the city; this artistic exercise provides the framework for the aesthetic and ideological contradictions that the novels face.

That the plots that bring international characters together also threaten the proper functioning of the nation-state is indicative of James' and Doyle's underlying unease with a world made smaller. While both novels suggest at various points that international conspiracy is the form which brings the world together, they both eventually retreat from the realm of politics to that of the personal. Holmes reads his mystery as a romance, and Hyacinth, refusing to become part of a larger political struggle, turns the excesses of that struggle on himself instead. If *The Princess Casamassima*, like *A Study in Scarlet*, ends up positing art as a separate place, though, it does so with a greater sense of the sacrifice entailed in such a necessarily violent separation.

A Study in Scarlet finally fails to provide, both literally and figuratively, a realistic basis for the cosmopolitan outlook that Holmes seems to personify, resorting instead to the vexed conflation of empiricism and spiritualism that characterized much mystery writing of the period. By using "providential" coincidences to bring about the redemption of Jefferson Hope at the novel's close, Doyle ends up absorbing the cultural dissonance so evident at its beginning into a familiar Manichean morality tale – one that sits uneasily with Holmes' skepticism and the atmosphere of imperial degeneration that pervades the novel but that has mysteriously evaporated by its end. *A Study in Scarlet*, then, enacts the problem of "bad" cosmopolitanism by reducing the political to the cultural. However, in the means by which it does this, it foregrounds the artifice involved in such an elision. The "finishing touches" that the policeman bestows on his report, and the distortion of the story that Watson reads to Holmes in the daily newspaper at the novel's end, self-consciously echo the work that Doyle has done to reconcile the cultural *and* political dissonances readily visible in other parts of the novel.

Hyacinth's more historicized vision of the world does not attempt to round off the ragged edges of narrative. His aestheticism is necessarily political because his version of aesthetic spectacle is simultaneously a view from above and below. Due to his mixed identity and experience of the city, Hyacinth cannot gloss over the suffering of the city's people even as he admires the art that posterity has bestowed on the world. His view of the city is sublime precisely because it is produced by the irreconcilability and significance of this vision. Never a complacent vision – a voyeuristic thrill at the spectacle of the world's suffering – Hyacinth's spectacle reveals a truth that he cannot ignore. While the action he takes is finally self-destruction, James' ending testifies to the aesthetic problem of representing not just the city but historical change itself. Rather than an attempt to encompass the world through the medium of the imperial archive (though the novel never entirely relinquishes its investment in this idea) or an effort to transcend it, aesthetic cosmopolitanism in James' novel, both an eloquent rendering of ideological complicity and a utopian refusal of it, is incarnated in the bloody, aestheticized excess of Hyacinth's corpse.

CHAPTER 4

Ethnography and allegory: Socialist internationalism and realist utopia in News from Nowhere and In Darkest England

> A map that does not include Utopia is not worth even glancing at, for it leaves out the one country at which Humanity is always landing.
>
> Oscar Wilde, "The Soul of Man under Socialism"[1]

As part of its strategy of provocation, Oscar Wilde's essay "The Soul of Man under Socialism" (1890) perversely suggests that utopia – a term derived from the Greek words for "no" and "place" – might be anchored at a specific point on a map. Wilde's essay makes the case for the compatibility of socialism and aesthetic individualism, arguing that true artistic self-expression can only occur in society as a whole after socialism has solved the problem of poverty and released individuals from the material constraints that dull their sensibilities. His impossible map of utopia is one of many characteristic paradoxes Wilde uses to confound Victorian norms of liberal, gradualist reform. But the idea of materializing utopia by mapping it on to a contemporary landscape, thus transporting its idealism from nowhere to the "here and now," was attempted in earnest by two other socialist works published in the same year as Wilde's: William Morris' *News from Nowhere* and General William Booth's *In Darkest England and the Way Out*. These works use intriguingly analogous utopian "mapping" schemes to address the desperate condition of London's urban poor. Because both argue for the necessity of confronting national problems with global solutions and use realist conventions to make their highly idealistic ventures seem viable, they should be seen as part of the literary tradition of cosmopolitan realism.[2]

They take that tradition to its logical conclusion, however, not only by positing the inseparability of urban and global space, as many other authors did, but by showing how those spaces might fundamentally renovate each other. In their futuristic visions, London no longer stands in for a global whole but is shown to be an integral part of a unified world. If aesthetic cosmopolitanism draws attention to the artifice of realist form and the tenuousness of the collectivities that narrative forms might shape, the socialist cosmopolitan utopias of Booth and Morris – with their determination to posit strong communitarian ties and to level out cultural differences and economic inequality – mark the limits of realism. *News from Nowhere* and *In Darkest England* generate a series of irresolvable tensions between secular and religious modes of explanation; ethnic essentialism and universal brotherhood; nature and nurture as contexts for social difference; and between the embedded present of urban squalor and the messianic future of global union. This chapter sees those tensions as emblematic of the Victorian global imagination at its most radical.

At first glance, of course, the writings of Booth and Morris are startlingly dissimilar. Morris' novel, for all its nostalgia, is an avant-garde work, equally indebted to Marxist ideas of social revolution and the Aesthetic Movement. It addresses problems of class conflict in England by using the romance novel to imagine a future in which all forms of social inequity have been resolved by the redistribution of wealth and aestheticization of work. Booth's work, by contrast, is at once a sociological study and a solicitation to the middle and upper classes to fund the Salvation Army. Influenced by Owenite collectivism, Henry Mayhew's study of the London poor, and H. M. Stanley's ethnographic travel narratives, it combines its communal work ideals with aggressively imperialist ones, evoking fears of "heathens and savages in the heart of our capital" to muster support for a scheme that promises economic and spiritual regeneration on both micro- and macro-levels.[3] While it imagines workers living and working together in small-scale, local communes, it also promises the eventual amalgamation of these communes into a Christian empire. In Booth's formulation, the spread of Salvation Army work-colonies across the globe will prevent Malthusian chaos at home – but only if British cultural values and administrative savvy are used to control the colonies from the center.[4]

Booth and Morris, then, seem to epitomize dichotomous strands within the discourse of cosmopolitanism. Booth's racist and imperialist utopianism fits the mold of the "bad" cosmopolitanism described by critics such as Simon Gikandi and Peter Van der Veer, who stress cosmopolitanism's affiliation with imperialism, missionary work, and Eurocentrism.[5] Morris' cosmopolitanism, however, is more likely to be seen as a critical and radical version, as it explicitly seeks to sunder global ideals from capitalist relations between nations by championing internationalism as the precondition for self-sufficiency on the local level. Regenia Gagnier, for example, states that "Morris was equally committed to a nativist love of the land and socialist internationalism: his is what we would call a situated cosmopolitanism." Pointing to his translation of world literatures and his emphasis on the figure of the "Guest" and hospitality in his own writing, Gagnier argues that Morris united openness to difference and a practice of transcultural exchange with a desire for worldwide revolution, thus exhibiting a cosmopolitanism more radical than some forms today.[6]

Looking at these texts in the context of cosmopolitan realism, however, allows us to see how writers as ideologically incompatible as Booth and Morris are engaged in the same generic task: one that entails similar challenges to the integrity of their visions.

Both Booth and Morris want to see London as the ground zero for social change on a global scale, and both draw upon similar components of the realist tradition in order to do so. Each writer invents a utopian future in which the city has been thoroughly reshaped by a global revolution in which the nation-state has either withered away (in Morris' case) or become largely irrelevant (in Booth's); both depict London as a New Jerusalem, revitalized and physically transformed by the overhaul of labor conditions. Both, moreover, are motivated by their anathema for global urban modernity and a compensatory turn to agrarian forms of communal life. They also share the sense that if systemic change is to occur successfully it must take place on an international scale; each regards the interdependence of London and the wider world as an ethical necessity and economic inevitability. Their works thus demonstrate the appeal of cosmopolitan representation across the political spectrum and the way in which its manifold generic challenges could expose overlaps between purportedly opposed ideologies, as well as inconsistencies within them.

Significantly, the utopias of Booth and Morris also overlap in their innovative use of the print medium to emphasize the global frame of their missions. At the *fin de siècle*, the international framework of socialism first articulated in Marx's *Communist Manifesto* was revisited by progressive writers such as Olive Schreiner and Edward Carpenter.[7] Booth and Morris inherit not only the *Manifesto*'s internationalism, however, but also Marx's notion that revolutionary ideals must circulate differently, registering newness on the level of the printed text itself, as well as on the level of content and form. Thus Marx's *Manifesto*, as we saw in Chapter 1, was translated into a number of languages and circulated transnationally, exemplifying the new "world literature" that it described. Like Marx, Booth and Morris conceived of their texts as international manifestos and published them accordingly. *News from Nowhere* and *In Darkest*

England use extra-textual materials, such as maps, advertising, illustrations, and statistical supplements, to position their works not only as cosmopolitan texts but as cosmopolitan objects. These materials do part of the formal work of mediating between urban and global scales. On the textual level, this mediation requires both writers to amplify a central tension within cosmopolitan realism between allegoric and scientific modes of description.

In my usage of the term "realism" thus far, I have understood it as both a moral project and a sustained attempt to conjure up a recognizable picture of the contemporary world. To borrow George Levine's influential formulation, realism is a "self-conscious effort, usually in the name of some moral enterprise of truth telling and extending the limits of human sympathy, to make literature appear to be describing directly not some other language but reality itself (whatever that may be taken to be)."[8] Mid-century *cosmopolitan* realism, I argued in Chapter 1, combined the anthropological and allegorical epistemologies of the visual sketch and panorama in order to marry the fact-finding, differentiating mission of urban investigation with a compensatory vision of human kinship. In reconciling local with global scales, writers such as Wordsworth and Dickens adapted the religious language of allegory to a secular understanding of community, privileging the panoramic "mind of man" as the locus of their unifying vision of urban space.

In the writing of Booth and Morris, though, the disjunction between the secular context of anthropology and the religious context of allegory becomes more apparent and more fraught. Ethnographic discourse in Morris' text makes the case for essential differences between cultures; in Booth's, it makes the case for essential differences *within* them. To imagine the transcendence of these seemingly irreconcilable divisions, they both draw upon the religious resonances of allegory. As Ruth Livesey argues, "the 'religion of socialism' in the 1880s and 1890s was articulated in a variety of non-realist literary forms such as romances, utopias, parables and dreams." For Livesey, allegory helps link utopia to the everyday, making its ideal seem, in effect, more realistic: "the very form of allegory, as opposed to utopia, is concerned with the parallel mapping of the place of the abstract and the unfamiliar onto daily experience; with finding the key that matches the reader's place and destiny to the collective map of the allegory."[9]

Christian allegory, in particular, is important to socialist utopia because of its universalist idealism. John Bunyan's influential *Pilgrim's Progress* (1678), for example, posited the overcoming of hierarchical distinctions in the afterlife emblemized by the Heavenly City; Booth and Morris use the form and language of such allegories to imagine a socialist utopia of the near future in which London serves as a type of Heavenly City in its embodiment of the global "brotherhood of man." They thus take the magical thinking and aesthetic artifice of James and Doyle a step further away from the Enlightenment epistemology and secular vocabulary of political community that characterized earlier cosmopolitanisms such as Kant's. In doing so, they provide a new cosmopolitan context for the turn from realism by the end of the nineteenth century and also prefigure, and help to explain, the success of religious cosmopolitanisms such as Islam and Christian evangelicalism a century later.[10]

LOCATING UTOPIA

How do the different epistemologies of allegory and ethnography come together in these narratives to imagine utopia as simultaneously global and locatable on a map? According to Northrop Frye, allegory is a term that could be applied to all literature in the sense that "a writer is being allegorical when it is clear that he is saying 'by this I also mean that' [but if] this seems to be done continuously, we may say, cautiously, that what he is writing 'is' an allegory."[11] Frye's circumspect definition gives us some indication of the difficulties inherent in characterizing allegory generically. Yet what allegorical writing *does* do, in making consistent reference to another field of meaning, is create unified fields of meaning – or "worlds" – that map on to each other. Because Booth and Morris wish to overcome the divisive logic of *fin-de-siècle* ethnography and promote London's potential to become a New Jerusalem, allegory's historical association with religious exegesis plays a central role in their work.

In his study of allegory's contribution to the moral project of the realist novel, Barry Qualls argues that because they were "[l]acking Bunyan's assurance, readers and writers held all the more tenaciously to his language. They were determined to shape the facts of this world into a religious topography, making a path towards social unity in this world an analogue to Christian's progress towards the Celestial City."[12] The difference between earlier types of religious allegory and its deployment in realism was that the novel internalized the world of salvation. Realists, Qualls notes, "use language both to create a mimetic image of the sordid realities of their world and to illuminate the process of 'salvation' by which the 'inward world' might survive this reality."[13] By imagining the world as a space capable of being re-shaped by the utopian imagination, however, Booth and Morris seek to re-exteriorize salvation. They thus use allegory much more explicitly than mid-century authors such as Charlotte Brontë, Eliot, and Dickens. Booth deploys religious language throughout his text and supplies his readers with a physical map of utopia that asks us to read the salvation of London in the allegorical terms of Renaissance emblem books. Morris, on the other hand, borrows both the dream trope and the parallel structure of the literal and spiritual journey from Christian texts such as Dante's *Divine Comedy* or Bunyan's *Pilgrim's Progress.* Further, in the 1892 Kelmscott Press version of his book, he uses the visual apparatus of medieval illuminated manuscripts, associated predominantly with religious content, to accentuate the messianic tone of his narrative. In both texts, allegory imparts a sense of moral urgency to the depiction of the present and allows for the positing of a radically different future. To imagine themselves as part of the utopian future, readers are asked to identify with Christian-like "pilgrims" – the soldiers in a worldwide Salvation Army, or Morris' Everyman narrator, Guest – in order to achieve temporary release from contemporary social hierarchies and national loyalties.

Alongside allegory, ethnographic method plays a more explicit role in Booth's and Morris' texts than in earlier cosmopolitan works. Booth's study, for example, is composed largely of statistics, charts, and the reported speech of workers interviewed on the street (a style of proto-anthropological evidence popularized by Mayhew). Morris, meanwhile, puts his main character, Guest, in the role of ethnographer. So alienated from the condition of utopia as a member of the Victorian bourgeoisie that he is unable to recognize his own country, Guest interrogates the "native informants" he encounters on his journey with the goal of understanding the sociological structure of the compelling civilization he find himself in and importing its lessons to contemporary England.

Booth and Morris wrote at a time when anthropological conceptions of culture were shifting from that of a single human culture with different developmental stages to that of plural cultures. In *Primitive Culture* (1871) E. B. Tylor defined culture as "a single domain shared by all the world's people ... the ways and institutions of each human group may be compared and assessed using a single developmental scheme."[14] Yet by the beginning of the twentieth century, "a new conception of object-like, mappable, and incommensurable social totalities" emerged that stressed insuperable differences between cultures, which were now understood as discrete entities with distinct historical trajectories.[15]

In *fin-de-siècle* narratives, the plural and the singular concepts of culture often vie for predominance. Booth's work, for example, rife with images of racial degeneration, tends to fluctuate wildly between the two ideas, depicting the "degenerate" poor either as devolved, or unevolved, aspects of a unitary civilization, or as a race unto themselves. In terms of the structure of their work, however, both Booth and Morris use an ethnographic methodology associated more readily with the twentieth-century concept of cultural plurality than with Tylor's understanding of culture. They therefore gesture forward to a new understanding of cultural difference even as they reach back to a religious vocabulary for a sense of human unity. In his study of "metropolitan autoethnography," discussed earlier, James Buzard uses ethnography "in the twentieth-century sense of a study of a people's way of life centering on the method of 'immersion' in extensive fieldwork and raising the issue of how, and how far, the outsider can become a kind of honorary insider in other cultures."[16] It is precisely this kind of study that Booth and Morris embark on, determined to render their utopias with a thickness of cultural description that makes them seem both habitable and possible.

If allegory maps one field of meaning on to another *vertically*, gesturing always to a "higher" plane of meaning, ethnography is a way of mapping the world in general, *horizontally*. Yet despite their different generic histories, ethnography and allegory are mutually implicated, both in their use by Booth and Morris, and more generally. James Clifford, in a famous critique of modern anthropology, has pointed out that "ethnographical texts are inescapably allegorical." Even if they are not full-fledged allegories, the "stories" told by ethnographers "simultaneously describe real cultural events and make additional moral, ideological, and even cosmological statements." Citing the early history of ethnographic writing in which "more or less explicit biblical or classical allegories abound," Clifford draws attention to the "inescapably" narrative nature of cultural description.[17] Because they borrow explicitly from both allegorical and ethnographic modes, the socialist utopias of Booth and Morris elucidate some of the ways in which the two forms became connected at a key moment in the development of anthropology. Yet in drawing together pronounced versions of realism's idealist and empiricist epistemologies, these texts also show how the underlying problem of cosmopolitan realism – its ambition to unite universalist and particularist views – had reached a point of *aporia*.

PUBLISHING UTOPIA: NEWS FROM "COMMONWEAL" AND THE
KELMSCOTT PRESS

Morris' *News from Nowhere* depicts a utopian world in which egalitarian
ideals prevail, work is a source of aesthetic pleasure, and strife is unheard
of. The first-person narrative tells of the imaginary journey of its protagonist William Guest, who is a member of the Socialist League to which
Morris himself belonged. After leaving a fractious League meeting, Guest
is on the verge of becoming terminally disaffected with the political
process. He falls asleep and wakes up in a familiar yet transformed world.
There, he is able to communicate with the inhabitants but unable to
understand their ways, restricted by his narrow Victorian individualism.
He pretends to be a traveler and quizzes the "natives" he encounters on
their modes of existence. His chief informants are a friendly boatman,
Dick, and his great-grandfather, Hammond. A librarian at the British
Museum, Hammond preserves the history of Nowhere – a narrative in
which few of its inhabitants are interested due to their sense of fulfillment
in the present – and is able to tell Guest about the revolution that
produced Nowhere's utopia. Since the "plot" of the novel consists simply
of the narrator's journey up the river to London and out to the country,
its main interest lies in the Socratic-style dialogues Guest has with
Nowhere residents, in which the utopic condition – a non-state-based
communitarian society – is delineated. Although Guest eventually wakes
up back in his own time, his conversations and observations in Nowhere
have converted him back to a faith in political action.

The novel is both anti-imperialist and cosmopolitan in outlook. Written largely as a response to his own disenchantment with piecemeal
reform and socialist in-fighting after the events of "Bloody Sunday," *News
from Nowhere* was Morris' attempt to win new support for international
socialism and write a materialist prophecy of history-to-come within the
tradition of utopian literature. Morris' cosmopolitan stance in the novel
was also partly a response to Edward Bellamy's *Looking Backward.* First
published in America in 1888, Bellamy's work, like that of Morris, is a
utopian novel that deals with urban and class crisis. Yet though it is
socialistic in its view of labor relations, *Looking Backward* is profoundly
nationalistic in its view of the state and of international relations – so
much so that it played an influential role in the American nationalist
movement of its period.

In contrast, the residents of Morris' utopia pride themselves on their
withdrawal from nationalist ideologies and from the exploitative

dynamics of the capitalist-imperialist "world-market." The revolution that leads to utopia is precipitated by a Bloody-Sunday-like episode that leads to a workers' strike and then civil war, eventually won by the workers; once power has changed hands, the government is dismantled and agrarian communism prevails. Although the novel is circumspect about how the revolution spread outside England, it represents utopia as a worldwide phenomenon and a withering away of the nation as a viable political category. "[T]he whole system of rival and contending nations which played so great a part in the 'government' of the world of civilization has disappeared along with the inequality between man and man in society," Guest is informed.[18] According to the logic of Nowhere, all individuals are citizens of the world without allegiance to countries or creeds. Nowhere is aptly named not only because of the word's relation to "utopia," but because the place Guest visits is no longer a nation in the modern sense: it lacks a government, no longer participates in a world economy, and functions as a decentralized, demodernized communal space. Goods and services still exist, but are exchanged freely between individuals whose reward is the pride they take in their craftsmanship and their "conscious sensuous pleasure in the work itself" (123).

The cosmopolitanism of Morris' socialist agenda was supported by extra-textual elements in both the serialized and printed forms of the novel. Morris' utopian narrative first appeared in serial form in *Commonweal*, a weekly periodical published by the Socialist League and largely run and funded by Morris; it disintegrated soon after he left the League, the same year in which *News from Nowhere* was published. *Commonweal* was dedicated to the idea of global workers' solidarity and thus, as a platform for the novel, would have allowed readers to equate the ethos of Nowhere with the ideology of the League. Its "Statement of Principles" announced that "Revolutionary Socialism must be International. The change which would put an end to the struggle between man and man would destroy it also between nation and nation."[19]

Commonweal attempted not only to understand socialism as international but, correspondingly, to position itself as a nexus of international ideas about socialism. It thus made socialist literature from other countries available to its readers at low cost; contained ads for periodicals in other languages (a typical ad page in *Commonweal*, for example, featured notices for German, French, and Danish radical newspapers); and kept a weekly tally of socialist periodicals around the world (countries listed include England, India, the United States, France, Holland, Belgium, Spain, Austria, Germany, Hungary, Denmark, Sweden, and the West Indies). It also published articles on the social condition of workers in other national contexts besides Britain and had a recurrent section, "International Notes," which summarized noteworthy radical actions in different countries. While more attention was paid to European nations, *Commonweal,* like *News from Nowhere,* was bitingly anti-imperialist and carried articles on colonized regions as well, noting the adverse effects of empire and the "civilizing mission" on workers and colonial subjects in general.

*Commonweal'*s serialization of Morris' novel did not do as much as the Kelmscott Press edition (discussed below) to accentuate the importance of allegory to its meaning and rhetorical effect, but it did include an allegorical element absent from the Kelmscott version. "Labour's May-Day," an illustration by the famous socialist artist Walter Crane, accompanied one of the serial episodes of the novel in *Commonweal* and was also used as the frontispiece to an 1890 US edition of the novel (see Figure 4.1).[20] An allegory of the international unity of labor, the illustration's massive globe would have functioned as a defamiliarizing device for readers used to associating the novel with a national framework and moral. Crane's cartoon serves as a sign that Morris' text demands both an allegorical and an internationalist reading. The image of unity between the continents – with representatives of each holding hands – signals a rejection of imperialist hierarchy and holds out the promise of global democracy.

While evoking a prelapsarian time of feudal peasant costumes and harvest festivals in its representation of the workers, the etching also looks forward to a future of international workers' solidarity in which representatives from Africa, America, Europe, Australia, and Asia are watched over benignly by Enlightenment ideals: "Fraternity," Freedom," and "Equality." The image thus not only signals the different kind of reading that Morris' novel requires, but also encapsulates its Janus-faced structure: both the illustration and the novel show that the coming of a utopian future is premised on the recovery of an idealized past.

In the novel itself, the allegorical structure allows Morris to set up an elaborate series of resonances between the real and ideal condition of England. Morris maps the latter squarely over the former: his house in Hammersmith, the British Museum, and his country residence, Kelmscott Manor in Oxfordshire, all appear in the novel as recognizable geographical indicators that make the connection between the two worlds unavoidable in the reader's mind and allow the world of Nowhere to serve as a commentary on the shortcomings of nineteenth-century liberalism. Allegory's association with religious narrative – its use of the visible world

Figure 4.1 Walter Crane, "Labour's May-Day."

as a revelation of the invisible – also provides a formal basis for Morris' messianic tone. Here what is prophesied is not divine redemption but a less secure, secularized faith in a transformative historical dialectic.

Morris' recourse to allegory is most immediately evident in the overall structure of the story, which takes the form of a conversion narrative overtly indebted to John Bunyan's *Pilgrim's Progress*. As in Bunyan's narrative, the protagonist dreams of a different world and a holistic moral universe. He is gradually converted to a "faith" in utopia, performs a journey that parallels a moral awakening, and then literally awakens to bestow the "lesson" of the dream on the reader. The majority of *Nowhere's* characters function allegorically as well. Dick, Clara, and the other workers are distinctly flat in their characterization and serve as ideal versions of Everyman and Everywoman, while Dick's great-grandfather Hammond, a living link between past and present, is the embodiment of History.

Morris' use of allegory not only turns to socialist ends the "conversion" trajectory common to many religious allegories, but also serves as a corrective to what he saw as the decadence of the novel form.[21] The realist novel, as residents of Nowhere see it, belongs to a time of pernicious individualism, when it served as a placebo for social ills by obfuscating class conflict: "towards the end of the story we must be contented to see the hero and heroine living happily in an island of bliss on other people's troubles" (176).

Though strategically reductive, Morris' description of realism draws attention to the relationship between form (the "happy ending" of the majority of nineteenth-century novels, their often superficial attention to the details of the lives of the poor) and ideological content (bourgeois individualism) in order to explicate his own formal choices. In other words, the allegorical elements of his novel are juxtaposed with its potential realism. In deliberate contrast to other Victorian novelists, Morris undermines the individuality of his characters, de-emphasizing interiority and introspection so as to privilege the notions of community over the individual, action over self-consciousness, and universality over particularity.

Yet Morris has a realist project as well, for he strives simultaneously to produce a detailed portrait of Nowhere as a specific kind of culture and to map that culture on to English land so that the novel might seem a realistic foretelling of the future rather than a fanciful pastoral idyll. Ethnographic methodology, in the form of autoethnography, plays a central role in his advancement of these goals. In his work on Morris' autoethnography, James Buzard argues that Morris uses Participant Observation to create a sense of a knowable utopian community that Guest both does and does not belong to. Delineating the similarities between the techniques of *News from Nowhere* and the methodology of twentieth-century ethnography, Buzard notes that the novel "presents us with a single fieldworker 'immersed' in the visited culture, . . . joins roles of fact-gatherer and synthesizer of data, . . . analyzes the particular customs of a single culture, . . . employs a holistic, parts-for-the-whole approach, . . . [and] envisions the study of one culture as a relatively autotelic enterprise."[22] In Buzard's reading, Morris' use of autoethnography is a culmination of the "self-interrupting, culture-seeking" impulse of the mid-Victorian novel, with its goal of establishing a "counterimperial narrative of English or British identity."[23]

Morris' use of ethnographic method is counter-imperial in the sense that it sets up the idea of a retrievable, archaic English culture against the dispersions of contemporary British imperial identity. But it might be seen as counter-imperial*ist* in its use of ethnography as well. Like Booth's text, which explicitly compares itself to *In Darkest Africa*, that of Morris is in dialogue with Stanley's popular travel narrative. That Morris had a bone to pick with Stanley is evidenced by the fact that the explorer is cited by name in *News from Nowhere* as an example of the depravities of nineteenth-century imperialism.[24] Two critiques of the explorer, moreover, appeared in the same issues of *Commonweal* that carried the serialization of *News from Nowhere*, attacking him for his "brutal carelessness of human life" and hypocritical piety.[25] One of these articles, "Stanley's Exploits, or Civilizing Africa," draws attention to the structural problem of anthropological narratives: "whenever I produce any evidence against Mr. Stanley, it is always taken from his own works and his own words. The unfortunate natives who have come in contact with the valiant explorer cannot tell us their side of the story."[26] Morris' use of ethnography, then, addresses itself to the problems posed by narratives such as Stanley's and attempts to redeem anthropological discourse from its use in imperialist contexts.

First, while Guest is learning about a "different" culture, he is making it clear – through the allegorical structure – that the lessons to be learnt from this culture are about his own; in other words, there is none of the illusion of objective scrutiny for which anthropologists have been subject to criticism. Second, Morris positions Guest, through his name, as a welcomed traveler rather than unwelcome colonizer: one willing to engage in the ethical reciprocity of guest–host relations. Despite the friendliness of his hosts, however, Guest is fated to return to the present because of his cultural incompatibility with Nowhere. In the logic of the narrative, he cannot think outside of the terms of his own Victorian context. As the natives of Nowhere keep pointing out to him, it is impossible for him to separate his identity and thought process from the material conditions in which they were produced; hence, he must go back and struggle to change

them. Third, Guest is different from other nineteenth-century ethnographers because he is shown, over the course of the narrative, to have a
right to speak for the "different" culture he finds himself in, unlike
Stanley when he speaks for African natives. By the time the narrator
recounts his travels to his friend at the League, he has covered enough
historical and geographical ground to ascertain that the land he visited
was, in fact, his own and that he, or at least his successors, might inherit it
if he tells his story convincingly enough.

Morris' use of ethnography is thus a parable about how and when
writers should speak for other cultures. Yet it also has an empirical role to
play, providing an experiential base to the allegorical structure of his tale
which the narrator can exploit to make an argument for the viability of
Utopia. Upon awakening from his dream, he evokes positivist reasoning
through images of vision and knowledge to convince readers to digest
what "[their] outward eyes have learned" (22). "If others can see it as
I have seen it," Guest argues, then they too may be converted to a belief in
utopia. What, then, does Guest's "vision" of the new society reveal? Like
the nineteenth-century ethnographer he both does and does not resemble,
Guest is led up the river by a representative "native." The first part of his
journey takes him to London, where he is astonished to find that "the
modern Babylon of civilization" (99) has vanished. In place of the "brick
and mortar desert" (102) of the city, London has become green and
pleasant: so green, in fact, that the distinction between town and country
has virtually disappeared. The second stage of his journey takes him out of
London to the rural countryside. Upon his arrival, he observes the
satisfied lives of individuals in self-contained communities living in
harmony with the land, wonders at their creative engagement with
everyday life, and joins in medieval-style festivities that celebrate the cycles
of nature.

For Morris, as Guest's journey demonstrates, the countryside *is* the
country.[27] The rural traditions of fourteenth-century England rather than
the cosmopolitan modernity of London define Nowhere's character, and
the problems of urban degeneration are eradicated along with urban
existence itself. Traditional customs such as harvest festivals have been
restored, and older forms of language usage have returned as well. Residents of Nowhere demonstrate their status as citizens of the world by
speaking German, French, Greek, and Latin, as well as English and local
dialects and idioms. In a vivid instance of the latter, Guest's guide in
Nowhere, Dick, diverging from the subject during conversation, uses a
translation of a quaint French expression – "I am wandering from my

lambs" (67) – to acknowledge his digression. This attempt to provide a
referential basis to metaphor by using a phrase drawn from rural work
experience follows from Morris' conception of labor and life in Nowhere
as an organic relationship to land and environment.

While autoethnography works as a way to defamiliarize Victorian
culture from itself, it also, as Buzard points out, allows the genealogy of
Nowhere to be traced to a distinctly English past, thereby undermining
the cosmopolitan notion that Nowhere could be anywhere. Instead, the
regeneration of London and the country at large depends on the revival of
rural traditions and a more "authentic" native culture. One implication of
this figuring of utopia as a reversion to authenticity and the natural
rhythms of the land and seasons is that there is little reason for cultural
exchange in this version of cosmopolitanism. Living in harmony with the
land implies that each "land" keeps to itself, so that even while many
inhabitants of Nowhere are multi-lingual, they are only superficially multi-
cultural: cultures, in fact, remain implicitly separate in Morris' framework.
Morris retrieves the idea of "primitive culture" and "barbarism" from
writers like Stanley and Booth, reclaiming it for higher moral values.
In 1885 he wrote: "how often it consoles me to think of barbarism
once more flooding the world, and real feelings and passions, however
rudimentary, taking the place of our wretched hypocrisies."[28] But in
doing so, he enacts some of the more pernicious consequences of the
twentieth-century idea of "separate" cultures. Hammond, speaking
against nationalism, ridicules the notion of coercing "certain families
or tribes, often heterogeneous and jarring with each other, into certain
artificial and mechanical groups, [to] call them nations," and says that
only by avoiding this form of grouping can "the different strains of blood
in the world ... be serviceable and pleasant to each other" (117). What this
implies, though, is that these "different strains" do not, or should not,
mix. While "guests" like William are welcome, the focus on archaic local
customs, dress, and language means that the local transcends the global,
place and race become fixed, and cultural and ethnic diversity are
precluded.

Furthermore, by linking his definitions of freedom to ideas of what is
"natural," Morris traps himself within the logic of degeneration discourse even while he is trying to shift the debate about England's future
away from it. In *News from Nowhere*, the nineteenth century is described
as a time of "self-inflicted diseases" (92), defined in opposition to the
images of health and vigor that permeate Nowhere. Guest finds its
inhabitants spectacularly beautiful and is informed that their robust

and fulfilling lifestyles made them so. This claim, clearly meant as an endorsement of Nowhere's work-for-work's-sake credo, operates by inverting Lombroso-esque ideas about the physically and morally degenerate lower classes. A holistic idea of well-being that relies on Lamarckian logic, the idea that beauty follows freedom is only one of many ways in which the novel conflates questions of biology and environment. Women, for instance, tend to perform domestic duties and wait on men in Nowhere, not because they are forced to, Guest is told, but because they are drawn to what they are good at. Anticipating criticism of his female characters from contemporary New Women (referred to deprecatingly in passing), Morris has Guest voice concern about the role of women in Nowhere. The rebuttal to Guest's nascent critique silences him with the supposedly irrefutable logic of its essentialism: "don't you know that it is a great pleasure to a clever woman to manage a house skilfully, and to do it so that all the house-mates about her look pleased, and are grateful to her?" (94).

In Nowhere, the longing for change that characterized the pre-revolutionary period is "akin to the unreasonable passion of the lover" (134), and once the change has come, a sexual satisfaction is used to describe the utopic condition: an "intense and overweening love of the very skin and surface of the earth on which [he] dwells, such as a lover has in the fair flesh of the woman he loves" (158). Thus Guest's growing desire for Ellen famously mirrors his desire for the freedom Nowhere represents: a passion for transformation and revolution that will stay with him after his visit. The fact that something akin to Hegel's world-spirit depends on the structure of heterosexual romance is not accidental, nor is the idea that the men and women in Nowhere are ideally complementary to each other.[29] A robust heterosexuality is represented as a crucial guard against the entropy generated by the masturbatory self-consciousness of modern life. Morris' Carlylean representation of work in Nowhere is also a guard against this self-consciousness. If, as in Nowhere, work is for art's sake and art is for work's sake, then each has a determinate, more utilitarian meaning that opposes the non-reproductivity of "art for art's sake." Because this is true for the residents of Nowhere, they are able to "live amidst beauty without any fear of becoming effeminate" (105).

Morris' representational strategies are overdetermined by his fears that culture inevitably degenerates when it is separated from the land by modernization: hence the importance of his idea that culture and land are inseparable. Just as the allegorical features of the text help to map Morris' world on to a utopic one, they also remove it from the complex web of imperial relations that Morris found so troubling by creating a synchronous universe in which a "purer" culture – both racially and morally – can abide peacefully. The text's ethnographic features perform a second mapping of a holistic culture on to English land and history in a way that circumscribes Morris' purportedly cosmopolitan vision. His view of democracy spreading across a world stage, then, co-exists uncomfortably with his ahistorical depiction of a timeless rural order – one that owes more to the tropes of Romantic nationalism than to the forward-looking cosmopolitanism which Morris sought to promote. The premium he places on cultural and racial purity, in other words, butts up against the global solidarity his text must *also* champion so that the revolution he wishes to imagine into being might occur on an international scale.

These paradoxes might have weighed on Morris' mind when he chose to produce a Kelmscott Press version of *News from Nowhere* in 1892. This rendition of the novel markedly played up its allegorical properties through its resemblance to a medieval religious manuscript. Printed on vellum, the Kelmscott edition used a Gothic script and elaborately decorated capital letters. Etchings of leaves and vines around the sides of the pages invoke the symbiotic relationship between word and image commonly found in medieval texts, where the images often elucidated, or at least illustrated, the words' meanings. In Morris' text, however, these etchings are only relevant to the text insofar as they stress the importance of nature to the author's vision. Beyond that, they seem to draw attention away from the words by overwhelming the reader visually – the letters, decorative in themselves, are of a piece with the illustrations, so that text and image seem continuous.[30] The sheer volume of undifferentiated organic matter depicted in the margins, claustrophic in its materiality, draws our focus to the "here and now" of the aesthetic, rather than diegetic, experience of reading. The narrative is also broken up differently than in the serial or regular bound version of the novel; chapters start in the middle of pages, for instance, so that white space is kept to a minimum, accentuating the illustrations' effect.

That Morris sought to produce a kind of reading experience with the Kelmscott text different from that of the serialized novel is also indicated by his use of medieval-style glosses in the margins of the book's pages. Because they appear in red, and contrast with the uniform black of the main text and the decorative margins, they divert the reader from the continuity of the narrative with condensed versions of it: the words "Help yourself!" for example, appear at the moment that Guest enters a market and realizes he doesn't have to use money to acquire possessions. The cumulative effect of the glosses is to provide a snapshot view of Utopia from outside of the narrative itself. Phrases like "A frank and joyous people," "A Market and its beauty," "Where are the prisons?," "Where are the factories?," "Where is the smoke?," and "Pictures of the world's childhood" condense the narrative to its bare bones, allowing the reader to skim over parts of the text or remind themselves of highlights.

In this edition, then, Morris emphasizes the allegorical nature of his novel over the ethnographic features that connect it to English culture. The Biblical aspect of the Kelmscott edition underscores the novel's moral import and the vivid red glosses summarize the key elements of utopia. But because the narrative itself is de-emphasized by the visual demands of the text-as-object, the Kelmscott edition seems designed to serve as a record of the tale's redundancy; it is a book that imagines utopia has already been instantiated, and that this secular Bible is a relic, there to remind us of an unfortunate past rather than point us towards the future.[31] By emphasizing the text's physical form over its ethnographic content, the Kelmscott edition helps to circumvent the troublesome problem of how to concurrently promote cultural difference and global brotherhood. Allegory makes the reader Everyman and, in the Kelmscott book, draws attention not to English narrative but to the lingua franca of its visual aesthetics.

MAPPING UTOPIA: GLOBALIZING THE SALVATION ARMY

If Morris borrowed from the Christian conversion narrative to make his utopian scheme compelling, Booth, an evangelical missionary, chose the opposite tactic. Though his narrative is equally one of progress from the "Darkness" of despair to the "Deliverance" of his idealistic solution, he is responsive to the fact that, for his middle-class audience, "sociology was replacing fiction as the layman's guide to social issues" and stresses his secular, positivistic approach to gathering knowledge about the working classes.[32] Written with the help of social critic and journalist W. T. Stead, Booth's text draws directly on the social investigation tradition pioneered by Mayhew, using statistics, charts, and ethnographic interviews to convince readers of the enormity of London's problems and the viability of his solution. Despite the fact that his scheme imagines, ultimately, the simultaneous religious and social redemption of nothing less than the entire face of the globe, Booth denied the utopian overtones of his text: "In this and in subsequent chapters, I hope to convince those who read them that there is no overstraining in the representation of facts, and nothing Utopian in the presentation of remedies" (17). Arguing for the unmediated (rather than "overstrained") nature of his factual evidence, Booth stresses his project's realism over its idealism in order to convince his audience that it is worthy of investment.

While part of its ambition was to stand as a sociological study in its own right, *In Darkest England and the Way Out* was also an elaborate subscription scheme that sought to encourage its readers to donate to the Salvation Army and thus to underwrite Booth's plan of global expansion. The appendices that accompanied Booth's narrative highlighted the purported practicality of his scheme. A chart entitled "The Position of our Forces," for instance, showcases the headway the Army had already made in establishing a worldwide presence: seventeen different countries are listed as having Salvation Army bases, including those as far from England as Tasmania, Ceylon, and "The Argentine Republic." Other appendices include forms which gave readers a sense of the range of the Army's activities and which they could presumably use themselves: a letter to "Employers of Labour," for example, solicits information about job vacancies, while another form could be used to recruit "local agents" who might "regularly communicate useful information respecting the social condition of things generally in their neighbourhood." Yet another form was addressed to the unemployed themselves, encouraging them to detail their employment history and register at a local labor bureau.

Booth was motivated to write *In Darkest England* by the failure of the Salvation Army to establish an evangelical presence in London's urban slums. By the 1880s, his Army had spread across the UK and set up missions in the USA and Europe, as well as in a number of British colonies. However, the fact that what he called his "Christian Imperium" had not yet taken hold in London, the symbolic heart of the empire, was particularly irksome to Booth. He eventually decided to try a tactic that would make urban and global reform inseparable. This venture, the Darkest England scheme, was a grandly ambitious one and explicitly international in its vision: "in its ramifications and extensions," he stated enthusiastically, "it embraces the whole world" (90). The narrative *In Darkest England*, the vehicle for his plan, was also conceived as cosmopolitan in scope. Booth hoped that it would be "read all over the world" by "practical men of every Colony in the Empire" (149).

The first segment of Booth's book, entitled "Darkness," describes the problem of urban blight that his scheme sought to address. Drawing on the popularity of Stanley's *In Darkest Africa* to critique the telescopic philanthropy of the Victorian middle class, Booth urges his readers to turn their attention back to the "horrors" of "Darkest England" instead.[33] These are detailed, ethnographically, through the reportage of Booth's Salvation Army officer-reporters: men and women who roamed the streets looking for potential converts to Salvation Army life. Details of street-life and mini-biographies of the working-class and indigent subjects that Army officers interviewed are inserted throughout this section, and its chapters draw upon this sociological "evidence" to divide the poor into different social "types," such as "The Vicious," "The Criminals," and "The Homeless."

The second part of his book, "Deliverance," delineates the "practical" measures by which he hopes to redeem the poor and, in turn, "Darkest England." An elaborate tripartite scheme is revealed that will allow the country to absorb and reclaim the degenerate masses. "City colonies," composed of self-subsisting workshops for the hitherto unemployed, would be set up to absorb a number of the working poor. The rest would move on to "country colonies" to work on farming cooperatives. A third stage of his scheme extends this logic further by proposing overseas colonization. Lastly, his "Practical Conclusion" ends the book with a plea for "subscriptions" to his scheme: donations that would serve as consent to his vision and provide the material base for its execution.

Unlike Morris' more self-conscious use of ethnography, Booth's attempt to understand what he saw as the distinct characteristics and cultures of different sections of the working class was in earnest, and purported to add to a body of sociological knowledge while simultaneously serving as evidence for his argument. Indeed, his identification of a "respectable" stratum, a liminal group teetering on the edge of dissolution, and a "submerged," barely salvageable, tenth of the population, played a significant role in the growing body of Victorian social investigation: "Booth's text, with its determination to distinguish between 'an uppercrust and a submerged tenth,' is among the most influential turn-of-the-century contributions to this construction."[34] The reappearance of this concept in the work of twentieth-century sociologists such as W. E. B. DuBois, who used it in *The Philadelphia Negro* (1899) and "The Talented Tenth" (1903), is a testament to its tenacity.

Booth's attempt to understand and dissect working-class culture was inseparable from his Arnoldian cosmopolitanism – the idea that the exchange of the best ideas of each nation is the ultimate basis for progress.[35] Describing how his officers will be well placed to take advantage of local knowledge for British interests, he states that "One advantage of the cosmopolitan nature of the Army is that we have officers in almost every country in the world" (133). In a chapter entitled "Our Intelligence Department," he imagines a future in which his understanding of London's working class becomes the center of an "imperial archive":

This Intelligence Department, which I propose to found on a small scale at first, will have in it the germ of vast extension which will, if adequately supported, become a kind of University, in which the accumulated experiences of the human race will be massed, digested, and rendered available to the humblest toiler in the great work of social reform. (227)

Yet despite this purported faith in the accumulation of knowledge, the anxieties evoked by the urban degeneration Booth charts are more visible in his work than in that of Morris. Even as he strains towards a Christian universalism in his promise of redemption for all, the opening imagery of his work, with its ethnographic delineation of the poor into different groups, uses ethnic difference as a metaphor for social disintegration. The plight of the poor in England, according to his account, involves their falling away not only from the church, but from English civilization.

Stanley's *In Darkest Africa* thus becomes, in Booth's text, the basis of an extended comparison between barbarism at home and abroad and an occasion to point out the threats that both pose to the possibility of human progress:

the two tribes of savages, the human baboon and the handsome dwarf, who will not speak lest it impede him in his task, may be accepted as the two varieties who are continually present with us – the vicious, lazy lout, and the toiling slave. They, too, have lost all faith of life being other than it is and has been. (12)

Here, Booth's evocations of the "vicious, lazy lout" and "toiling slave" are clearly ironized versions of contemporary stereotypes of the poor, meant to dispute the notion these different "types" are fixed in their degrading roles. But by insisting on the comparison of different "savage" species – dwarf and baboon – with different classes of the poor, he characteristically wavers between determinism and essentialism in his understanding of cultural difference.

For this reason, it is not surprising that, like Morris, Booth sees the country as the solution to urban degeneration. He argues that it removes the environmental factors, such as public houses and slums, that degrade the poor, and undoes the proliferation of types generated by city life by restoring a healthier, more holistic mode of existence. "[T]he country is the breeding ground of healthy citizens" (62), he argues, for it reverses the "hereditary weakness of body and hereditary faults of character" (66) that he ascribes to the city's "undigested and indigestible masses of labor" (62). A healthy social body, for Booth as for Morris, is one operating under the conditions of the traditional rural village, where the "natural cycle of the day" is not perverted by technology and where there is "swift ... means of communication between the community as a whole" (115). Apart from the "country colonies" which would help to unmake what he saw as the disastrous overcrowding of the cities, Booth's "overseas colonies" would provide yet another outlet and resource for Britain's surplus labor and "so [lay] the foundations, perchance, of another Empire to swell in vast proportions in later times" (93).

This empire, Booth assures his middle-class potential contributors, would be built on the "family idea" (218), with strong autocratic control of the colonies centered in England (hence the militarism implicit in the Salvation Army name and the hierarchical titles of its followers). Booth's cosmopolitan scheme for a global federation of Salvation Armies was thus unabashedly imperial in its imagination of the relationship between center and periphery. The end goal of "universal brotherhood" that he imagines through the democratizing structure of the Army (in which everyone is a "comrade") and the communal structure of his work colonies is always glaringly at odds with the imperial and autocratic imagery he uses to delineate his vision.

While Morris' novel attempts to resolve problems of degeneration by reversion to the local and rural, thereby weakening the global frame of his argument, Booth's narrative generates the opposite problem. Placing himself at the center of his scheme and imagining its global expansion, Booth imposes the local on the global, eradicating diversity rather than ignoring it. But because his ethnographic analyses toy with the idea of hereditary degeneration as the cause as well as the symptom of poverty, correlating the poor with "savage" races, they raise the specter of types ("the baboon" and "dwarf") that will never be able to help themselves and be worthy of inclusion in Booth's Christian brotherhood. In the face of this problem, Booth strategically supplements his scientific discourse with the language and imagery of religious allegory. Thus his narrative is organized as a progress from "Darkness" to "Deliverance" and its text is accompanied by running titles on each page that offer minute exegeses of the "meanings" of each page, much like the glosses in Morris' Kelmscott Press *News from Nowhere*. The apocalyptic language he uses, moreover, draws on the Christian imagery of *Pilgrim's Progress*: London, for instance, is described as "the Slough of Despond" (13).

Booth's use of allegory, however, is most strikingly evident in his visual representation of the "Darkest England" scheme (Figure 4.2). This richly colored and carefully detailed illustration functions as the frontispiece to the book and is meant to act as an incentive to change. The frontispiece caption reads: "the more the Scheme contained in this book is studied and assisted, the more will the beautiful prospect held out on the Chart be likely to be brought into reality." Produced as a fold-out map, the drawing is a minutely rendered microcosm of Booth's plan that manages to capture both its large-scale temporal and spatial dimensions. Clearly meant to evoke the functional maps used in Charles Booth's sociological work, in guidebooks, and in travel narratives such as Stanley's, Booth's map may well have been part of the ongoing parallel he sought to draw between Stanley's work of exploration and his own social investigation. Like the archival, mapping work of missionaries and explorers in Africa, his scheme promises a future of progressive enlightenment inseparable from imperialist expansion.

The map announces its ethnographic project of mapping culture horizontally by describing sociological particulars of Darkest England. Meant to resemble a "real" map, it is covered with facts and figures that, drawn into the pillars that act as a gateway into Booth's vision, literally support his vision. Yet, as the metaphorical as well as literal function of the figures suggests, the map draws heavily upon allegory as well. In particular, it summons up for its Victorian readers the allegorical tradition of Renaissance emblem books that many mid-century writers, such as Dickens and George Eliot, found useful in their attempts to superimpose a spiritual layer of meaning on everyday facticity.[36] The lower part of the map depicts a shipwreck, representing the capsizing of man's soul on the River of Life. The cruel waves responsible for the wreck are named after the city-based problems that plague the wreck's victims: among the many urban blights identified are "Jack the Ripper," "gin," "prize fighting," "brothels," and, of course, "slums." Borders surrounding the image bear statistics designed to authenticate its grim vision, such as the stark revelation: "In London, there are over 30,000 prostitutes." Victims are rescued from their plight by the capable hands of uniformed Army workers, while the lighthouse shining above them represents God's grace and the "salvation" that the Army's name guarantees. The lighthouse serves as the visual center of the illustration, pointing towards the glorious future that follows Salvation Army intervention; it can also be seen as a signifier for the despotic figure of General Booth himself, who is notably absent from the picture and thus easy to project on to it in the panoptical role of the "all-seeing" lighthouse.

Figure 4.2 "In Darkest England, and the Way Out"

With London at its center, Booth's map encapsulates the world. The city colonies lead out to farm colonies, and tiny boats leave those to go on to "British colonies" and "Foreign lands." The colors of the map lighten as the eye moves along it, signaling a move from present to future and from despair to salvation. The drawing also becomes more abstract and idealized as the eye moves upward, suggesting the increasingly utopian nature of the colonized future. Every inch of the globe is accounted for in Booth's plan; there is an absolute fit between the plan and the space available for its representation. In order to impose the immensity of the plan on to the page, however, and account for both the fallen present and the heavenly future represented by the colonies, most of the map is taken up by images of the city: both the shipwreck that is London and the city colony that serves as Booth's idealized version of it. The visual hierarchy that ensues from this arrangement reflects that of Booth's scheme in general. By imposing itself on the world, London will be redeemed and the diseased and dying bodies in the water at the bottom of the map regenerated as the robust, idealized male and female workers in its uppermost corners.

These workers, with their generically English appearance, demonstrate the way in which allegory helps Booth to circumvent the problems raised by his ethnographic study of the poor. If, in Coleridge's famous definition, allegory is "difference presented to the eye, likeness to the mind," Booth covers both bases.[37] Because his ethnography reveals an uneasiness about the poor's potentially irredeemable backwardness, the allegorical structure suggests a "likeness to the mind" by evoking Christian salvation as the progressive force that will inevitably override degeneration. Mapping the world vertically in an allegory of redemption, the illustration accents the fact that his plan is not only cosmopolitan in its global scope but also cosmological: a sign of a universal, heavenly order. However, by simultaneously mapping the world horizontally as the British empire and literally turning the world and its peoples (as the figures at the top suggest) British, the map proffers a likeness to the *eye* as well.

Once it has been ratified by monetary support from his readers, Booth states at the narrative's end, his plan will be manifested as part of a divine progress: "if it is His will – and whether it is or not, visible and manifest tokens will soon be forthcoming – who is there that can stand against it?" (277). Contributions ("tokens") thus become religious signs that verify Booth's claim that his plan is inseparable from a larger, celestial one and that he has adequately interpreted God's ways to man. The emphasis at the close of his book, then, shifts notably from the cultural particularity of

"Darkness" to the religious universality of "Deliverance." Through this trajectory, Booth is able to bypass the disturbing ethnographic questions of racial and cultural difference that trouble his vision of the Salvation Army's undisturbed global expansion – and his utopian ideals of undifferentiated world brotherhood. Flattening out difference as a solution to its inevitable presence, Booth's imperialist utopia enacts a violent erasure that poses a similar but opposite problem to Morris' socialist one.

News from Nowhere and *In Darkest England* appear at the end of this account of the Victorian global imagination for good reason. In many ways the most ambitious cosmopolitan works profiled here, these texts draw out the vexed logic – whether socialist or imperialist or both (in Booth's case) – that underlay much cosmopolitan thought of the period as it sought to reconcile changing ideas about culture with a growing sense of cultural permeability and interconnection. In exacerbating realism's inner tension between scientific and moral epistemologies, and local and global paradigms, Booth and Morris seem to exhaust its potential for cosmopolitan representation and pave the way for the space-clearing anti-realism practiced by many modernist writers.

CHAPTER 5

The moment and the end of time: Conrad, Woolf, and the temporal sublime

> The mask fell off the city, and she saw it for what it really is – a caricature of infinity . . . She went for a few moments into St. Paul's, whose dome stands out of the welter so bravely, as if preaching the gospel of form. But within, St. Paul's is as its surroundings – echoes and whispers, inaudible songs, invisible mosaics, wet footmarks crossing and recrossing the floor. Si monumentum requires, circumspice: it points us back to London.
>
> E. M. Forster, Howard's End¹

Cosmopolitanism has more often been associated with modernism than with Victorian literature, and for good reason. The broadness of the term in its quotidian usages encompasses the expatriate ennui of Isherwood and Hemingway; the colonial cross-cultural encounters portrayed by Forster, Orwell, and Woolf;[2] and the global reach of literary references in the epic stylings of Joyce, Eliot, and Pound. It was in the modern period that empire moved from the background to the foreground of national consciousness and British identity began to change incontrovertibly as colonial subjects demanded the rights of citizenship.[3] In the wake of growing doubts about empire, and the sense of global political crisis that prevailed immediately before and after the First World War, internationalism acquired a new visibility among intellectuals, and a number of modernist writers engaged global ideals both in their writing and through political activism. Leonard Woolf's *International Government* (1916), for instance, influenced the establishment of the League of Nations; H. G. Wells addressed the Reichstag on the topic of "The Common Sense of World Peace" (1929); and Virginia Woolf became involved with the Women's Cooperative Guild, an internationalist socialist organization.[4]

Recent critical attention to the cosmopolitan politics of the early twentieth century has been a necessary corrective to the tendency of earlier critics to ignore these politics or dismiss them as elitist, and has provided illuminating connections between different literary contexts.

Brent Edwards' work on black internationalism, for instance, enhances existing understandings of the Harlem Renaissance as well as of European modernism, as does Laura Winkiel's work on modernism, race, and internationalism.[5] Jessica Berman and other recent writers who work on modernist feminism and "global aesthetics," such as Holly Henry and Deborah Parsons, also offer a revisionist view of the period's literature. Contesting the familiar alignment of high modernism with elitist quietism, they show how intimately writers like Woolf, Gertrude Stein, and Dorothy Richardson engaged questions of civic and global belonging in their politics and literature.[6] Focusing on cosmopolitanism and urban writing respectively, both Berman and Parsons demonstrate how modernists construct imaginative communities that emphatically reject the universalism for which cosmopolitanism is often indicted. As Berman puts it, "Radical community [figures] as an antidote to the consolidation of social identity rather than its reason for being, and comes to demand a cosmopolitan perspective as a function of its very refusal of universality."[7] Rebecca Walkowitz's *Cosmopolitan Style* makes a similar case by focusing on literary technique. She argues that innovative elements of modernist style – Woolf's parataxis, for example, or Conrad's delayed decoding – might be reconceptualized as attempts to stage a "critical cosmopolitanism": one that asserts the "often-invisible connections between personal and international experiences."[8]

By highlighting modernism's contribution to internationalist and cosmopolitan ideals, this body of criticism has significantly challenged older arguments about modernist autonomy. Because these works focus on twentieth-century texts, however, they abbreviate the longer history of literature's engagement with cosmopolitanism that a Victorian perspective brings into view. The cosmopolitan realism of the Victorian novel was, in fact, the precondition for the more explicit political discourse of the modern era. While my emphasis on the relationship between urban and global community differs in some respects from the political stance other critics highlight, the Victorian framework I use demonstrates how both the formal and discursive changes the novel undergoes between the nineteenth and twentieth centuries have much to do with its response to cosmopolitan realism.

To put it differently, the modernist critique of nineteenth-century forms of knowledge results in a formal and ideological rejection of the kinds of imaginative totality that Victorians envisioned. In the passage from *Howard's End* cited above, St. Paul's no longer offers a clarifying view of London, as it did in the Colosseum panorama or in Dickens' evocation of the "Heart of London."⁹ Instead, "point[ing] us back to London," it serves only as a "caricature of infinity": formlessness without the redemptive sublimity of infinity. In city novels such as *The Secret Agent* (1907) and *Mrs. Dalloway* (1925), London defies unifying overviews such as that of Wordsworth's poet-impresario or the all-seeing, all-knowing scrutiny of Sherlock Holmes. Instead, it is thoroughly discontinuous, amorphous and alienating. The airplane that effortlessly traverses national borders in *Mrs. Dalloway* and the labyrinthine streets of *The Secret Agent* that harbor the irresolvable "secret" plots of international unrest signify the city's porosity and its consequent vulnerability.

Conceived as an imaginative relation between city and world, cosmopolitanism becomes more elusive within the increasingly secular and politically skeptical outlook of modernist writers. This chapter analyzes modernist novels set in the imperial city before and after the war to explain why the imagined communities of Victorian urban literature were no longer viable by the early twentieth century, and to show how a more tenuous cosmopolitanism took its place. My purpose is to delineate the formal properties of the global imaginary in modernist literature but also to elucidate, through the retrospective view from this period, how essential realism's amalgamation of scientific and moral modes of knowledge was to Victorian cosmopolitanism. In jettisoning Victorian epistemologies modernist writers simultaneously abandoned the totalized view of urban space as a figure for global community. By doing so, they liberated themselves from the ideological contradictions and representational aporias of urban realism but also surrendered a robust fictive vocabulary for large-scale community. This is not to say that modernist novels are no longer cosmopolitan, but that the idea of human interconnectedness across space no longer shapes the fictive world of the text. Within the works of Conrad and Woolf, totality – in the form of conspiratorial connections and standardized time – is the source of anxiety rather than the solution to it.

In their rejection of nineteenth-century visual epistemologies and spatial overviews, then, modernist novels turn to new perceptions of time as a means of imagining a common humanity. The famous city novels of Conrad and Woolf use two distinct modern temporalities that, paralleling the simultaneously detailed and distanced views of realist literature, involve the balancing of antithetical scales. In place of the sketch, both writers use dilated moments of mutual recognition as ways of registering connections between individuals; in place of the panorama both compose an overarching sense of evolutionary time that makes evident the finitude of human history. These temporalities, the moment and the "end of time," produce a new kind of cosmopolitan sublime: one that jettisons the centrality of the human subject crucial to Romantic versions of sublimity but that offers in its place a tentative vision of species-being as a site of identification. The concept of humanity composed in this manner is no longer a liberal one, for it is based on the notion of survival rather than a shared consciousness or set of ideals. Moments of empathy occur when characters viscerally imagine each other's deaths (or Stevie feels the pain of cab-horses), while the demise of humanity as a whole is the precondition for a post-humanist form of species-identification in each novel.

COSMOPOLITANISM AND MODERNIST FORM

Fredric Jameson's essay "Modernism and Imperialism" provides a different explanation for the spatial crisis faced by the modernist novel. Its inability to produce a unified sense of imagined community, he argues, is related to the entrenchment of imperialism in the early twentieth century, when it became fully incorporated into the political, economic, and cultural forms of the nation. Because a vast portion of an imperial nation's capital was located outside the nation itself, "daily life and existential experience in the metropolis – which is necessarily the very content of national literature itself, can now no longer be grasped immanently."[10] Given the absent-centered nature of empire, modernism cannot reproduce realism's "intention towards totality"; both the form and content of modernist literature, according to Jameson, reflect these changes.

Modernism's departure from the overview of the realist novel, however, can also be attributed to a number of other historical factors that Jameson overlooks: the increased unviability of a progressive and unifying world-historical vision in light of the national rivalries leading up to the First World War; the unprecedented devastation of the war itself, which seemed to writers to defy representation; and, as I argue above, modernists' sense of the complicity between realist forms and the coercions and exclusions of nationalism and imperialism.

Jameson's argument is useful, then, in its description of how the imagination of space changes after the turn of the century rather than in its claim about imperialism's relationship to novelistic form *per se*. As he points out, novels such as *Heart of Darkness* no longer pose a dichotomous relationship between "home" and "abroad." Instead, London spills out on to Africa via Conrad's metaphoric connection between the Thames and

Congo rivers, posing an insurmountable challenge to realism's totalizing, cartographic impulse. What takes the place of the totalizing gesture in modernist narrative, Jameson suggests, is style which, in its aesthetic density and artificiality, "becomes the marker and the substitute of the unrepresentable totality."[11]

My analysis, however, focuses not on style at the level of language but on a different way of conceiving form, in terms of the novels' deployment of time, as a substitute for totality. Momentary encounters between strangers in the city, and the apocalyptic sense in both novels of the shared fate of humanity, unite characters in novels that otherwise stress discontinuity between individual perspectives. In the Victorian novel, as I argued in the Introduction, it is precisely the non-coevalness of different societies within anthropological and economic theories of development that makes metaphors of spatial unity essential to the realist novel's interconnection of city and world. By bringing disparate peoples in the same visualizable space (such as the Crystal Palace), Victorian utopias sought to represent a common human project.

Modernist disenchantment with the implicit politics of spatial unification, however, helps to explain how cosmopolitanism, along with the novel itself, changed shape after the Victorian period, and why notions of time in the novels of Conrad and Woolf take on a quality of transcendence previously the prerogative of the realist overview. Because their notions of humanity are constructed at the limits of human life, they circumvent the problem of disparate temporalities within anthropological thought without capitulating to the homogenizing view from above.

THE FAILURES OF COSMOPOLITAN REALISM

Despite the fact that a progressive cosmopolitanism is more often linked with modernist than with Victorian literature, the word "cosmopolitan" and its variants are often used pejoratively in the early twentieth century, as in the nineteenth. In E. M. Forster's *Howard's End*, it is sometimes positively associated with the open-minded Schlegels and their mixed German-English heritage which makes them like "tourists who pretend each hotel is their home."[12] But it is more often linked to urban sprawl and a correspondent loss of shared values: "London was but a foretaste of this nomadic civilization, which is altering human nature so profoundly, and throws upon personal relations a stress greater than they have ever borne before. Under cosmopolitanism, if it comes, we shall receive no help from this earth."[13]

The negative valences of cosmopolitanism in modernist literature reflect both an intensification of anxieties about urban diversity, as well as a new level of cynicism about Victorian liberal ideals and the national and imperial politics that accompanied them. In *The Secret Agent*, the international tensions that prefigured the First World War underlie the novel's plot, while *Mrs. Dalloway* demonstrates how these tensions have played out to their logical, terrible conclusions. The utopias adumbrated in both novels are thus sinister or fallen ones. When Clarissa Dalloway reflects on the Edwardian twilight of Bourton, when she and Sally shared an Edenic love, read William Morris' utopian writings, and dreamt of a socialist future, she marks the absence of such idealism in the present. In *The Secret Agent*, utopic thinking is equally blighted. Those utopias imagined by Verloc's gang of socialist co-conspirators – bleak, hierarchical, and mechanistic – are far from the idealistic cosmopolitan spaces conjured up by earlier thinkers such as Morris and Booth.[14]

More significantly, both writers cast a jaundiced eye on the forms of knowledge that underwrite cosmopolitan realism. *The Secret Agent*'s detectives, like Inspector Bucket and Sherlock Holmes, are savvy but their self-interested machinations are indistinguishable from those of the criminals. In *Mrs. Dalloway*, "Dr. Holmes" has metamorphosed from a brilliant all-seeing detective into a dense and unperceptive physician. Furthermore, unlike in earlier narratives of "urban investigation," the characters of these novels refuse to fit neatly into occupational, ethnic, racial, or criminological types. When one of Conrad's anarchists, Ossipon, attempts to use Lombroso's theories to understand Stevie, he does so at his own expense – Conrad coyly depicts Ossipon himself as a negroid "degenerate."

Indeed, in *The Secret Agent*, difference fails to fit on to a scale at all; it is either absolute, meaningful only as stereotype (Verloc insists that he will never understand Winnie because of her gender, for instance), or entirely meaningless. The Assistant Commissioner, snooping around a seedy side-street in search of clues to the novel's mystery, is both assimilated into the city and objectified by it: "the genius of the locality assimilated him. He might have been but one more of the queer foreign fish that can be seen of an evening there flitting around dark corners."[15] Later, entering an Italian restaurant, he notes that its patrons were "as denationalized as the dishes set before them ... They seemed created for the Italian restaurant, unless the Italian restaurant had been perchance created for them" (149). Ethnicity, like all other forms of identity in the novel, is thoroughly distorted by urban commerce. The Italian restaurant is no longer Italian, the agent of

British government recognizable only as a "queer foreign fish." Rather than an indication of progress or at least an awe-inducing spectacle, the city's cosmopolitan landscape is a sign of modernity hurtling relentlessly towards homogeneity, corroding identities and relationships along the way.

In *Mrs. Dalloway*, the city's population is not as international, and Woolf focuses on class and gender difference rather than national identity as a source of alienation. Yet she dwells upon the seeming impossibility of a utopian cosmopolitanism as well. Rezia, the most conspicuous non-English character in the novel, is a war-bride, whom Septimus has transplanted to England. Her alliance with Septimus, whose mental illness makes him a social outsider as well, increases her self-consciousness and alienation. In one scene, she demonstrates how urban spectatorship might have an alienating rather than unifying effect when she differentiates herself from those around her in a park: "[They were] English people, with their children and their horses and their clothes, which she admired in a way; but they were 'people' now, because Septimus had said, 'I will kill myself'; an awful thing to say. Suppose they had heard him."[16] Unable to find solace in those around her, Rezia comes to see her fellow city-dwellers as a mass of indifference and potential censorship, recognizable only as a conglomerate of possessions: "children," "horses," and "clothes."

Despite their evident pessimism about the possibility of empathy beyond or even across the nation, however, both Conrad and Woolf are critical of the exclusionary nationalism that came to define the early part of the century. After the real-life attempted bombing of Greenwich in 1894, propagandists used the event to foment support for the anti-immigration Aliens Act that successfully passed in 1905.[17] The newspaper reports that fed the anti-immigrant sentiment following the Greenwich explosion exploited "overlapping discourses of racial difference and degeneration" so that *The London Times* presented "the blond, underdeveloped, effeminate and definitely 'foreign' body of Martial Bourdin, the Greenwich bomber, as a generalized trope for anarchism."[18] Septimus in *Mrs. Dalloway* and Stevie in *The Secret Agent* are not technically "foreign," but are both outsiders because of their mental fragility and compromised masculinity – their inability to successfully perform the work of war and of social conformity so central to national belonging. By having the tragedies of these anti-heroes reverberate at the absent center of their novels, Woolf and Conrad render the violence inherent in the cohesion of imagined communities explicit.

SECULAR TIME AND THE URBAN IMAGINATION

Early twentieth-century scientific and philosophical ideas about time abound in the works of both Conrad and Woolf. The second law of thermodynamics, often cited as an influence on Conrad's work, infected the *fin-de-siècle* imagination with fears of heat-death, while developments in astronomy, a particular interest of Woolf, made finite the scale of human and planetary life.[19] At the same time, studies of the city that combined sociological and psychological epistemologies, such as those of Georg Simmel, provided new ways of thinking about subjective time. Simmel suggested that the city's numerous forms of stimulation accelerated an individual's "nervous life," producing both over-sensitivity (neurasthenia), and a blasé indifference to the fate of others: a shriveling of empathy.[20]

Degeneration theories thrived upon such notions of the corrosive effects of modernity. If Victorian anthropological writing about colonial cultures situated them in the past, at a temporal as well as a spatial distance from the metropolitan center, early twentieth-century scientific thought made it harder to fathom this distance. Instead, the primeval past identified with the colonies, and a machine-dominated future identified with the march of capitalism, co-exist in modern versions of the city. In *The Secret Agent*, for instance, an office scene is described in both the language of the jungle and that of the cyborg: "Speaking tubes resembling snakes were tied by the heads to the back of the Assistant Commissioner's wooden arm-chair, and their gaping mouths seemed ready to bite his elbows" (97).[21]

Another significant scientific context for modernist urban writing is time standardization. In *Einstein's Clocks, Poincaré's Maps*, Peter Galison demonstrates that the late nineteenth and early twentieth centuries were characterized by the "materialization of simultaneity."[22] The Great Exhibition put the ideas of global trade and international solidarity on display, but also demonstrated that when it came to the calculation of time "'chaos' reigned between national systems."[23] For the next half-century, governments, scientists, metrological societies, and clock-makers tried to bring the management of time into sync with the needs of modern commerce and empire: "Time coordination . . . was not merely an arcane thought experiment; rather, it critically concerned the clock industry, the military, and the railroads as well as [being] a symbol of the interconnected, sped-up world of modernity"[24] (Figures 5.1 and 5.2).

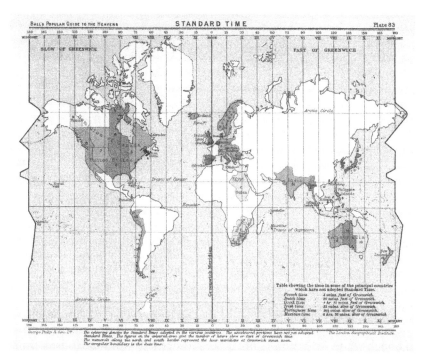

Figure 5.1 "Standard Time," map.

Time coordination has both positive and negative symbolic resonances in modern literature because it arose from competing impulses: "Synchronized time remained hypersymbolized. *Einheitszeit* emerged from contestation among imperial empire, democracy, world citizenship, and antianarchism."[25] Thus while Conrad has little sympathy for the anarchists who attempt to blow up the Greenwich Meridian (the *ur*-symbol of standardized time, according to them), the impossibility of escaping the homogenizing forces of modern urban life defines his novel's baleful outlook. In Woolf's work, the chimes of Big Ben serve to unify the thoughts of its characters, creating the "simultaneity across time" that Benedict Anderson famously argues is central to the novel's imagined community.[26] But while this sense of community is sometimes salutary in the novel, it is also painfully exclusionary and alienating. As a result, Woolf devotes as much imaginative energy to dismantling a sense of shared time in the novel as she does to constructing it.

Also influential on the modernist literary imagination was the idea of relativity. According to Galison, this was not antithetical to the notion

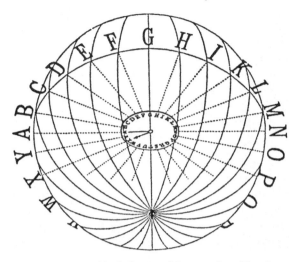

Figure 5.2 Sandford Fleming, "Cosmopolitan Time"

of standardized time but emerged dialectically from Einstein's work on clock coordination during the scientist's time in a Geneva patent office. Though relativity has more often been associated with modernist writing than time standardization, both concepts feature prominently in *The Secret Agent* and *Mrs. Dalloway*. Subjective time is connected in both novels to urban isolation and the fragmentation of community, but also, in more utopian terms, to a new biological concept of human empathy and community.

PREMONITIONS OF THE POST-HUMAN IN "THE SECRET AGENT"

The Secret Agent's conspiratorial plot revolves around the seedy world of Adolf Verloc, a double agent who pretends to sympathize with a group of international anarchists but reports on their activities to both the Russian embassy and the British government. His British contact, Inspector Heat, reports in turn to an Assistant Commissioner and ultimately Sir Ethelred, a prominent politician. The action begins when Vladimir, the First Secretary at the Russian embassy, demands that Verloc step up his lackluster conspiratorial activities by bombing the Greenwich Meridian. In Vladimir's mind, this act will cause the otherwise overly tolerant British to crack down on anarchists, allowing him to argue for greater restrictions on political activism at the upcoming International Conference in Milan. Verloc's wife, Winnie, who has married him for the financial safety-net he offers her and her family, has a "simple" younger brother, Stevie, who is intensely sensitive to the suffering of those around him. Stevie worships Verloc, whom he sees as a revolutionary hero; he becomes Verloc's assistant in the plot to bomb the Meridian, which he believes is a protest on behalf of the working poor. En route to the bomb site, however, he trips – and blows himself up instead. Inspector Heat manages to trace Stevie to Verloc's house (thanks to an address Winnie has sewn into his coat) and Verloc resigns himself to a period in jail. Before his arrest, however, Winnie murders him in a rage over his exploitation of Stevie and later commits suicide.

The Secret Agent seems at first to support conventional wisdom about the modernist novel's cosmopolitanism. First, it takes the city's diversity for granted. Rather than imagining the urban multi-culture as a new subject for aesthetic contemplation (as James and Doyle do), the novel uses it as the underlying premise of its international conspiracy plot.[27] Moreover, in his creation of Vladimir, the novel's most sinister character, Conrad seems explicitly to be indicting anti-immigration sentiment. Vladimir is sinister precisely because he is anti-democratic as evidenced by his cynical exploitation of the International Conference in Milan. By plotting to blow up the Meridian and blame a group of international socialists for the deed, Vladimir hopes to turn the Conference against Britain's "sentimental regard for individual liberty" (29) – its relatively open borders and political tolerance – and thus to engineer a Continental backlash against liberal democracy. This subplot reflects on the fact that the real Greenwich bombing was used to support a successful anti-immigration lobby in Britain in 1904. In February 1894, Martial Bourdin, the ill-fated inspiration for Stevie, died of shrapnel wounds in an apparent attempt to bomb the Meridian. Though the press was not excessively alarmist, fears of international working-class solidarity were prevalent, and Bourdin's association with French anarchists through the Autonomie Club, his immigrant status, and an almost synchronous anarchist bombing in Paris, made his failed act of violence adequate fodder for anti-alien sentiment.[28]

Anarchism in Britain during this period was seen as a foreign export as so many political exiles from the Continent made their way there.[29] Ironically, English tolerance towards political groups of all leanings (the "sentimental regard for individual liberty" that Vladimir reviles) led to the myth "that London was the secret international headquarters of the (anarchist) movement, where its horrible crimes were planned."³⁰ Consequently, anti-immigrant leaders argued that the British working class was being led astray by foreign conspirators; conservatives such as Lord Salisbury, who supported an Aliens Bill in 1894, attempted to single ethnic groups out for blame even when members of these groups were not "aliens" but British subjects.

The effect of the 1905 Aliens Act on British liberalism in the new century was profound:

> Prior to 1905, the laws preventing immigrants from settling in Britain had been applied intermittently and selectively, in response to political expediency rather than as a coherent attempt at social policy, and even the practice of deportation had often been viewed with suspicion ... After 1905, however, one begins to see an important shift of emphasis as "the protection of refugees" is ... increasingly displaced by "the 'protection' of borders."³¹

By debunking the notion of international conspiracy from below (it is, in fact, the heads of national governments, such as Vladimir and Sir Ethelred, who are ultimately responsible for the "political" activities of Verloc), and reserving the greatest portion of sympathy for Stevie (the actual bomber), *The Secret Agent* seems to be writing against the racism of the Aliens Act supporters and in favor of greater national permeability.

Given its cynical vision of human agents and their agency, however, critics of the novel have seldom argued for its utopianism. On the contrary, recent criticism of Conrad's work has focused chiefly on the novel's morbid, stultifying preoccupation with heat-death, degeneration, and panoptical power.³² This criticism sees the novel as, at worst, counter-revolutionary in its indictment of "terrorists" for their acceleration of social disintegration, or, at best, irredeemably apocalyptic in the virulence of its social critique. Conrad seems more truly anarchic than his anarchists (except perhaps the Professor), for he posits no way of transcending the all-consuming capitalism he derides, nor does he take refuge in the redemptive power of art.

Though Conrad was himself an émigré and a new British national (he became a citizen in 1886), his association of cosmopolitanism with the pernicious effects of capitalism and imperialism generates a nostalgia for national belonging or older forms of community so profound that it seems to override the compassion for the victims of modernity also evident in his novel. The novel's plot demonstrates the negative reper-cussions of the city's diversity through its depiction of the violent impact of the global (Vladimir's political machinations at the Russian embassy) on the local (Verloc's family in Soho).

Conrad's anti-cosmopolitanism thus often seems as virulent as Vladimir's. His portrayal of the city as both the sign and cause of degeneration dismantles the Victorian idea of London as an "imperial archive" of intellectual and artistic riches; instead his description of the British capital as "the very center of the Empire on which the sun never sets" (214) is heavily ironic. If General Booth, as I argue in Chapter 4, employed the imagery of an "urban jungle" to advocate for a systematic and purportedly humane approach to empire and reform, Conrad's more generalized use of the "urban jungle" motif fashions a world beyond reform.[33] Winnie, after murdering Verloc, is depicted as the degenerate hybrid offspring of city life and cave life: the narrator's explanation for the murder is "the inheritance of her immemorial and obscure descent, the simple ferocity of the age of caverns, and the unbalanced nervous fury of the age of barrooms" (163).

The question of how to define the "human" in a cosmopolitan era, as Conrad's preoccupation with animalism demonstrates, is a central concern of the novel, and one which seems to impel it irresistibly towards the issue of national identity, for the entropic lack of distinction between man/animal, margin/center, city/jungle is coupled to the novel's portrayal of the city's diverse population. English characters are in the minority. Verloc is part French; Winnie, too, claims to be "of French descent"; the Assistant Commissioner, the chief representative of British government, is constantly described as foreign; and Vladimir, the novel's chief villain, is "not only utterly un-English, but absolutely un-European, and startling even to [Verloc's] experience of cosmopolitan slums" (24–5). In a scene where the conspirators take their leave from a bar after learning of Verloc's betrayal, a player piano (a recurrent symbol of urban alienation in the novel) underscores the tragedy of this pervasive absence of national identity:

The lonely piano, without as much as a music stool to help it, struck a few chords courageously, and beginning a selection of national airs, played [Ossipon] out at last to the tune of "Blue Bells of Scotland." The painfully detached notes grew faint behind his back while he went slowly upstairs, across the hall and into the street. (79)

Mocking the "lonely" departure of Ossipon by dredging up the national belonging he has renounced through his work, and underscoring the post-lapsarian state of the city with its evocation of pastoral "blue bells," the piano demonstrates that even the most powerful tools of national cohesion – anthems – have become sterile. The "painful" cosmopolitan detachment that enables the conspirators to work together serves, in Conrad's rendering, as an indication of their work's futility.

As many critics have noted, the personification of the player piano is only one of the ways in which the novel alludes to the interchangeability of animate and inanimate objects. Significantly, the loneliness and pain in the passage above are attributed to the piano rather than to Ossipon, suggesting a correlation between the loss of national, and human, identity. Verloc, in his ability to be manipulated by those around him, including his employers and Winnie, is described as an "automaton": "this resemblance to a mechanical figure went so far that he had an automaton's absurd air of being aware of the machinery inside him" (197), while the Professor is on a quest to turn himself into "[a] variable and yet perfectly precise mechanism. A really intelligent detonator" (67).

Donna Haraway's work famously appropriates the idea of the post-human, whose history she locates in "the 'West's' escalating dominations of abstract individuation," for a utopian progressivism, arguing that "a cyborg world might be about lived social and bodily realities in which people are not afraid of their joint kinship with animals and machines, not afraid of permanently partial identities and contradictory standpoints."[34] Evaluating the repercussions of the demise of humanism almost a century before Haraway, Conrad portrays the advent of the post-human with horror. The animal and inanimate imagery that pervades the novel reflects his fear that humans have been transformed by the city's corrosive effects on identity into both "simians" and "cyborgs," at once prey to their primitive instincts *and* reduced by the effects of urban commercialism to the level of the objects around them.

The fact that cosmopolitanism has overwhelmingly negative implications for Conrad is visible, as we have seen, on the level of the content, with Verloc switching national allegiances at will; the international conspirators demonstrating their haplessness through their *lack* of will; and the International Conference in Milan serving as a platform for the quashing of working-class resistance. The idea of human solidarity is raised only to be mocked. The narrator, satirizing the Professor, says that he is "perhaps doing no more than seeking for peace in common with the rest of mankind – the peace of soothed vanity, of satisfied appetites, or perhaps of appeased conscience." All humanist resonances of the word "peace" (that which could be shared "in common with the rest of mankind") are eroded in Conrad's prose by the conjunction of the word with "soothed vanity" and the alliteration that links the baser words "appetite" and "appeased."

On the level of form, too, the novel rejects the imagination of London as a continuous space or community. Instead, Conrad describes the city in his "Author's Preface," and throughout the novel, in terms of obfuscation, much as Dickens does in *Bleak House*:

> the vision of an enormous town presented itself, of a monstrous town more populous than some continents and in its man-made might as if indifferent to heaven's frowns and smiles; a cruel devourer of the world's light. There was room enough there to place any story, depth enough for any passion, variety enough there for any setting, darkness enough to bury five millions of lives. (xxxvi)

Unlike Dickens' city, though, this one cannot be redeemed by domestic devotion, nor does it ultimately reveal its mysteries. Rather than suggesting a unified whole, the city is an unimaginable void: a "devourer of the world's light," infinitely wide, deep, and various, hence "dark" and "monstrous." Far from the repository of anthropological information it served as for writers such as Mayhew and Dickens, London is a place where lives are "buried" rather than explicated and strangers traversing the city "would never be heard of again" (150).

Though some critics have pointed to Conrad's specific references to streets and destinations in London in the novel, his emphasis on the city's unfathomable size and shifting shape stresses its unknowability.[35] Stevie, destined to exemplify the fate of the modern urban individual in his literal fragmentation by the bomb, does not know his own address (hence the Inspector's ability to trace his body to Verloc via the address that Winnie has stitched into his coat). Verloc, who is described as being "cosmopolitan enough not to be deceived by London's topographical mysteries," visits streets inscribed with evidence of the city's shape-shifting. No. 10 Chesham Square is located between No. 9 and No. 37 and "the fact that this last belonged to Porthill Street ... was proclaimed by an inscription placed ... by whatever highly efficient authority is charged with the duty of keeping track of London's strayed houses" (14). As Martin Ray notes, "Conrad immediately stresses in the opening page that the London he depicts has vanished: Verloc's house was 'one of those grimy brick houses which existed in large quantities before the era of reconstruction dawned upon London.'"[36]

If the city eludes representation or comprehension in the novel, so does a larger global totality. In *The Secret Agent*, the clarifying map of the world imagined in the works of Doyle or Booth is gone, replaced by a haunting image of multiple worlds, abstract, meaningless, and chaotically inter-twined. Stevie's bizarre drawings of "innumerable circles, concentric, eccentric; a coruscating whirl of circles that by their tangled multitude of repeated curves, uniformity of form, and confusion of intersected lines suggested a rendering of cosmic chaos, the symbolism of a mad art attempting the inconceivable" (45) render a terrifying interplanetary system in which the earth is lost amidst the chaos of space. As I argued in Chapter 3, web or fabric imagery in earlier Victorian writing often facilitated the imagination of an interconnected world because, while it typically focused on a particular part of the whole, it suggested a larger network of cultural relations. *The Secret Agent* and *Mrs. Dalloway* make reference to webs of connections too, but these webs, rather than encom-passing the world, are filled with holes and loose ends. Connections between people and places taken for granted in Victorian writing are here depicted as weak and susceptible to rupture.

Thus *The Secret Agent*'s narrator, referring to the moments in which anarchism can occur without being detected, states that "in the close-woven stuff of relations between conspirators and police there occur unexpected solutions of continuity, sudden holes of space and time" (85). In this rendering, the web of relations is a cloth prone to rip unexpectedly, producing "sudden holes." Another image of an incomplete web is supplied by the Assistant Commissioner who, expressing frustra-tion about his unsolved crime, exclaims: "Here I am stuck in a litter of paper ... supposed to hold all the threads in my hands and yet I can but hold what is put in my hand, and nothing else. And they can fasten the other ends of threads where they please" (115). Unlike the fortuitous web of connections in *A Study in Scarlet* which enables Holmes to solve the mystery, *The Secret Agent*'s web is saturated with the menace of panoptical power.[37] Inspector Heat is connected to the criminals he pursues because he blackmails them privately for information; Verloc links the Russian embassy to the conspirators through his spying activities. The most intimate affiliations are those that knit together people plotting against each other, but even these are liable to break apart. In *The Secret Agent*, connections between people lead directly to complicity in the deaths of individuals and the tragedy of modern war: a coming calamity which Stevie's bomb and Vladimir's deadly political tactics seem always to foreshadow.

Conrad's portrait of urban cosmopolitanism seems devoid of any basis for moral decision, political action, or empathetic connection. The dire implications of this are exemplified by Verloc's disenchanted marriage and his failure to understand Winnie's grief for Stevie. Beyond the animal-like maternal instincts of Winnie, empathy in the novel is fundamentally "impossible": "it was impossible for [Verloc] to understand [Winnie's mourning] without ceasing to be himself" (233). Stevie, seemingly the only character capable of empathetic, even altruistic, emotion, suffers unendingly because of it – "he contemplated open-mouthed . . . the dramas of fallen horses, whose pathos and violence induced him sometimes to shriek piercingly in a crowd" (9) – and ultimately is destroyed by it (by agreeing to the bombing because of his loyalty to Verloc and spontaneous sympathy for the working classes). In light of this, the novel might be seen as an extended protest against "bad" cosmopolitanism: the moral and affective detachment which Conrad connects to the city's simultaneous overproduction and obliteration of difference.

Yet, while often reactionary in its recourse to the language of racial degeneration to describe this difference, Conrad's portrait of cosmopolitanism is also a powerful denunciation of its imbrications in global capitalism and imperialism. If the novel shuns the panoptical overview of the realist novel, it also registers hostility towards the notion of global homogeneous time. Despite Conrad's lack of sympathy for Vladimir and the socialists behind the bombing plot, the novel's sense of tragedy stems not only from the death of Stevie but also from the failure of the plot to blow up Greenwich: an act of nihilism that is utopian in its impossibility (one can't throw a bomb into time or into "pure mathematics," Vladimir laments in proposing his plan to Verloc).

Greenwich is a symbol both for the machine-like world that should be "smashed" and of time coordination, a concept singled out for critique by many modernist writers because of its reifying, homogenizing role in national life, and its connection with capitalist efficiency. Georg Simmel, for example, states that "If all clocks and watches in Berlin would suddenly go wrong in different ways, even if only by one hour, all economic life and communication of the city would be disrupted for a long time."[38] Vladimir's attack on the symbolism of the Greenwich Meridian reflects this widespread modernist assumption, for his plan assumes that the "bourgeois worship" of science and progress will be assaulted by the bombing of the Observatory. In a letter to R. B. Cunninghame Graham, Conrad's own investment in the idea of "smashing" the system is made clear, as well as his sense of the idea's futility. Comparing the world to a machine, he says that it has "made itself without thought, without conscience, without foresight, without eyes, without heart" and laments the fact that: "You can't interfere with it. The last drop of bitterness is the suspicion that you can't even smash it."[39]

Juxtaposed to the notion of public standardized time is that of "private time," time perceived relatively and subjectively. Henri Bergson, among other modernist thinkers, argued that private time could be liberating in its defiance of the oppressive influence of social systems such as Greenwich Time, and its possibilities for self-determination. In "Time and Free Will," he argues that time, rather than space, offers an unmediated experience of subjectivity and thus the potential to perceive duration and harness the process of becoming. Conrad's representation of "private time" shares at least a portion of Bergson's optimism. In their ability to manipulate time by mentally accelerating and decelerating it, characters in the novel briefly have the luxury of identification with their own humanity and mortality, and that of others.

Inspector Heat's investigation of Stevie's death-scene exemplifies this manipulation of time, for his experience of it changes radically in his contemplation of Stevie's abject end. Surveying Stevie's body, the Inspector "rose by the force of sympathy, which is a form of fear, above the vulgar conception of time ... The inexplicable mysteries of conscious existence beset Chief Inspector Heath till he evolved a horrible notion that ages of atrocious pain and mental torture could be contained within two successive winks of an eye" (88). Even while Stevie is, for him, a terrorist and an enemy, the Inspector's will to live here – "a form of fear" – overcomes his will to power, provoking "sympathy" with Stevie through an act of imaginative identification.

Similarly, the Professor, describing the twenty seconds he must wait before an explosion after detonating the bomb he carries, fills Ossipon with horror at the thought of the eternity that those seconds would last. Ossipon's sense of time is also altered by the notion of Winnie's death once he reads about it in a newspaper. The very presence of the newspaper in his pocket transforms his heartbeat ("His heart was beating against it") and his mental rhythms: "the mystery of a human brain pulsating wrongfully to the rhythm of journalistic phrases" (311).

Conrad's novel itself functions as an elongation of private time, for his motivation to write *The Secret Agent*, he claimed, arose from his outrage that the death of the real Greenwich bomber had been reduced to a footnote in newspaper history.[40] Blaming mass forms such as the newspaper for urban alienation, Conrad protested that:

In this age of knowledge our sympathetic imagination, in which alone we can look for the ultimate triumph of concord and justice, remains strangely impervious to information, however correctly and even picturesquely conveyed.[41]

"Great art," he argued, offers a "more indirect method" for imagining human sympathy because it allows for a sense of the duration of a person's life through the intensity of fictionally reconstructed moments of it. Similarly, the Inspector can sympathize with Stevie's death because he can imagine it as "ages of atrocious pain" rather than the "two successive winks of an eye" in which it happened, and in which a newspaper might record it.

Conrad's idea of what "human" might mean in the modern world is also conveyed through the novel's evocation of a nonhuman future. The return of the swamp that lies just beneath the surface of the city is ominously foretold by Conrad's insistence on the possibility of human self-annihilation. *The Secret Agent* ends with the Professor, the real secret agent, whom the police seem powerless to stop. Walking anonymously through the crowd, he is "terrible in the simplicity of his idea calling madness and despair to the regeneration of the world" (311). This "regeneration," Conrad's irony implies, might mean the end of human life. The Greenwich bomb plot, futile though it turns out to be, also gestures towards this idea, for it represents the violent lengths to which nations will go in the interests of policy.

The novel thus fluctuates between two different notions of time: time on a grand scale (human history) and time on a micro-level (the moments in which the value of individual lives are contemplated by one of the characters). The impossible imaginative leap required by both these perceptions of time is depicted by Conrad as the experience of a temporal sublime in which humanity is reaffirmed in the face of its absence. One life, no matter how circumscribed or marginalized (Stevie's is, tragically, both), can contain "ages of atrocious pain" but the empathetic consideration of such local cases might renovate human sympathies. As Ossipon comes to realize in the wake of Winnie's death, "Mankind wants to live – to live" (305).

This version of empathy requires a cosmopolitan imaginary because it depends on the very diversity that Conrad seems continually to decry. Inspector Heat's response to Stevie, and Stevie's to the horse and cabman, are unsolicited responses to difference in the kind of encounter that could only take place in urban space, where radically unassimilable lives are closely and violently interconnected. In spite of his antipathy for the city, Conrad's most powerful renderings of human consciousness connect its "sordidness" to the utopian ability to transform it imaginatively. Inspector Heat finds that "The murmur of town life, the subdued rumble of wheels in the two invisible streets to the right and left, came through the curve of the sordid lane to his ears with a precious familiarity and an appealing sweetness. He was human" (94).

Over the course of the novel, and the chaotic downward spiral of its plot, the categories "human" and "community" take on new meanings. Stevie suffers equally in sympathy for the horse that the cabman beats, and for the cabman who is driven to beat him by his need to make money. His initial response to their plight is depicted as almost grotesquely inappropriate: "the tenderness to all pain and all misery, the desire to make the horse happy and the cabman happy, had reached the point of a bizarre longing to take them to bed with him" (167), but the fleeting and tiny community that he creates in this vision allows for his own transcendence from the resignation that surrounds him. The fact that his ongoing "tenderness" leads to his death might suggest the unviability of Stevie's solutions to human and nonhuman suffering alike. Yet through the *duration* of Stevie's reaction – the time that he takes to consider a solution to the suffering he recognizes – Conrad also shows that this response is the novel's only appropriate one in its "tenderness of ... universal charity" and its refusal to succumb to the overwhelmingly "anaesthetic" effect of city life.

"LIFE, LONDON, THIS MOMENT IN JUNE": COSMOPOLITAN TIME IN "MRS. DALLOWAY"

Woolf's internationalism, her scorn for empire and her love of the city have all been amply vouched for in recent analyses of her writing and political life.[42] While these aspects of her intellectual outlook are all important to her cosmopolitan imaginary, I focus in particular on how it was structured as a response not only to Victorian ideals, but to the formal project of cosmopolitan realism. Woolf's famous critique of realism, "Life is not a series of gig-lamps symmetrically arranged ... life is a semi-transparent envelope surrounding us from the beginning of consciousness to the end," indicts its linearity and allegiance to systematic order.[43] The "semi-transparent envelope" she erects in its place confounds traditional notions of space and time by collapsing them. In her formulation, life is presented as a unification of both space and time but hers is a unity, significantly, that is permeable or "semi-transparent." This permeability is necessary to Woolf's use of narration to imagine community in ways that elude normative spatial configurations.

Mrs. Dalloway and *The Secret Agent* share a vision of the city as a discontinuous and unassimilable space in which the threat of violence lurks menacingly beneath the surface of everyday life. The fears of degeneration and anomie that inform Conrad's plot also underwrite Septimus' war-inspired, cataclysmic hallucinations in *Mrs. Dalloway*, while a preoccupation with death, emphasized by Clarissa's and Septimus' repetition of the line, "Fear no more the heat of the sun," is palpable throughout the novel. Woolf's representation of the city, however, is notably less dystopian than Conrad's and moments of redemption in her novel are intermittent rather than elusive. While Conrad depicts the city as the vacuous nadir of modern depravity, Woolf celebrates the ways in which it allows for the unmaking and remaking of identity and community.

While *Mrs. Dalloway* does not share Conrad's negative association of cosmopolitanism with the destructive energies of global capital, Woolf's London seems, anomalously, ethnically and racially homogeneous, suggesting, at first glance, a national rather than cosmopolitan or international canvas. The immigration issues that provide the impetus for the plot of *The Secret Agent* are conveniently elided by Woolf's focus on a city made up almost exclusively of the limited perspectives of Clarissa's inner circle. Since virtually all of the characters, with the notable exception of Rezia, are British, part not only of the same class but of the same social set, their narratives delineate a relatively insular and parochial perspective on urban experience.

Woolf's cosmopolitanism, then, takes a form unlike that employed by Victorian novelists. Rather than representing difference with reference to the varied "types" in the city (a mode Conrad preserves through irony), Woolf focuses on difference as experienced in time. While the "outsider" status of her characters depends on cultural and relatively ineluctable factors such as class, gender, and ethnicity, these identities are depicted as being experienced in, and changing over, time, while other kinds of particularity and perceptions of otherness are equally important: Septimus' acute sense of alienation from those around him because of his combat experience, for instance, or Miss Kilman's sense of her exclusion not only because of her class and religious beliefs, but because of her inability to hate Germans.

Cosmopolitanism in *Mrs. Dalloway* also takes shape through Woolf's critique of the oppressive and exclusionary nature of national belonging, particularly that generated by urban spectacle. In the famous episode where a crowd is drawn together by the spectacle of a motor car containing a VIP, Woolf notes the nationalistic pull of the idea of "the dead, the flag, empire" (18) and the reflexive way in which the mass participates in what Conrad called the "quiet enjoyment of the national spectacle."[44] Though the spectacle of the car creates a pleasurable experience for many in the crowd who feel interpellated into a larger whole – "strangers looked at each other" (18) – others are excluded. Moll Pratt, a bystander, is denied participation because of her class and ethnicity: "[she] would have tossed the price of a pot of beer – a bunch of roses – into St. James's Street out of sheer light-heartedness and contempt of poverty had she not seen the constable's eye upon her, discouraging an old Irish-woman's loyalty" (19).

Similarly, the experience of shared national identity that the dignitary inspires is torture to the sensitive Septimus, whose madness is visionary in its indictment of modern disciplinary practices: in particular the normative and narrow-minded approach to mental health prescribed by Bradshaw. Like Stevie, who "shrieks piercingly into the crowd" at the sight of fallen horses, Septimus rejects the moment of cohesion offered by national spectacle: "this gradual drawing together of everything to one centre before his eyes, as if some horror had come almost to the surface and was about to burst into flames, terrified him. The world wavered and quivered and threatened to burst into flames. It is I who am blocking the way, he thought" (15). In this moment, Septimus' paranoia associates the "drawing together of everything" (which in Wordsworth's and Hyacinth's vision of London had revolutionary implications) with the violence and destruction of war: the threat of everything "burst[ing] into flames" which the passage underscores through obsessive repetition. Septimus stands outside the spectacle, observing the observers rather than abandoning himself to the pleasures of collective identification, thereby "blocking the way" to national cohesion. This scene's dramatic irony resides in the fact that Septimus, in his post-traumatic state, is once again a victim of the nationalism that he once celebrated: "he went to France to save an England which consisted almost entirely of Shakespeare's plays and Miss Isabel Pole in a green dress walking in the square" (86).

If, as Susan Stanford Friedman among others has argued, *Mrs. Dalloway* can be read as a successful attempt to show the ways in which public and private "are inseparably connected," Woolf's other challenge in the novel, in light of her critique of "tyranny," is to represent the utopian ideal of "one world, one life," while rejecting the "passive specta[cle]" that so often draws people together into a destructive sense of cohesion (like the passing motorcade that unites the crowd in the novel while alienating

Septimus and Moll Pratt).[45] If Conrad uses Stevie's drawings as an objective correlative for the anomie depicted in the rest of the novel, Woolf, too, uses an outsider's art to draw attention to the problem of representing community. Septimus' drawings of "the map of the world" recall (and perhaps refer to) Stevie's in their suggestion of radical chaos: "Diagrams, designs, little men and women brandishing sticks for arms, with wings – were they? – on their backs" (147).

Yet unlike Stevie's, Septimus' drawings suggest the possibility of connection even within fragmentation: "Circles traced around shillings and sixpences – the suns and stars; zigzagging precipices with mountaineers ascending roped together, exactly like knives and forks; sea pieces with little faces laughing out of what might perhaps be waves: the map of the world" (147). The circles are grouped together as a galaxy of "suns and stars," the mountaineers perform an impossible ascent, yet are "roped together" for safety, while the "little faces" laugh, held together by the wave currents which in this novel (and, more famously, in *The Waves*) signify cohesion as well as dissolution. Woolf acknowledges the oppressive potential of totalizing representations by dismantling the idea of the city as bounded space, but posits a new version of community through the notion of provisional and continually re-made web-like connections. While any whole in the novel is necessarily exclusionary (Clarissa's party, for instance, excludes Miss Kilman and Rezia, even though she imagines herself connected to Septimus), *Mrs. Dalloway*'s narrative innovations suggest that the form of an unbounded web, constantly in process, allows for new inclusions. The novel itself includes the characters that Clarissa's party excludes and connects them to individuals at the party at other points.

Instead of a panoramic view of the city, then, London is represented through the disjointed perspectives of the novel's characters. As in Septimus' drawings, however, continuity and discontinuity co-exist. The characters are drawn together, despite their radically different thought processes, by the overarching "weave" of the narrative and the repetition of key images and phrases. If images of connection in Conrad's novel stress disjuncture and displacement, those in *Mrs. Dalloway* are more positive. Even as some strands are severed, others are re-attached, as part of a continuous process of re-weaving. Lady Bruton, for example, is connected to her unofficial political aides, Richard Dalloway and Hugh Whitbread, by "a thin thread ... which would stretch and stretch, get thinner and thinner as they walked across London" (112); Richard, thinking of Clarissa, to whom he has never fully expressed his love, is linked to her by a thread as well: "as a single spider's thread after wavering here and there attaches itself to the point of a leaf, so Richard's mind, recovering from its lethargy, set now on his wife" (114). Individual threads also attach people to strangers and to the phenomenal world. Clarissa, feeling a momentary connection to an old woman in a window across the street, sees her move away after Big Ben strikes "as if she were attached to that sound, that string" (127). Septimus, plagued by his hallucinations, is helpless in the face of the demands made on him by external phenomena and painfully unable to determine the limits of his subjectivity: "they beckoned; leaves were alive; trees were alive. And the leaves being connected by millions of fibres with his own body, there on the seat, fanned it up and down; when the branch stretched he, too, made that statement" (22).

Septimus' madness and pain, both in this moment and when he is overwhelmed by the "drawing together" of the crowd watching the car, suggest that a sense of ongoing connection with the web of the world is untenable. One can only conceive of the whole in moments but then must let go in order to retain subjectivity and sanity, and leave oneself open to new attachments (such as Clarissa's feeling for the old woman at the window). Apart from Septimus, Clarissa is the character most associated with empathy and connection: "What she loved was this, here, now, in front of her; the fat lady in the cab" (9). She, too, sees herself spread out like a web, or a "mist," over the world:

Somehow in the streets of London, on the ebb and flow of things, here, there, she survived, Peter survived, lived in each other, she being part, she was positive, of the trees at home ... part of people she had never met; being laid out like a mist between the people she knew best, who lifted her on their branches as she had seen the trees lift the mist, but it spread ever so far, her life, herself. (8)

Clarissa's empathetic expansiveness is such that she feels connected, like Septimus in his hallucinatory states, to the human and nonhuman alike: "Odd affinities she had with people she had never spoken to, some woman in the street, some man behind a counter – even trees, even barns" (153).

But unlike Septimus, who cannot protect himself from an overwhelming sense of universal empathy, Clarissa can pull herself back together from the disembodiment that accompanies empathy to guard her inner privacy and individuality, hence protecting herself from the totalizing, totalitarian will of figures like Bradshaw. While the random connections that Clarissa feels for strangers imply a cosmopolitan embrace of the city, her sense of the essential "privacy of the soul" (126) is part of Woolf's attempt to achieve a representational tension between universality and particularity, public and private. For Clarissa, life's "supreme mystery" is the fundamentally solitary and impenetrable nature of consciousness even while connections between people are momentarily possible:

> That old lady ... whom she would see going from chest of drawers to dressing-table. She could still see her. And the supreme mystery which Kilman might say she had solved, or Peter might say he had solved, but Clarissa didn't believe either of them had the ghost of a chance of solving, was simply this: here was one room; there was another. Did religion solve that, or love? (127)

Clarissa invades the old woman's inner sanctum but remains irreducibly a stranger.

By celebrating Clarissa's talents at connecting people, the novel suggests that the ability to form community is necessary and ethical, but that the capacity to draw apart is both these things as well. Richard must snap the thread of his connection to Lady Bruton to embrace his far more meaningful love for Clarissa; Septimus is only able to express affection for Rezia when he manages to separate himself from the overwhelming call of the world around him; Clarissa must step away from her unifying role at the party to acknowledge Septimus' death.

Woolf's cosmopolitanism, then, forfeits the spatial imagining of the city as a figure for the world in exchange for a temporal flux between human connection and disconnection. Her use of free indirect discourse creates another level of fluctuation as well, in the narrator's close identification with the viewpoint of each character but residual difference from them. By following the characters' streams of consciousness we perceive their individuality and alienation, even while the continuous flow of the novel posits ongoing connections between character and character, and narrator and character. As Ann Banfield puts it, "Shifting from perspective to perspective, the novel's language constructs a public world which 'enables us to pass beyond the limits of our private experience.'"[46] If Clarissa's party brings together a certain community, the novel as a whole reminds us of those outside it: Septimus, Rezia, the old woman singing, the Germans with whom Miss Kilman sympathizes.

The use of free indirect discourse in portraying a character such as Rezia is particularly important to this dimension of the novel's cosmopolitanism. As the only non-British character, Rezia's perspective on Britain is truly that of the "outsider," and her interiority decisively breaks open the hermetic whole that the novel sometimes seems to create in its focus on English viewpoints. Septimus' insanity, meanwhile, makes his grip on both personal and collective identity all but non-existent; Moll Pratt, the "old Irishwoman," and another peripheral character, Maisie Johnson, both experience exclusion from the collective identity they perceive in formation around them. Maisie's sense of the strangeness of the city is induced by her observation of Rezia and Septimus in particular – "the young woman seeming foreign, the man looking queer" – but her perception of them is extended to the crowd of English people as well, whom she sees as radically different from herself: "and now all these people ... the old men and women, invalids most of them in Bath chairs – all seemed, after Edinburgh, so queer" (26). In perceiving Rezia and Septimus' alienation, Maisie discovers her own. Paradoxically, though, she is still connected by the "web" of the narrative to the "foreign" woman she observes (Rezia) who, like her, is struck more by the quotidian suffering of the old people in Bath chairs than by the national grandeur of Regent's Park.

Yet the experience of oneself as a stranger within the nation extends to the novel's English characters as well. As Susan Squier points out, Clarissa (unlike Peter, Hugh, or Richard) imagines herself as a ghost on the streets of London because of her gendered disempowerment in public; "this body, with all its capacities, seemed nothing – nothing at all. She had the oddest sense of being herself invisible; unseen; unknown" (11). Suddenly, Clarissa is reduced to "Mrs. Dalloway" and those around her to "the rest of them" (12). Even Peter, though, is subject to alienation because of his expatriate status: "the earth, after the voyage, still seemed an island to him, the strangeness of standing alone, alive, unknown, at half-past eleven in Trafalgar Square overcame him"(52). While free indirect discourse always underscores the degree to which characters are atomized, Woolf posits this problem specifically in relation to city-living and national belonging. In urban space, where everyone has the capacity to perceive themselves a "stranger" or a "secret agent," forms of belonging and sensations of unity are always provisional.

Time is important not only to Woolf's cosmopolitan experiments with identity but also because moments in the novel, rather than bounded space, produce an experience of unity. For the reader, characters are connected through the suggestion that their actions and thoughts occur simultaneously in time. The chimes of Big Ben or another city clock often generate the narrative connection between two characters even as they break the stream-of-consciousness of one to allow the narrative to shift to another. The national symbol of Big Ben, however, serves both to unify and dismantle any imaginable space, national or otherwise – unlike the chimes in Dickens' "Master Humphrey's Clock" it highlights the radical distance between characters even as it imposes a provisionally unifying form on them.[47]

The oft-cited aeroplane scene in *Mrs. Dalloway* is one of the most notable points at which characters' consciousnesses are drawn together in a briefly utopian moment: "As they looked the whole world became perfectly silent, and a flight of gulls crossed the sky, first one gull leading, then another, and in this extraordinary silence and peace, in this pallor, in this purity, bells struck eleven times" (20–21). Although the "whole world" has not literally become silent, it is possible to imagine a "whole world," Woolf suggests, in moments like this, whose inevitable transience is marked by the chiming of the bells. As Gillian Beer has argued, this particular moment of unification also demonstrates how the shared space of the nation, fleetingly brought into being by the passing motor-car, is dispersed by the effortless passing of the airplane across borders.[48]

While *Mrs. Dalloway* is less preoccupied than *The Secret Agent* with the mechanization of modern life, Woolf, like Conrad, locates a new kind of agency in the imaginative manipulation of time. Clarissa's talent, the novel suggests, is her ability to make the most of the transient moments of connection offered by the city by inhabiting each moment intensely: "Lolloping on the waves and braiding her tresses she seemed, having that gift still; to be; to exist; to sum it all up in the moment as she passed" (174). The recurrent image of her pausing on the threshold or on top of a staircase indicates her knack of drawing out time to experience "an exquisite suspense" (30). The perception and appreciation of the passing of time is crucial to the experience of moments of connection to which Clarissa, more than the other characters, is privy. Her celebration of urban existence is depicted as a heightened temporal experience: "in the triumph and the jingle and the strange high singing of some aeroplane overhead was what she loved; life; London; this moment of June" (4).

Clarissa links "life," "London," and "this moment of June" metonym-ically. Her existence in the city, and her ability to experience it fully, depend on a compressive movement towards an appreciation of "the moment." If Victorian representations often moved from the details of urban life out into the world at large, Woolf moves from the general to the particular instead, through temporal rather than spatial metaphors. Clarissa's ability to "love life" and elongate time carries ethical connota-tions because of its association with her empathic abilities. Bradshaw is unethical, we are to assume, because he is associated with the regimentation of time rather than a playful subjective experience of it. In Rezia's mind, his prescriptions for Septimus become synonymous with the demands of Harley Street clocks: "Shredding and slicing, dividing and subdividing, the clocks of Harley Street nibbled at the June day, counseled submission, upheld authority, and pointed out in chorus the supreme advantages of a sense of proportion, until the mound of time was ... diminished" (102). Clarissa, however, can "create ... every moment afresh" and this ability is available to others as well: "the veriest frumps, the most dejected of miseries sitting on doorsteps (drink their downfall) do the same; can't be dealt with, she felt positive, by Acts of Parliament for that very reason; they love life" (4).

As in *The Secret Agent*, then, the drawing out of time suggests a primal identification with human rather than national life. Just as the Inspector feels empathy for Stevie upon examining his body in *The Secret Agent*, Clarissa feels empathy for Septimus, whom she has never met. Like the Inspector, Clarissa spontaneously draws out the moment of Septimus' death, forming an imaginative connection that is corporeal as well as emotional: "Up had flashed the ground; through him, blundering, bruising, went the rusty spikes. There he lay with a thud, thud, thud in his brain, and then a suffocation of blackness" (184). Her contemplation of his death leads to a graver response to her own death – "They (all day she had been thinking of Bourton, of Peter, of Sally), they would grow old" (184) – and a renewed appreciation of her remaining life.

Septimus' death, for Clarissa, is the ultimate form of communication because it posits an end to the contingency that inevitably separates people: "Death was defiance. Death was an attempt to communicate; people feeling the impossibility of reaching the centre which, mystically, evaded them; closeness drew apart; rapture faded, one was alone. There was an embrace in death" (184). By erecting a paradox in which complete identification with the other can only occur in death, Woolf circumvents the pitfalls of humanist notions of connection by refusing to provide a facile solution to the problems of difference that Clarissa identifies with such finality: "here was one room; there another."

Like Conrad's novel, *Mrs. Dalloway* also suggests that an elongated sense of historical time may draw the connection between individual death and the possible threat of species-death. This connection provides a basis for the kind of global unity that "the dead bodies, the ruined houses proves" in *Three Guineas*. Woolf refers repeatedly in *Mrs. Dalloway* to a world, either primeval or post-apocalyptic, from which humanity has been removed.[49] Rezia, in her isolation, imagines a ghostly London in which "perhaps at midnight, when all boundaries are lost, the country reverts to its ancient shape" (24). The old woman singing incoherent words is described as singing "through all ages ... when the pavement was grass, when it was swamp" (81). Septimus sees a future world in which "dogs will become men? It was the heat wave presumably, operating upon a brain made sensitive by eons of evolution. Scientifically speaking, the flesh was melted off the world" (68). Through these visions of a nonhuman world, Woolf evokes the necessity and basis for global community. The airplane, Beer proposes, performs the same function; "the dallying light aircraft represented the reassuring triviality of peace after the war, which is still melting and freezing the consciousness of Septimus Smith. Here the aircraft ... also presages the future: a future that may not exist" (284).

Woolf's essay "Flying over London" (1950) makes more urgent and explicit both the premonitions of species-death in *Mrs. Dalloway* and the utopian potential of the airplane. The view from the airplane in the imaginary flight described in her essay is one in which geographical borders and the divisive markings of capitalism disappear simultaneously:

One could see through the Bank of England; all the business houses were transparent; the River Thames was as the Romans saw it, as paleolithic man saw it, at dawn from a hill shaggy with wood, with the rhinoceros digging his horn into the roots of rhododendrons. So immortally fresh and virginal London looked and England was earth merely, merely the world. (132)

Traveling back in time from the era of banks and business houses to the world of the Romans, then to that of paleolithic man, and finally to the nonhuman world of the prehistoric rhinoceros, Woolf creates a perspective that allows her to see England as "merely the world." Here the panoramic overview unifies both space and time yet humbles rather than aggrandizes the observing human subject. "Merely" undermines the arrogance and artificiality of national identity, but its repetition, and the transformation of "earth" to "world" in the sentence's chiasmatic structure, also has ironic connotations. The temporal overview reveals that merely *everything* is at stake: "It was the idea of death that now suggested itself ... not immortality but extinction."[50]

In this passage, cosmopolitanism takes shape around humanity imagined finitely in time. As with Septimus, though, full identification with the idea of "the human" relies on the limit-case of death – a vision of unity that must, the novel suggests, be assembled and disassembled in the lived experience of contingency. In Clarissa's contemplation of Septimus' death, however, this paradoxical experience of "cosmopolitan time" is liberating. The temporal movement from universal empathy to the particularity of selfhood is an affirmation of the self and its inevitable relation to others: "She felt somehow very like him – the young man who had killed himself. She felt glad he had done it; thrown it away ... He made her feel the beauty, made her feel the fun" (186). Clarissa's strange exhilaration at the suicide is not a distanced callousness, as some have argued, but a temporary yet complete identification with Septimus that is liberating in the freedom it allows her – to choose differently from him – and in the meaning that it bestows on Septimus himself, who would otherwise remain a stranger ("the young man who had killed himself" [186]) to the distracted urbanites at the party.

That *Mrs. Dalloway* manages to recover a utopianism all but obliterated in Conrad's novel is attributable in part to Woolf's feminism, which motivates her critique of separate-sphere ideology and hence her representation of communities that permeate boundaries and defy them. Perhaps even more important is her concrete sense of the possible freedoms mobilized by a globalizing society. The image of Elizabeth boarding the bus to explore London while fantasizing about her future associates urban living with the will to transform self and society:

She would become a doctor, a farmer, possibly go into Parliament, if she found it necessary, all because of the Strand ... It was the sort of thing that did sometimes happen, when one was alone – buildings without architect's names, crowds of people coming back from the city having more power than single clergymen in Kensington, than any of the books Miss Kilman had lent her, to stimulate what lay slumbrous, clumsy and shy on the mind's sandy floor to break surface ... an impulse, a revelation, which has its effects for ever. (136–7)

Unaffected by the forces of "conversion" (here symbolized by the clergymen and Miss Kilman's books) so relentlessly satirized by Woolf throughout the novel, Elizabeth is instead "for ever" changed and empowered by the city's energy – even the capitalist energies of the Strand and of people coming back from "the city," London's financial center.

The potential rewards for feminism still latent in the Janus-faced formations of modernity also explain why Haraway can welcome a posthuman future as liberating, while Conrad finds it horrifying. Both Woolf and Haraway embrace the flux that accompanies global identities because of its prospective benefits to women and other "outsiders" never fully included in the conceptions of national belonging whose disintegration Conrad contemplates with dismay. Haraway, by now more often associated with the utopian potential of the cyborg future, is well aware that post-humanism does not guarantee progress: "From one perspective, a cyborg world is about the final imposition of a grid of control on the planet, about the final abstraction embodied in a Star War apocalypse waged in the name of defense, about the final appropriation of women's bodies in a masculinist orgy of war." Yet the political struggle, she argues, is to "see from both perspectives at once because each reveals both dominations and possibilities unimaginable from the other vantage point."[51] The cosmopolitan practice of seeing "from both perspectives at once," indeed from multiple perspectives, is exemplified by Woolf's narrative experiments.

While Woolf is markedly more optimistic than Conrad about the utopian potential of urban experience, their projects have more in common than the imaginative space of London. Both novelists rely upon a critical tension between difference and identity in constructing their global cities, wherein the assertion of a common humanity is regularly called into question by a somber sense of intractable national conflict and individual alienation. A sense of alienation in *The Secret Agent* and *Mrs. Dalloway* erupts most frequently in fragmented urban spaces where characters trace out private and desolate paths through the cityscape. Characters identify and connect with strangers, however, in extended moments of time in which they contemplate the duration and value of an individual life, and in accelerated mental journeys to a future in which humans have vanished, or ceased to be recognizably human. This sublime apprehension of the time of individual and species life, the novels presciently advise us, is an imperative response to the possibility of their potential annihilation in a newly incendiary world. What we have in common is simply – and only – what we have to lose.

Conclusion
"A city visible but unseen": Cosmopolitan realism and the invisible metropolis

> It seemed to me that . . . [the London Indian community] really was unseen. It was there and nobody knew it was there. And I was very struck by how often, when one would talk to white English people about what was going on, you could actually take them to these streets and point to these phenomena, and they would somehow still reject this information.
>
> Salman Rushdie, "Interview" (1996)[1]

In contemporary London, on the bank of the Thames, tourists line up to ride on a giant observation wheel that offers a panoramic view of the city (Figure 6.1). The London Eye was built in 1999 to commemorate the millennium, capitalize on Britain's recent success in the global economy, and cement the country's image as "Cool Britannia" (a 1990s media catchphrase that succinctly evoked the country's imperial past and Britain's newly successful exports in the "cool" worlds of fashion, film, and music). With its sleek, futuristic design, the London Eye embodied the promise of the new century but also looked back to the glory of the Victorian era, deliberately referencing visual spectacles such as the Crystal Palace and the Colosseum panorama that imagined the city as the center of the world. Like the rhetoric that surrounded the Great Exhibition, the Eye's advertising slogan – "the way the world sees London" – marked the capital's prominence and visibility in a globally conceived landscape.

As Figure 6.2 illustrates, the view from the top of the Eye, like the view from the top of St. Paul's so important to Victorian conceptions of the city, emphasizes both the city's buildings and the semblance of organic form lent by the curve of the river. The experience of the Eye does not immediately resemble that of panoramic paintings, of course, as the circle the viewer traverses is vertical (as they are lifted around by the wheel), rather than horizontal (the 360-degree canvas of nineteenth-century panoramas). But because the visitor makes the journey in a glass, eye-shaped pod that they share with other passengers, the ferris-wheel offers a

Figure 6.1 The London Eye

contained experience of the crowd just as panoramic paintings did, and bestows form on the experience in similar fashion – though here it is the glass circularity of the pod, rather than that of the panoramic canvas, that provides a bounded horizon.

Booklets sold in the tourist-booths surrounding the Eye also reference the nineteenth-century spectacles, for they provide detailed information

Figure 6.2 Panorama of London from the top of the Eye

about the sights visible from the wheel, much as the "Descriptions" that accompanied panoramas identified objects in the painted landscape did. In the case of the Eye, the booklets give the viewer an instant touristic overview of "official" London by highlighting commercial, administrative, and historical landmarks visible at various points in the ride (such as Battersea Power Station, MI6 Headquarters, the Ministry of Defence, Downing Street, Buckingham Palace, the Houses of Parliament, and Tower Bridge, among others).

While the example of the London Eye shows how some aspects of contemporary visual culture hark back to London's imperial heyday, the postcolonial context of late twentieth- and early twenty-first-century London has inspired a wealth of narratives that run counter to nostalgic versions of the city, while still evoking its global significance. In his study of the transnational metropolis in postcolonial fiction, John Clement Ball points out that "any hyperindustrious reader who undertook to survey all English-language fiction would find London to be the single most frequently used geographical signifier and setting." Ball attributes London's popularity as a setting in postcolonial writing to its historic function as a symbol of the world and its ongoing status as an immigrant city: the destination, in particular, of many settlers from former British colonies.

Due in part to its centrality in the cosmopolitan realist writings of the Victorian period, London functions in many postcolonial texts "as both a site and an object of resistance."[2]

The title of this chapter – "a city visible but unseen" – is borrowed from one of the most influential of these resistant narratives, Salman Rushdie's *The Satanic Verses* (1988), which uses the phrase to draw attention to London's non-white communities and position the capital within a transnational historical frame. Rushdie is now part of a growing body of contemporary writers and film-makers who seek to supplement or supplant earlier urban narratives by bringing new visibility to the city's minority populations and to its unofficial spaces.

If the first half of the nineteenth century witnessed the stupendous rise in London's population that fueled the Victorian literary imagination, the period of decolonization, from the 1940s on, gave rise to equally dramatic changes in the urban landscape that called for its reimagining:

In the half-century from 1947 (India) to 1997 (Hong Kong), as England gradually withdrew its imperial tentacles, hundreds of thousands of former subjects went along for the ride ... With over two million non-white residents in the year 2000 ... London has been transformed; demographically it is becoming more and more global (or transnational) and less and less traditionally – that is ethnically, racially, or even nationally, – English or British.[3]

In the wake of these historic changes, writers continue to use London as a way to examine multi-cultural community and global citizenship but do so from perspectives that challenge the imperial outlook of Victorian city writing.

Thus while Rushdie makes a point of showing the South Asian community's formative influence on London in *The Satanic Verses*, his incendiary critique of Islam in the novel and his conception of character and history rely centrally on his depiction of the city as a radical challenge to stable notions of the self or nation.[4] Zadie Smith's debut novel *White Teeth* (2000) famously takes its cue from Rushie in its postmodern critique of identity and playful riffs on magical realism. Instead of focusing in on one ethnic community, however, Smith stresses the city's eclectic international population, tracing the connections among white British, South Asian, Jamaican, and Jewish city-dwellers of different class backgrounds across two generations of geographic displacement and historical upheaval.

Gautam Malkani's more recent novel *Londonstani* (2006) takes the postcolonial urban novel's destabilizing of identity one step further still.

Written entirely in a South Asian-English urban vernacular, it follows the misadventures of a group of South Asian youths who are equally at home in, and able to manipulate, the rough streets of the city and the complex networks of global commerce, culture, and crime. The dramatic twist at the end of the novel is that the protagonist (Jas) is not, in fact, South Asian and lower middle class, as his narration leads us to believe, but white and bourgeois ("Jas" turns out to be short for Jasper rather than Jasbinder). The "Paki" identity he assumes throughout the course of the story, however, is shown to be central both to Jas' understanding of urban authenticity and to ours. The point of Malkani's elaborate ruse is clear: urban narrative is no longer the unquestioned prerogative of the white bourgeois writer and claims to representational authority must therefore be staked in terms that openly grapple with the city's internal differences.

In Chapter 5, I argued that modernist writers shun Victorian methods of representing totality because of their distrust of nineteenth-century religious and scientific norms. For contemporary writers with a stake in the city's cosmopolitan population, however, certain realist techniques, such as the use of the vernacular, a focus on quotidian lives, and the cumulative effect of representative detail, assume a certain political urgency. Serving a vital documentary function, postcolonial urban novels provide a record of the city's rapidly changing composition and help to situate the temporally and spatially far-reaching histories of its increasingly diverse communities within localized and individuated portraits. This is one of the reasons, no doubt, that so many reviewers have compared Rushdie and Smith to Dickens.

The form that might best be seen as inheriting the legacy of cosmopolitan realism, however, is contemporary urban film, for it is in this medium that the importance of the visible remains as trenchant as it was in the Victorian period. Patrick Keiller's *London* (1994) and Stephen Frears' *Dirty Pretty Things* (2002) are evidently indebted to cosmopolitan realism but also seek to revise and re-use Victorian representations of the city. While Keiller's film is self-consciously artistic and Frears' caters to a mainstream movie-going audience, both directors create a visual record of London that challenges dominant ways of recording and celebrating urban space – Keiller, by using a highly individual and unfamiliar version of the city as a backdrop for a rant about urban corporatization in the post-Thatcher era, and Frears by focusing on the invisible city of undocumented immigrant workers.

SKETCH AND PANORAMA IN PATRICK KEILLER'S "LONDON"

Keiller's dreamy quasi-documentary trains its camera both on official sites, like Buckingham Palace, and on unrecognizable urban trivialities, such as street-corners, ditches, and walls. Using an effect that recalls nineteenth-century travelogue narratives, magic lantern shows, and early cinema, Keiller's experimental film is made up of a series of still shots. People move through the space shown on the camera, leaves rustle, but the camera itself holds our gaze on one spot while the narrator tells us of the musings and complaints of his erstwhile lover, Robinson, and of a journey the two take through the city. We do not exactly travel with them, however; sometimes the shots we see connect to the narrative and sometimes they don't. The effect is supremely disorienting; what are we to make of the often dreary and uninteresting sights we are shown? Are they the narrator's memories? Robinson's? Are they meant to recall the sensations the narrator ascribes to Robinson – his feelings of alienation and nostalgia in a city that seems to him to have been thoroughly appropriated by a malign government and global corporations?

Though it leaves these questions unanswered, the film asks us to see each of the sights it shows us as unorthodox postcards of the city, meant to represent parts of urban experience not often depicted visually but nonetheless impossible to avoid: the banal (a giant inflatable Ronald McDonald rolls around on a drive-in roof), the squalid (a recurring shot of a dirty patch of river), and the fleetingly picturesque (flowers growing on a brick wall). These images are at once highly individual, attached to the disaffected thoughts of Robinson, and impossibly, and meaninglessly, general, for the correspondence between what we see and what we hear on the soundtrack (either the narrator's account of Robinson or mournful music) is often so vague that we might have found these snapshots in an antique store, devoid of referent (the manner in which W. G. Sebald reportedly found the equally cryptic photos that appear in his own quasi-travelogue, *Rings of Saturn* [1999]).

The film thus makes new use of the sketch and panoramic modes. On the one hand, Keiller's work is made up of a series of aural–visual sketches; strange images accompanied by impressionistic, individualized micro-narratives. Robinson and the narrator are *flâneurs*, wistfully referencing nineteenth-century versions of themselves: Rimbaud, Verlaine, Baudelaire, Poe's "man of the crowd," and other "exiles" who wandered cities. But the sketches have none of the authority or empirical value of Victorian ones. Instead, they remain mysterious; the narrator even references Sherlock Holmes and the neighborhoods he was meant to have traveled through and then states "Everywhere we went there was an atmosphere of conspiracy and intrigue." This evocative phrase is left hanging, however, stranded against the backdrop of a dark, whirling eddy in the Thames. The main intrigues here, the film's narrative suggests, are the profoundly uninspired ones of corporate finance. The Victorian urban references the film playfully throws out, then, are instantly ironized, rendered devoid of the scientific and moral frameworks that once made them meaningful.

London makes allusion to the panoramic tradition as well, through some of the shots it uses (such as views of the Thames and its bridges); its travelogue style and reference to a wide range of London neighborhoods and suburbs; and its account of recent historical events, such as IRA bombings and a general election: all of which suggest that the series of shots it displays will add up to some kind of overview of contemporary London. As with the film's sketches, however, its panoramic narrative remains inconclusive by the film's end, not least because the shots we see are both visually discontinuous, with the film shifting abruptly from one to the next, and unconnected metonymically as well. There is no larger urban whole to which the film refers: only a series of loosely connected memories, associations, and cryptic declarations, such as the film's opening one: "It is a journey to the end of the world."

The film's references to Victorian urban realism seem, for the most part, to ironize its surety and utopianism. The narrator and Robinson follow in Guest's footsteps in *News from Nowhere* by heading upstream to Hammersmith, but Morris' idyllic country escape inspires only a bitter exclamation, "London is all waste ... a stage set for the spectacle of nineteenth-century reaction, endlessly re-enacted for television." Even the city's international character is little cause for celebration, for Robinson associates it primarily with symbols of global commerce and finance, such as products in the supermarket and buildings that have been taken over by foreign companies.

Yet despite its satire of urban realism, the film does not completely abandon the utopian tenor of the tradition. Notwithstanding his dark view of the city, Robinson insists on seeing aspects of it, such as a Roman milestone, in terms of myth and magic. The narrator reports that "Robinson believed that if he looked at it hard enough the city would reveal to him the molecular basis of historical events ... and in this way he hoped to see into the future." While this statement is largely nonsensical in light of Robinson's inability to predict the Conservative election victory that so disheartens him halfway through the narrative, and thus seems to partake in the film's satire of Victorian urban rhetoric, it also serves as part of the film's oblique promise that the visual modes of urban realism might open up on to something impalpably consequential. For Robinson's nostalgia, the film's music, and the often haunting beauty of Keiller's cinematography, even when trained on the most quotidian urban scene, make the film deeply pleasurable in spite of its aura of depression. Part of this effect stems from the fact that Robinson, even as he epitomizes urban alienation, is never alone. Instead, he is always in conversation with the narrator and other urban dwellers who temporarily inspire him – Peruvian musicians who briefly accompany the narrator and Robinson on their journey, Caribbean immigrants celebrating carnival, a "man of the crowd" who rails at him the way Robinson himself rails at the narrator, and a man reading Walter Benjamin in a shopping center. Though these figures offer Robinson only temporary solace, he seems enchanted with them and, indeed, with his own deep ambivalence for the city.

Keiller's London is no doubt a purgatory – a "city full of interesting people like Robinson who would prefer to be elsewhere" – but his film insists on the value of the city as a record of what the narrator evocatively calls "psychic landscaping," even if that landscape chiefly records the ongoing assault of poorly conceived urban development and global trade on the city's quirky charms. While Robinson claims to hate the nineteenth century for starting London on the downward trajectory that he helps to chronicle, he cannily comments on the sketch, the panorama, and the utopian framework of the urban realist tradition in order to record complaints about the city not as dissimilar to those of Victorian writers as he might think.

THE HOTEL AS COSMOPOLIS IN "DIRTY PRETTY THINGS"

The title of *Dirty Pretty Things* promises that the film will portray a landscape rife with filth and materiality and its visuals uphold this pact: a large part of the film takes place at night, in seamy, confining locations, shot to claustrophobic effect. The camera leads the audience through unidentifiable back alleys, immigrant markets, tiny apartments, sweat-shops, taxicab offices, and hospital morgues, reflecting its director's determination to "find bits of London that hadn't been in every other film."[5] Part of Frears' investment in the project of urban realism stems from his interest in representing an aspect of the city largely unfamiliar to the middle-class eye.

Whereas Victorian urban investigators and novelists drew attention to the British working class and the crowded and unhealthy circumstances of their life and work, Frears focuses on London's immigrant underclass. Following in the footsteps of postcolonial texts like Rushdie's and Smith's, and building upon his own earlier films about London, *My Beautiful Laundrette* (1985) and *Sammy and Rosie Get Laid* (1987), Frears puts non-white characters at the center of his text. A heterogeneous assemblage of working-class characters, including ones from the Middle East, Nigeria, Somalia, Turkey, South Asia, Spain, Eastern Europe, and China, take center stage and are shown to be a vital though unacknowledged part of the city's operations.

Dirty Pretty Things chronicles a black-market trade in organs that exploits the legal and financial vulnerability of this growing class. The Baltic Hotel is a key node in the network of the grisly trade; its manager Juan arranges for "donors" to surrender their organs in illegal, risky operations, offering them forged passports and immigration papers in exchange. The film's hero, Okwe, a Nigerian refugee, was once a doctor but now moonlights in the hotel after his day job as a taxi driver. He becomes aware of the organ trade after finding a human heart, the result of a botched operation, in one of its toilets. The discovery prompts moral outrage on Okwe's part and sets up the film's central questions: can Okwe translate this response into action, given the fact of his non-existence in the eyes of the authorities? Can he save himself and his friends from being literally and existentially dismantled by the depravities of global capitalism and the exclusions of the nation-state?

In the end, Okwe cannot challenge the organ trade, or the other global economic systems in which he is enmeshed, but is able to manipulate them to his advantage with the help of an ad hoc community of the disenfranchised: Juliet, a savvy prostitute; Guo Yi, a hospital worker who gives Okwe medical supplies; and Ivan, the hotel's cynical doorman. Okwe is initially able to brush off Juan's attempts to corrupt him by offering him a stake in the organ business in exchange for his services as a surgeon, but Senay, Okwe's Turkish Muslim roommate who works as a chambermaid, is particularly vulnerable to exploitation because of her gender. Though she has left Turkey to live the life of an independent modern woman, Senay attempts to hold on to parts of her Muslim identity as well, shunning pork and priding herself on her virginity. Like Okwe's moral integrity, though, Senay's "honor" is constantly under attack. After the immigration authorities learn of her illegal labor at the hotel, she is forced to work in a sweatshop, where her boss extorts oral sex from her by threatening to report her to the state.

Desperate to escape, Senay makes a deal with Juan to trade both her virginity and her kidney for a passport and ticket to New York, where she will be able to live with her sister. Okwe, however, is determined to save her from this objectifying bargain. Taking advantage of Juan's weakness for alcohol, Okwe manages to turn the tables on him at the last minute by taking *his* kidney when he has passed out, and exchanging it for Senay's papers – his intervention comes too late, though, to save her from being forced to have sex with Juan. Yet the film ends on a subtly hopeful note. Senay motivates herself to escape to New York by visualizing it as an enchanted land of cabhorses and snow (even though she admits to knowing better), while Okwe decides to risk persecution in Nigeria and return home to the daughter he left there. Though their romance has been forever deferred and their values compromised (Okwe becomes a link in the chain of the organ trade that so horrified him and Senay loses her prized virginity), the two immigrants have managed to carve out their own trajectories in a global landscape where individual narratives and interpersonal transactions seem exclusively determined by material forces.

Dirty Pretty Things most resembles the tradition of cosmopolitan realism in its use of the city as a symbol of the world, and its simultaneously dystopian and utopian view of this urban–global nexus. In Victorian narratives, the capital city is depicted as cosmopolitan but is still nestled within a recognizably English landscape that reminds us of its British identity.[6] As I have argued, some novels (*Bleak House* and *News from Nowhere*, for example) work to rearticulate and retrench this identity over and against the international landscape they delineate. Even *The Secret Agent*, which anticipates Frears' film in depicting a London more foreign than British, still evokes an abiding Britishness in the form of the tranquil English countryside to which Michaelis can retreat from anarchist activity. But in *Dirty Pretty Things*, the only signifiers of Britishness are the (South Asian) immigration officials who ineffectually attempt to police the country's borders and, in doing so, emphasize the irrelevance of the nation to the immigrants and refugees they pursue, who are buffeted about the film's global landscape by forces beyond their control.

Writing of the global city, Saskia Sassen argues that it is characterized by extremes of power and of poverty:

There is an interesting correspondence between great concentrations of corporate power and large concentrations of *others*. Large cities in both the global South and global North are the terrain where a multiplicity of globalization processes assume concrete, localized forms. A focus on cities allows us to capture ... not only the upper but also the lower circuits of globalization. These localized forms are, in good part, what globalization is about, pointing to the possibility of a new politics of traditionally disadvantaged and excluded actors operating in this new transnational economic geography.[7]

Frears' film, as we have seen, is centrally interested in the relationship between both the upper and lower circuits of globalization identified by Sassen. It focuses on the city's "others" to show the different ways in which they are impacted by its concentrations of corporate power. It gives us glimpses of London's international elite culture – the luxury hotel, the business people who use the taxis Okwe drives – but dwells upon what Sassen describes as the "concrete, localized forms" of invisible global processes and points to their unacceptable costs, such as the heart in the toilet and the sexual abuse of Senay.

The main characters' lack of agency and their vulnerability to the forces of globalization are emphasized by their inability to control boundaries themselves, particularly those between private and public. Just as their bodies are under threat of unwanted penetration (sexual or surgical), their local spaces are not their own. Guo Yi sleeps in the morgue where he works, while Okwe sleeps in Senay's living room. When he uses the tap in the kitchen, he disrupts her bath; "Everything here is connected to everything else," she tells him, driving home the film's theme.[8] Recalling works like *Bleak House* and *A Study in Scarlet*, the film stresses the interconnectedness of the very different people and parts of the city that it depicts, but it also shows these connections to be arbitrary and fleeting.

The Baltic Hotel is another architectural space in which the plumbing (where the heart gets stuck) serves an allegorical function. Crucial to the film's ability to make connections between local and global scales, the hotel serves as an even more condensed image of the world than London itself. Of the postcolonial London novel, Ball argues that "there is a recurring impulse to create microscopic images of a smaller, more manageable city, which take many metaphorically suggestive forms: a house, a club, a family, a community, a neighborhood, a shop, a body of water, a ride on the tube."[9] In *Dirty Pretty Things*, the hotel is a metonymy of the global city, demonstrating the proximity between the international business elite and the immigrant workers who tend to them, as well as the paradoxes generated by the disparities between them. The workers are meant to be "invisible," contributing to the hotel's veneer of luxury by deflecting attention from their own subjectivity or labor, yet they are constantly under surveillance by security cameras.

A space of transience and transaction, the hotel is a fitting, if dystopian, symbol of the global city. At one point, Juan makes a jaded comment that explains the movie's title: "The hotel business is a business of strangers. Strangers always surprise you. They come to the hotel at night to do dirty things; it's our job in the morning to make it all look pretty again." As the movie's plot repeatedly emphasizes, people's identities, within the logic of the hotel and the world it stands in for, are subordinate to their bargaining power. Once he makes his abusive deal with Senay, for instance, Juan tells that she can choose for her passport to make her either "Spanish, Greek or Italian." The film asks us to read the hotel as a desperately unhealthy global body politic. Within the logic of this metaphor, the immigrants both supply organs and serve as the hotel's, and society's, unseen and, in this case, abused vital functions. Correspondingly, the dramatic discovery of the heart jamming the toilet literalizes the idea of bodily dysfunction.

Alongside its allegory of the diseased body, though, *Dirty Pretty Things* also offers a tentatively optimistic vision of human community. Okwe and his friends, through mutual assistance, solidarity, sympathetic identi-fication and affection, defy the mechanistic and predatory world of capitalist exchange. Ties of kinship ultimately propel Senay to her sister in New York and Okwe back to his daughter in Nigeria; romantic love underlies Okwe's good deeds on behalf of Senay; solidarity motivates his decisions to help both fellow cabdrivers with venereal disease, and the Somalian victim of a botched operation; while friendship and respect prompt Juliet, Ivan, and Guo Yi to help Okwe outwit Juan. These affective bonds, the film suggests, might – by allowing for moments of subversion, agency, and escape – overcome the financial and information networks that threaten to wholly circumscribe the lives of immigrants. Without suggesting what form it might take, the film gestures towards Sassen's idea that the global city provides "the possibility of a new politics of traditionally disadvantaged and excluded actors operating in [a] new transnational economic geography."

Yet even as it attempts to do justice to forms of alienation peculiar to a twenty-first-century landscape, the film's alternative vision still relies in telling ways on the narrative techniques and troubled humanism of Victorian cosmopolitan realism. Frears uses his immigrant protago-nists – the virginal Senay and the idealistic Okwe – to embody nineteenth-century values of moral and bodily integrity that the film's largely bourgeois and Western audience would find hard to associate with Western characters. With his instinctual kindness to strangers in the city, and his disgust at the commodification of human bodies, Okwe is an old-fashioned humanist. While the audience is often aligned with his view-point in the film (sometimes literally), his righteous indignation in the face of human suffering is rendered realistic only by virtue of his cultural difference from them – his relative unfamiliarity with the thoroughgoing materialism of Western culture. That the film itself does not believe in Okwe's humanism is evidenced by its focus on his gradual disillusion-ment, but it does have a stake in demonstrating how Victorian values we tend to dismiss or be suspicious of (virginity, anti-materialism) can become newly subversive in a globalized context. One could argue, vis-à-vis the film's use of Victorian values, that instead of reorienting them, it recapitulates them. Even as it forces its audience to witness the often invisible labor and lifestyles of urban immigrants, *Dirty Pretty Things* relies for its pathos on a romanticized sense of its protagonists' innocence that is implicitly condescending.

Nevertheless, if there is an essential difference between the middle-class viewpoint of the cosmopolitan realist text and that exemplified by the film's contemporary one, it resides not so much in the scopic authority of Frears' bourgeois audience but in its relative irrelevance. In *Bleak House*, middle-class agency is encroached upon by large bureaucracies such as the civil courts and criminal justice system. But because he closes in on key middle-class protagonists, Dickens can argue that bourgeois moral action in the private sphere might gradually radiate outwards to affect the nation as a whole. In *Dirty Pretty Things*, by contrast, all spheres – the home, the nation, the globe – overlap so completely that bourgeois agency is not only non-existent in the film but also unimaginable in the larger world to which it refers. Instead, the forces that propel the action are far more insidious and unfathomable than the Chancery Court in *Bleak House*, while the moral and social values that Okwe seeks to embody are shown to be largely illusory: so much so that he decides to risk imprisonment in Nigeria rather than continue his futile pursuit of safety and refuge in London.

For its middle-class audience, the only scope for action that Frears' vision provides is the narrative legacy of Victorian cosmopolitan realism itself. The film implies that we need these conventions not only so that we might recognize the deprivations and proximities of the world we live in, but also so that we might imagine reacting to them with an Okwe-like humanist indignation even if this means that, like Senay imagining New York, we are all too aware of the fictions this entails.

In the conclusion to his anthology *British Cultural Studies*, Kevin Robins points to the pervasive influence of cultural nationalism in current political debates about the challenges to British integrity posed by globalization and the European Union. Contesting these versions of nationalism, Robins proposes using London as a "cognitive model" for an alternative vision of community (much as Derrida uses a generic version of the city as a model for a state of asylum in "On Cosmopolitanism"): "London might allow us to think differently and more productively about issues and problems of multiculturalism ... the metropolitan city, Babylon–London, clearly poses the question of coexistence most profoundly and intensely. And, in the urban and metropolitan context ... it is a question that must necessarily be more grounded and more complex than the national imagination can accommodate."[10]

This short concluding chapter cannot, of course, do justice to the manifold connections between cosmopolitan realism and contemporary literary and filmic visions of the city. I end with Robins' evocation of London, however, to demonstrate how *Urban Realism and the Cosmopolitan Imagination* points forward not just to fictive and filmic images of the city but also to scholarly urban utopias such as those of Robins and Derrida. One of the aspects of intellectual culture that I hope to have illuminated is that ideas such as these owe much of their rhetorical force – and our ability to see this force with such clarity in the current moment – to the long literary history of London-as-cosmopolis that this book traces.

Notes

PREFACE

1 Charles Manby Smith, *The Little World of London: or, Pictures in Little of London Life* (London: Arthur Hall, Virtue, & Co., 1857), vi.

2 Henry Mayhew and John Binny, *The Criminal Prisons of London and Scenes of Prison Life* (London: Cass, 1968), 4. Subsequent references appear parenthetically. Though planned as a comprehensive study of London's peoples and institutions, Mayhew's "The Great World of London" eventually took shape as a part of this detailed study of the prison system.

3 On the conflation of race and class in Mayhew's writing, see "Mayhew's Cockney Polynesia" in Christopher Herbert, *Culture and Anomie* (University of Chicago Press, 1991).

4 See Anne Humpherys, *Henry Mayhew* (Boston: Twayne Publishers, 1984), 143–4.

5 Cited in Eric de Mare, *Victorian London Revealed: Gustave Doré's Metropolis* (London: Penguin, 2001), x.

6 Henry James, "London" in *The Portable Henry James*, ed. Morton Dauwen Zabel (New York: Penguin, 1977), 513–32 (520–1).

7 Raymond Williams, *The Country and the City* (New York: Oxford Univeristy Press, 1973).

8 Edward W. Said, *Culture and Imperialism* (New York: Knopf, 1993).

9 Ian Baucom, *Out of Place: Englishness, Empire, and the Locations of Identity* (Princeton University Press, 1999), 55.

10 *Ibid.*, 61.

11 See Vincent Pecora, *Secularization and Cultural Criticism: Religion, Nation, and Modernity* (Chicago University Press, 2006).

12 Immanuel Kant, "To Perpetual Peace: A Philosophical Sketch" in *Perpetual Peace and Other Essays on Politics, History, and Morals*, trans. Ted Humphrey (Indianapolis, IN: Hackett, 1983), 107–43.

13 Karl Marx and Friedrich Engels, *The Communist Manifesto* [1888], ed. Frederic L. Bender (New York: Norton, 1988).

14 See Pascale Casanova, *The World Republic of Letters* (Cambridge, MA: Harvard University Press, 2004), and Priya Joshi, *In Another Country: Colonialism, Culture, and the English Novel in India* (New York: Columbia University Press, 2002).

15 *Yahoo News,* Ben Silverman, "Playstation 2 component incites African war." July 22, 2008.

INTRODUCTION: COSMOPOLITAN REALISM

1 In Steven Vertovec and Robin Cohen, eds., *Conceiving Cosmopolitanism: Theory, Context and Practice* (Oxford and New York: Oxford University Press, 2002) 42.

2 In Amanda Claybaugh, *The Novel of Purpose: Literature and Social Reform in the Anglo-American World* (Ithaca, NY: Cornell University Press, 2006); Christopher Gogwilt, *The Fiction of Geopolitics: Afterimages of Culture, from Wilkie Collins to Alfred Hitchcock* (Stanford University Press, 2000); and Paul Young, *Globalization and the Great Exhibition* (Houndsmill, Basingstoke: Palgrave Macmillan, 2009).

3 Lauren M. E. Goodlad and Julia M. Wright, "Introduction and Keywords." Special Issue on "Victorian Internationalisms." *Romanticism and Victorianism on the Net* 48 (2007), para. 15. For other uses of *internationalism,* see Margaret Cohen and Carolyn Dever, eds., *The Literary Channel: the International Invention of the Novel* (Princeton University Press, 2002).

4 On Enlightenment uses of cosmopolitanism, see Thomas J. Schlereth, *The Cosmopolitan Ideal in Enlightenment Thought* (University of Notre Dame Press, 1977); on Romantic cosmopolitanism, see Jeffrey Cox and Jillian Heydt-Stevenson's special issue of *European Romantic Review* on "Romantic Cosmopolitanism," *European Romantic Review* 16: 2 (2005).

5 Roland Robertson, *Globalization: Social Theory and Global Culture* (London: Sage, 1991), 8.

6 "cosmopolitan, *a.* and *n.*" *Oxford English Dictionary,* 2nd edn., 1989. *OED Online* Oxford University Press, November 24, 2009, <http://dictionary.oed.com/cgi/entry/ 50051138>.

7 See Chapter 1 for a detailed discussion of the various uses of cosmopolitanism at the Great Exhibition.

8 See Timothy Brennan, *At Home in the World: Cosmopolitanism Now* (Cambridge, MA: Harvard University Press, 1997); Pheng Cheah, *Inhuman Conditions: On Cosmopolitanism and Human Rights* (Cambridge, MA: Harvard University Press, 2007); and Simon Gikandi, "Race and Cosmopolitanism," *American Literary History* 14: 3 (2002), 593–615.

9 See Amanda Anderson, *The Powers of Distance: Cosmopolitanism and the Cultivation of Detachment* (Princeton University Press, 2001) and *The Way We Argue Now* (Princeton University Press, 2005); Kwame Anthony Appiah, *Cosmopolitanism* (New York: W. W. Norton & Co., 2006); Bruce Robbins, "Introduction Part I: Actually Existing Cosmopolitanisms" in Pheng Cheah and Bruce Robbins, eds., *Cosmopolitics: Thinking and Feeling Beyond the Nation* (Minneapolis, MN: University of Minnesota Press, 1998), 1–20; and Rebecca Walkowitz, *Cosmopolitan Style: Modernism Beyond the Nation* (New York: Columbia University Press, 2007).

10 Anderson, *The Way We Argue Now,* 77.

11   I discuss this debate in more detail in my article "Cosmopolitanism and Literary Form," *Literature Compass* 7: 6 (June 2010), 452–66. See also the chapter on "The New Cosmopolitans" in David Harvey, *Cosmopolitanism and the Geographies of Freedom* (New York: Columbia University Press, 2009) for a useful critique of contemporary cosmopolitanism.

12   Though the nation has successfully asserted itself as the pre-eminent model of collectivity in modernity, it was not always seen as the inevitable telos of human government and social identity. Kant and Marx influentially conceptualized the nation as one stage in the unfolding of a cosmopolitan history. See, in particular, Kant's essays, "Idea for a Universal History with a Cosmopolitan Intent" (1784) and "To Perpetual Peace: a Philosophical Sketch" (1795) in *Perpetual Peace and Other Essays on Politics, History, and Morals*, trans. Ted Humphrey (Indianopolis, IN: Hackett, 1983); and Karl Marx and Friedrich Engels, *The Communist Manifesto* [1848], ed. Prederic L. Bender (New York: Norton, 1988).

13   Benedict Anderson, *Imagined Communities* (New York: Verso, 1983), 25, 30.

14   The essays in Homi Bhabha's anthology *Nation and Narration* (New York: Routledge, 1990), for example, examine the relationship between nationalism and literature in a range of different periods; Katie Trumpener's *Bardic Nationalism: the Romantic Novel and the British Empire* (Princeton University Press, 1997), which treats antiquarianism, cultural nationalism, and the rise of the novel in the context of imperialism, is another influential example of literary criticism that takes on the formative role of nationalism in the history of the novel.

15   James Buzard, *Disorienting Fiction: The Autoethnographic Work of Nineteenth-Century British Novels* (Princeton University Press, 2005).

16   *Ibid.*, 22.

17   James Buzard, "'Anywhere's Nowhere': *Bleak House* as Metropolitan Autoethnography," *Yale Journal of Criticism* 12: 1 (1999), 13.

18   Buzard, *Disorienting Fiction*, 50.

19   "Blank metaculture" is a term used by Jed Esty in *A Shrinking Island: Modernism and National Culture in England* (Princeton University Press, 2004), 21. Like Buzard, Esty sees the novel's focus on national culture as a reaction to the metropolitan anticulture created by Victorian imperialism. Esty examines this phenomenon at a later stage of the novel, however, and describes a diachronic dialectic at play, with the late modern novel reacting against the "metropolitan perception" of early modernism. Buzard, on the other hand, locates a synchronic dialectic in the structure of the novel itself, which sets up a constitutive tension between anticulture and culture.

20   Edward W. Said, *Culture and Imperialism* (New York: Knopf, 1993), cited in Buzard, *Disorienting Fiction*, 51.

21   In a recent essay for *Victorian Literature and Culture*, Buzard looks at the question of autoethnography from a different angle in an analysis of *Little Dorrit*, exploring the idea of cultural *outsideness* in Dickens' novel. Here he sees cosmopolitan and national paradigms as explicitly in dialogue. See James

Buzard, "'The Country of the Plague': Anticulture and Autoethnography in Dickens's 1850s," *Victorian Literature and Culture* 38: 2 (2010): 413–21.

22 Paul Gilroy deploys this term in *Postcolonial Melancholia* (New York: Columbia University Press 2007); I find it useful because it names a condition of society rather than the abstract principle associated with the term "multiculturalism." Gilroy discusses the vexed meanings of this term in *Against Race* (Cambridge, MA: Harvard University Press, 2002), 241–5.

23 Baucom, *Out of Place*, 33.

24 Amanda Anderson, *The Powers of Distance* (Princeton University Press, 2001). For other examples of recuperative cosmopolitanism, see Christopher Keirstead, "Stranded at the Border: Browning, France, and the Challenge of Cosmopolitanism in Red Cotton Night-Cap Country," *Victorian Poetry* 43: 4 (Winter 2005), 411–34; and "A 'Bad Patriot'?: Elizabeth Barrett Browning and Cosmopolitanism," *Victorians Institute Journal*, 33 (2005), 69–95.

25 Anderson, *Powers of Distance*, 21. For substantial critiques of cosmopolitanism's relationship to racism, imperialism, and globalization, see Brennan, *At Home in the World*; Cheah, *Inhuman Conditions*; and Gikandi, "Race and Cosmopolitanism," cited earlier.

26 Anderson, *Powers of Distance*, 30, 4.

27 *Ibid.*, 6, her emphasis.

28 As I argue in "Cosmopolitanism and Literary Form," Anderson pays particular attention to form in her chapter on Wilde's epigrammatic style but does not prioritize the relationship between cosmopolitanism and form in the rest of her book.

29 See Joseph McLaughlin, *Writing the Urban Jungle* (Charlottesville, VA: University Press of Virginia, 2000) and Jonathan Schneer, *London 1900* (New Haven, CT: Yale University Press, 2000).

30 Baucom, *Out of Place*, 55.

31 Northrop Frye writes that "[t]he symbol of conscious design in society is the city, with its abstract pattern of streets and buildings, and with the complex economic cycle of production, distribution and consumption that it sets up." "Varieties of Literary Utopias," *Daedalus* 94 (1965), 324.

32 *Ibid.*; Fredric Jameson, *Archaeologies of the Future* (New York: Verso, 2005), 4.

33 Louis Marin, *Utopics: Spatial Play* (Atlantic Highlands, NJ: Humanities Press, 1984), 201.

34 Jane Jacobs' *The Death and Life of Great American Cities* (New York: Vintage Books, 1992) is a famous early example of a work that celebrates the heterogeneity and spontaneity of urban space. More recent examples include David Harvey, *Spaces of Hope* (Berkeley, CA: University of California Press, 2000) and Jon Binnie *et al.*, eds., *Cosmopolitan Urbanism* (New York: Routledge, 2006).

35 Saskia Sassen, *Globalization and its Discontents* (New York: New Press, 1998), xxi. It is worth noting, given the ongoing contestation of the term *cosmopolitanism*, that Sassen uses the word "cosmopolite" negatively, to separate the

elitist outlook of privileged city-dwellers from that of the "disempowered actors" whose new connectedness across cities she celebrates. See "Global is Not Always Cosmopolite," interview of Sassen by Nina Fürstenberg in *Eurozine* (September 18, 2002).

36 Jacques Derrida, *On Cosmopolitanism and Forgiveness* (New York: Routledge, 2001); for Arendt on the displaced person, see "The Decline of the Nation-State and the Ends of the Rights of Man" in *The Origins of Totalitarianism* (San Diego, CA: Harcourt Brace Jovanovich, 1994).

37 See Michel Foucault, *Discipline and Punish: the Birth of the Prison* (New York: Vintage, 1995).

38 Kurt Koenigsberger, *The Novel and the Menagerie: Totality, Englishness, and Empire* (Columbus, OH: Ohio University State Press, 2007).

39 Simon Joyce, in *Capital Offenses: Geographies of Class and Crime in Victorian London* (Charlottesville, VA: University of Virginia Press, 2003) also applies Jameson's "cognitive mapping" to the work of nineteenth-century writers, though he is more interested in the national than in the global context of Victorian city writing: "the choice of appropriate spatial metaphors allows a writer to move back and forth between the local particularities of experience and the life of the nation, establishing a continuum within which the former necessarily serves as a condensed but representative example of the latter" (26).

40 Fredric Jameson, *Postmodernism, or the Cultural Logic of Late Capitalism* (Durham, NC: Duke University Press, 1992), 52.

41 Fredric Jameson, "Cognitive Mapping" in Cary Nelson and Larry Grossberg, eds., *Marxism and the Interpretation of Culture* (Urbana, IL: University of Illinois Press, 1998), 354.

42 David Harvey also sees a kind of utopianism in what he calls "the cartographic imagination" of the nineteenth century. Arguing that the city functions both as a spatial pattern and as a type of moral order in realist works, Harvey demonstrates that geographic knowledge, when combined with moments of novelistic mystery and sublimity, conjures an image of the city that allows for alternative visions that might "shape the city to human desires"; Harvey, "The Cartographic Imagination: Balzac in Paris" in Vinay Dharwadker, ed., *Cosmopolitan Geographies: New Locations in Literature and Culture* (New York: Routledge, 2001), 83.

43 I do not mean to imply that, when mapping the city, texts were performing the work of imperialism and bourgeois hegemony, and when imagining the invisible world, they were transcending these ideologies; by simultaneously imagining city and world, cosmopolitan realism made mapping and cognitive mapping inseparable. I therefore disagree with critics, such as Michel de Certeau, who decouple the antithetical scales of urban representation, opposing the "official" view from above to the "unofficial" view from the street to see the first as oppressive and the second as liberatory. In *The Practice of Everyday Life* (Berkeley, CA: University of California Press, 1984), de Certeau argues that a progressive image of the urban is located only in the lives of "ordinary practitioners" of city life and the "everyday strangeness"

that they encounter (93). In my argument, both views – from above and from below – are essential to the representation of the everyday and they operate together to create a variety of ideological effects.

44 Jameson, "Cognitive Mapping," 291.

45 George Stocking refers this way to mid-century ethnology in *Victorian Anthropology* (New York: Free Press, 1987), 47–8.

46 Anne McClintock, *Imperial Leather* (New York: Routledge, 1995), 49.

47 Johannes Fabian, *Time and the Other* (New York: Columbia University Press, 2002), 31.

48 *Ibid.*, 17.

49 Paul Young, "Mission Impossible: Globalization and the Great Exhibition" in Jeffrey A. Auerbach and Peter H. Hoffenberg, eds., *Britain, the Empire, and the World at the Great Exhibition of 1851* (Aldershot: Ashgate, 2008), 25.

50 For an overview of the nineteenth-century discourse of degeneration, see J. Edward Chamberlin and Sander L. Gilman, *Degeneration: the Dark Side of Progress* (New York: Columbia University Press, 1995), and Daniel Pick, *Faces of Degeneration: A European Disorder* (Cambridge University Press, 1989).

51 James Buzard and Joseph Childers, "Introduction: Victorian Ethnographies," *Victorian Studies* 41: 3 (Spring 1998), 351.

52 *Oxford English Dictionary.* 2nd edn, 1989. *OED Online.* Oxford University Press, October 26, 2009, <http://dictionary.oed.com/cgi/entry/50088508>.

53 See Levine's articles in successive issues of *Victorian Studies*, "Strategic Formalism: Toward a New Method in Cultural Studies" 48: 4 (Summer 2006), 625–57, and "Scaled up, Writ Small: A Response to Carolyn Dever and Herbert F. Tucker," 49: 1 (Autumn 2006), 100–105.

54 Caroline Levine, "Strategic Formalism," 626, 633.

55 Lauren Goodlad, "Cosmopolitanism's Actually Existing Beyond: Towards a Victorian Geopolitical Aesthetic" *Victorian Literature and Culture* 38: 2 (2010), 413–21.

56 René Wellek, "The Concept of Realism in Literary Scholarship" in Stephen G. Nichols, Jr., ed., *René Wellek: Concepts of Criticism* (New Haven, CT: Yale University Press, 1963), 229, 253.

57 George Levine, *The Realistic Imagination* (University of Chicago Press, 1981), 262, 267.

58 Alexander von Humboldt, *Cosmos: Sketch of a Physical Description of the Universe*, vol. I, trans. E. C. Otté (New York: Harper & Brothers, 1850), 53.

59 Though her focus is not on the techniques, such as synecdoche, whereby writers move from visible to invisible realms, Kate Flint also stresses the interplay of visibility and invisibility in realism, arguing that it allows writers to acknowledge the limitations of empiricism, and gesture at the larger truths that might lie beyond it. Realism, she argues, produces "a constant slippage from concern with viewing the material world to inner forms of vision" (*The Victorians and the Visual Imagination* [New York: Cambridge University Press, 2000], 9).

60 Johannes Fabian, for example, analyzes the hold of a "visual-spatial logic" on anthropology from its nineteenth-century origins to the present, while Michel de Certeau argues that optical knowledge is a means of reckoning with the difference within as well as outside of European nations: "The atopia–utopia of optical knowledge has long had the ambition of surmounting and articulating the contradictions arising from urban agglomeration" (Fabian, *Time and the Other*, 113; de Certeau, *Practice of Everyday Life*, 93). For analyses of visual knowledge that extend beyond the urban context, see Martin Jay, *Downcast Eyes* (Berkeley, CA: University of California Press, 1994) and Jonathan Crary, *Techniques of the Observer* (Boston, MD: MIT Press, 1992).

61 Jonathan Arac, *Commissioned Spirits* (New York: Columbia University Press, 1989), 3.

62 *Ibid.*, 22. Arac describes the adaptability of the realist novel in its efforts to construct an omniscient overview. Arguing that the visual was particularly important to the novel's experimentations, he points out that it had to "appropriate smaller forms and borrow from adjacent practices of discourse to make new forms in order to contain the mobility of its age in a new totality" (9).

63 See Chapter 2 on the relationship of the panorama phenomenon to literary realism.

64 See Peter H. Hoffenberg, *An Empire on Display* (Berkeley, CA: University of California Press, 2001); Koenigsberger, *The Novel and the Menagerie*; Timothy Mitchell, "The World as Exhibition," *Comparative Studies in Society and History* 31: 2 (April 1989), 217–36.

65 Richard Maxwell, *The Mysteries of Paris and London* (Charlottesville, VA: University of Virginia Press, 1992), 10, x.

66 Pecora, *Secularization and Cultural Criticism*, 195.

67 *Ibid.*, 20.

68 *Ibid.*, 22.

69 See Benedict Anderson, *Imagined Communities*, on how nationalism takes on the imaginative power of older religious identifications within secular modernity.

70 For a fuller account of discussions of cosmopolitanism in postcolonial theory specifically, see the chapter entitled "The Postcolonial Critique of Cosmopolitanism" in Harvey, *Cosmopolitanism and the Geographies of Freedom*.

71 *Ibid.*, 42.

72 See Harvey on "The Flat World of Neoliberal Utopianism" in *Cosmopolitanism and the Geographies of Freedom*.

73 See, for example, William Chapman Sharpe, *Unreal Cities: Urban Figuration in Wordsworth, Baudelaire, Whitman, Eliot, and Williams* (Baltimore and London: Johns Hopkins University Press, 1990), and David Pike, *Metropolis on the Styx* (Ithaca, NY: Cornell University Press, 2007).

74 See Chapter 5 for more on Jameson's version of this argument about modernism and how I seek to amend it.

75 Raymond Williams, "Metropolitan Perceptions and the Emergence of Modernism" in *The Politics of Modernism: Against the New Conformists*, ed. Tony Pinkney (New York: Verso, 1989), 44.

76 Kurt H. Wolff, ed., *The Sociology of Georg Simmel* (Glencoe, IL: Free Press, 1964), 418–19.

77 Williams, "Metropolitan Perceptions," 44. Subsequent references appear parenthetically.

78 Globalization's origins are less often identified with the nineteenth century than with early modern phenomena – such as European exploration, trade, and territorial appropriation in Asia and the Americas, the slave trade and transnational commercial entities such as the East India Company – or our current postcolonial moment and the late capitalist world-market. But the way in which empire expanded notions of Britishness in the Victorian period crucially changed British awareness of the rest of the world. Among others, Stuart Hall identifies the period of the British empire as a key moment in the history of globalization. For him, globalization has to do with "a nation's position as a leading commercial world power ... with its position of leadership in a highly international and industrializing world economy, and with the fact that this society and its centers have long been placed at the center of a web of global commitments": Stuart Hall, "The Local and the Global: Globalization and Ethnicity" in Anthony D. King, ed., *Culture, Globalization, and the World-System* (Minneapolis MN: University of Minnesota Press, 1997), 20.

79 Nick Merriman, "Introduction" in Nick Merriman, ed., *The Peopling of London: Fifteen Thousand Years of Settlement from Overseas* (London: Museum of London, 1993), 4.

80 On the correspondence between urban and imperial geography, see Simon Joyce, *Capital Offenses*, and Pamela K. Gilbert, *Mapping the Victorian Social Body* (Albany: State University of New York Press, 2004). On the way the imperial imagination affected urban representation, see McLaughlin, *Writing the Urban Jungle*; on correspondences between early anthropology, sociology, and ethnographic methodology, see especially "Victorian Cultural Ideology and the Image of Savagery" in George Stocking's *Victorian Anthropology* and the chapter on "Mayhew's Cockney Polynesia" in Christopher Herbert's *Culture and Anomie* (University of Chicago Press, 1991).

81 Sean Hutton, "The Irish in London" in Merriman, ed., *The Peopling of London*, 119.

82 Nick Merriman and Rozina Visram, "The World in a City" in Merriman, ed., *The Peopling of London*, 6.

83 On Irish stereotypes, see L. Perry Curtis, *Apes and Angels: The Irishman in Victorian Caricature* (Washington: Smithsonian Institution Press, 1971); on anti-Semitism, see Bryan Cheyette, *Constructions of "the Jew" in English Literature and Society* (Cambridge University Press, 1993).

84 See Merriman, ed., *The Peopling of London*, and Gretchen Gerzina, *Black London: Life Before Emancipation* (London: John Murray, 1995).

85 Gregory Anderson, *Victorian Clerks* (Manchester University Press, 1976), 61.

86 Antoinette M. Burton, *At the Heart of the Empire: Indians and the Colonial Encounter in Late-Victorian Britain* (Berkeley, CA: University of California Press, 1998), 171.

87 Rozina Visram, "South Asians in London" in Merriman, ed., *The Peopling of London,* 172.

88 The important work of fleshing out the histories of these varied urban popula-tions and exploring their own narratives of London life has only recently begun. See, for example, Sukhdev Sandhu, *London Calling: How Black and Asian Writers Imagined a City* (London: Harper Perennial, 2004); Burton, *At the Heart of the Empire,* C. L. Innes, *A History of Black and Asian Writing in Britain* (Cambridge University Press, 2008); Leela Gandhi, *Affective Communities* (Durham, NC: Duke University Press, 2006). The digital collections published by Adam Matthews Publications, *The Empire Writes Back* (Parts 1 and 2), make accessible a wide range of first-person narratives of colonial visitors to London.

89 Keith Hanley and Greg Kucich, "Introduction: Global Formations and Recalcitrances," *Nineteenth-Century Contexts* 29: 2 (2007), 76.

90 Richard Menke, *Telegraphic Realism: Victorian Fiction and other Information Systems* (Stanford University Press, 2008), 15.

91 *Ibid.,* 5.

92 Thomas Tobin, "A Method and Formula for Quantifying Timeliness in Nineteenth-Century Periodicals," unpublished conference paper, 1–3.

93 Benedict Anderson, "Exodus," *Critical Inquiry* 20. 2 (Winter 1994), 316–18. Ian Baucom makes a related argument about dislocation in *Out of Place,* as does James Buzard in *Disorienting Fiction.*

94 Williams' "Metropolitan Perceptions" and his book *The Country and the City* (New York: Oxford University Press, 1973) offer a broad, influential account of the social and literary transformations that resulted from London's growth and imperial significance in the nineteenth century.

95 In *The World Republic of Letters,* Pascale Casanova argues that Paris was thought to be the major center of the literary world in the eighteenth and nineteenth centuries, though she herself occasionally makes the case that London was more, or equally, important to the transnational exchange that her book charts: "London is, of course, along with Paris, the other great capital of world literature, not only by virtue of its accumulated literary capital but also owing to the immensity of its former colonial empire" (117).

96 The fact that a collection of essays on urban reform, Charles Frederick Gurney Masterman's *The Heart of the Empire* (London: T. Fisher Unwin, 1901), argues that domestic problems should be seen in the wider context of imperial policy, shows the degree to which urban and imperial space were seen as continuous by the end of the century.

97 Duncan Bell, ed., *Victorian Visions of Global Order* (Cambridge University Press, 2007), 3.

98 Lara Kriegel argues that the annexation of the Punjab was a critical event in changing ideas of empire at mid-century. See "Narrating the Subcontinent in 1851: India at the Crystal Palace" in Louise Purbrick, ed., *The Great Exhibition of 1851: New Interdisciplinary Essays* (New York: Manchester University Press, 2001).

99 Duncan Bell, *The Idea of Greater Britain: Empire and the Future of World Order: 1860–1900* (Princeton University Press, 2007), 1. Bell argues that

"the shifts in the perception of the planet that helped underpin the idea of an integrated global polity can be traced principally to the 1860s" (3). See also Lauren M. E. Goodlad, "Trollopian 'Foreign Policy': Rootedness and Cosmopolitanism in the Mid-Victorian Global Imaginary," *PMLA* 124: 2 (March 2009), 437–54: "In viewing settler colonies as organic extensions of the Anglo-Saxon metropole, Trollope anticipated the 'Greater British' imaginary of later thinkers such as Charles Dike and J. R. Seeley" (440).

100 P. J. Cain, "Economics and Empire: the Metropolitan Context" in Andrew Porter, ed., *The Oxford History of the British Empire*. Vol. III: *The Nineteenth Century* (Oxford and New York: Oxford University Press, 2001), 42, 51.

101 Anthony Howe, "Free Trade and Global Order" in Bell, ed., *Victorian Visions of Global Order*, 34.

102 See Cain, "Economics and Empire" and, for a literary analysis of these questions, Bruce Robbins, "Victorian Cosmopolitanism, Interrupted," *Victorian Literature and Culture* 38: 2 (2010), 421–7.

103 Paul Young, *Globalization*, 10.

104 *Ibid.*, 24.

105 Cain, "Economics and Empire," 39.

106 Howe, "Free Trade and Global Order," 31.

107 John M. Mackenzie, "Empire and Metropolitan Cultures" in Porter, ed., *The Oxford History of the British Empire*. Vol III, 280.

108 *Ibid.*, 282–3.

CHAPTER I: THE PALACE AND THE PERIODICAL

1 Charles Dickens, *Master Humphrey's Clock* (Philadelphia, PA: Jesper Harding, 1847), 215.

2 Robbins, "Introduction, Part One" in Cheah and Robbins, *Cosmopolitics*, 2.

3 Lauren Goodlad, "Trollopian 'Foreign Policy,'"439.

4 See "cosmopolitan, *a.* and *n.*," *Oxford English Dictionary*, 2nd edn, 1989. *OED Online*, Oxford University Press, November 24, 2009 <http://dictionary.oed.com/cgi/entry/50051138> and "cosmopolitanism," *OED*, 2nd edn 1989. *OED Online*, Oxford University Press, November 24 2009 <http://dictionary.oed.com/cgi/entry/50051389>.

5 See, for example, Anderson, "Cosmopolitanism, Universalism, and the Divided Legacies of Modernity" in her *The Way We Argue Now*, or Cheah's chapter on "The Cosmopolitical – Today" in his *Inhuman Conditions*. For historical uses of the word, see, for example, Robert John Holton, "Cosmopolitanism or Cosmopolitanisms? The Universal Races Congress of 1911," *Global Networks* 2 (2002), 153–8.

6 Immanuel Kant, "To Perpetual Peace" in *Perpetual Peace and Other Essays*, 125.

7 James Bohman contends that there are "many different and overlapping and transnational public spheres for world citizens and that public opinion rather than coercive law seems to be the sole mechanism for the enforcement of

human rights." James Bohman and Matthias Lutz-Bachmann, "Introduction" in James Bohman and Matthias Lutz-Bachmann, eds., *Perpetual Peace: Essays on Kant's Cosmopolitan Ideal* (Cambridge, MA: MIT Press, 1997), 12.

8 Kant, "To Perpetual Peace," 125.

9 *Ibid.*, 119.

10 Martin Puchner, *Poetry of the Revolution: Marx, Manifestoes and the Avant-Garde* (Princeton University Press, 2006), 57–8.

11 *Ibid.*, 61.

12 On the differences between Kantian and Marxist cosmopolitanism, see also Cheah, *Inhuman Conditions*, 21–9.

13 Judith Walkowitz's recent work on cosmopolitanism develops her earlier view. In "The 'Vision of Salome': Cosmopolitanism and Erotic Dancing in Central London, 1908–1918," *American Historical Review* 108: 2 (April 2003), 337–76, she argues that cosmopolitanism was "first, a pleasurable, stylized form of imaginative expatriation, associated with privileged mobility; and second, a debased condition of deracination, hybridity, displacement, and racial degeneration – all the dangers of the unplaced" (340), and shows how it was connected to both Jewishness and homosexuality. See also Walkowitz's article on "Cosmopolitanism, Feminism and the Moving Body," *Victorian Literature and Culture* 38: 2 (2010), 427–51.

14 See Bruce Robbins, "Telescopic Philanthropy: Professionalism and Responsibility in *Bleak House*" in Homi Bhabha, ed., *Nation and Narration* (London: Routledge, 1990); Amanda Anderson, *The Powers of Distance*, and James Buzard, "Anywhere's Nowhere" in *Disorienting Fiction*.

15 Dickens, *Bleak House*, 307.

16 Henry Cole, *On the International Results of the Exhibition of 1851* (London: David Bogue, 1852), 429.

17 *The Crystal Palace Exhibition Illustrated Catalogue* (New York: Dover Publications, 1970), xi. On the layout and organization of the exhibition space, see Jeffrey A. Auerbach, *The Great Exhibition of 1851: a Nation of Display* (New Haven, CT: Yale University Press, 1999); John R. Davis, *The Great Exhibition* (Stroud: Sutton, 1999); James Buzard, Joseph W. Childers, and Eileen Gillooly, eds., *Victorian Prism: Refractions of the Crystal Palace* (Charlottesville, VA: University of Virginia Press, 2007).

18 Recent noteworthy contributions to Exhibition scholarship specifically related to the question of global thought include Jeffrey A. Auerbach and Peter H. Hoffenberg, eds., *Britain, the Empire, and the World at the Great Exhibition of 1851* (Aldershot, Hampshire: Ashgate, 2008) and Paul Young, *Globalization*.

19 Young, *Globalization*, 7; Kylie Message and Ewan Johnston, "The World within the City: The Great Exhibition, Race, Class and Social Reform" in Auerbach and Hoffenberg, eds., *Britain, the Empire, and the World*, 28.

20 See Auerbach, *The Great Exhibition*, 151–8 on the attendance of different classes at the Exhibition.

21 Karen Chase and Michael Levenson, "Mayhew, the Prince and the Poor" in Buzard, Childers, and Gillooly, eds., *Victorian Prism*, 124.

22 Cited in Davis, *The Great Exhibition*, 44.

23 Cole, *On the International Results*, 420. Emphasis in the original.

24 Young, *Globalization*, 25.

25 Cited in C. H. Gibbs-Smith, ed., *The Great Exhibition of 1851: a Commemorative Album* (London: HMSO, 1950), 31.

26 Young, *Globalization*, 50, 59, 85.

27 Mitchell, "The World as Exhibition," 227.

28 *Ibid.*, 226.

29 Hoffenberg, *An Empire on Display*, 17–18.

30 Albert (Prince Consort) and Sir Arthur Helps, *The Principal Speeches and Address of His Royal Highness, The Prince Consort* (London: John Murray, 1862), 110–12. Emphasis in the original.

31 Cited in Ronald Pearson, "Thackeray and Punch at the Exhibition" in Parbrick, ed., *The Great Exhibition*, 194.

32 Cited in Davis, *The Great Exhibition*, 192.

33 *Northern Star*, June 14, 1851.

34 William Whewell. "The General Bearing of the Great Exhibition on the Progress of Art and Science" in *Lectures on the Results of the Exhibition, delivered before the Society of Arts, Manufactures and Commerce, at the Suggestion of H.R.H. Prince Albert, President of the Society* (London: David Bogue, 1851), 14.

35 Anderson, *Imagined Communities*, 7.

36 Cited in Asa Briggs, *1851* (London: Historical Association, 1951), 21.

37 Auerbach, *The Great Exhibition*, 159.

38 For more on the discourse of cosmopolitanism within Anglo-American slavery debates, see Edlie Wong, "Anti-Slavery Cosmopolitanism in the Black Atlantic," *Victorian Literature and Culture* 38: 2 (2010), 451–67.

39 *The Anti-Slavery Reporter* 6: 65 (May 1, 1851): 1.

40 William Wells Brown, *An American Fugitive in Europe: Sketches of People and Places Abroad* (Boston: J. P. Jewett, 1854), 196.

41 Elisa Tamarkin, "Black Anglophilia; or, the Sociability of Anti-Slavery," *American Literary History* 14: 3 (2002), 458–9.

42 *Ibid.*, 460.

43 *Ibid.*, 465.

44 Pascale Casanova, *The World Republic of Letters* (Cambridge, MA: Harvard University Press, 2004), 5, 12.

45 Sharon Marcus, "Same Difference? Transnationalism, Comparative Literature, and Victorian Studies," *Victorian Studies* 45: 4 (2003), 677–86.

46 While it is tempting to assume that circulation was not high for the short-lived titles (*Cosmopolitan Review, Cosmopolitan Critic and Controversialist,* and the 1887–9 *Cosmopolitan*), it might also be true that circulation figures haven't survived *because* they were short-lived.

47 *Cosmopolitan Review* (Feb. 15, 1861): 5.

48 *Philogene's Cosmopolitan Political and Statistical Review* 1: 1 (1839), 1.

49 The term "cosmopolitan" was employed similarly in a collection entitled *Cosmopolitan Essays* (London: Chapman & Hall, 1886) by Sir Richard

Temple, MP and Governor of Bombay. His works described the "globe-encircling British Empire," and aimed to educate the reader about the colonies and the "mother country" as well as other countries that affected British foreign policy, such as China, Turkey, Palestine, and Greece.

50 See J. Don Vann and Rosemary T. Van Arsdel, eds., *Periodicals of Queen Victoria's Empire: An Exploration* (University of Toronto Press, 1996).

51 Bruce Robbins, "Introduction Part I: Actually Existing Cosmopolitanisms" in Cheah and Robbins, eds., *Cosmopolitics*, 13.

52 Edited by Fernand Ortmans, *Cosmopolis* had a short-lived existence from January 1896 to November 1898 but its first issue was quite a success, with 24,000 copies sold. The available statistics on *Cosmopolis'* circulation tell us only about the sales of the first issue and that 18,000 copies of the second issue were printed. Alvin Sullivan, ed., *British Literary Magazines: The Victorian and Edwardian Age, 1837–1913* (Westport, CT: Greenwood Press, 1983–6), 91.

53 "Prospectus," *Cosmopolis* 1 (January 1896). I am indebted to Michael Black's website, "The Cosmopolis Archive" (www.clubi.ie/zoom/cosmopolis/index.html) for making available *Cosmopolis'* table of contents and prospectuses in three different languages, and for his extensive research on the journal's publication and circulation history.

54 Thomas Nagel used this phrase as the title for his book addressing philosophical debates on objectivity and detachment, *The View from Nowhere* (New York: Oxford University Press, 1986).

55 Between 1896 and 1899, over thirty references to *Cosmopolis* appear in *The Times*.

56 Amanda Anderson, for instance, argues for this view of cosmopolitanism in "Cosmopolitanism, Universalism, and the Divided Legacies of Modernity" in Cheah and Robbins, eds., *Cosmopolitics*.

57 *Cosmopolis* 2, 660–68, 719–38.

58 Alvin Sullivan, *British Literary Magazines*, 87.

59 Frederic Harrison, "The True Cosmopolis," *Cosmopolis* 3 (August 1896), 327.

60 In *Cosmopolis* issues for June, August, and September 1898.

61 Julia Reid, "*The Academy* and *Cosmopolis*: Evolution and Culture in Robert Louis Stevenson's Periodical Encounters" in Louise Henson *et al.*, *Culture and Science in the Nineteenth-Century Media* (Aldershot: Ashgate, 2004), 263–73.

62 Harrison, "The True Cosmopolis," 329.

63 *Ibid.*, 335, 337.

64 *Ibid.*, 330.

65 Frederick Greenwood, "The Safeguards of Peace," *Cosmopolis* 2 (May 1896), 353.

66 Edward Dicey, "Why England is Unpopular," *Cosmopolis* 4 (December 1896), 680.

CHAPTER 2: THE SKETCH AND THE PANORAMA

1 In *The Criminal Prisons of London and Scenes of Prison Life*, 7. All subsequent references in this chapter appear parenthetically.

2 Humpherys, *Henry Mayhew*, 143.

3   In his study of the role of the underworld and the devil in the imagination of urban culture, *Metropolis on the Styx: The Underworld of Modern Urban Culture, 1800–2001* (Ithaca, NY: Cornell University Press, 2007) David Pike demonstrates that "Two primary ways of approaching the modern city were codified in the nineteenth century, the view from above and the view from below" (36).

4   See Walter Benjamin, *Charles Baudelaire: A Lyric Poet in the Era of High Capitalism*, trans. Harry Zohn (London: New Left Books, 1973). All subsequent references will appear parenthetically.

5   Charles Dickens, *Dombey and Son*, 1846–8 (New York: Oxford University Press, 2001), 685.

6   Both Jonathan Arac and Richard Maxwell, in *Commissioned Spirits* and *The Mysteries of Paris and London* respectively, argue that a panoramic perspective is used in the Victorian novel to address the perception, endemic to the period, that urban space eludes conventional modes of order and representation.

7   Arac writes briefly on Dickens' sketches in relation to the panoramic mode of his novels but sees them as antithetical rather than related forms (see *Commissioned Spirits*, 120). In "The World in Images: Nineteenth-Century Picture Worlds and Modernist Ways of Seeing," however, Katie Trumpener points to the interrelation of the two forms in nineteenth-century picture books.

8   For Benjamin, the panorama literature is specific to Paris in the 1840s. The physiologists were soon "passé," he argues, surpassed by writers like Poe who encapsulated the city's "disquieting and threatening aspects" (40). In his account, the panorama literature serves more as an introduction to these darker genres than as an influential form in its own right.

9   See Lukács' *The Theory of the Novel* and *Studies in European Realism*.

10 George Eliot, *Middlemarch*, 1871–2 (New York: Penguin, 1985), 896.

11 Bruce Robbins, Mary Wilson Carpenter, and Helena Michie, focusing respectively on international investments, global diseases, and Continental travel, have each pointed to significant ways in which Eliot's novel evokes a wider world: Bruce Robbins, "Victorian Cosmopolitanism," 421–7; Mary Wilson Carpenter, "Medical Cosmopolitanism: *Middlemarch*, Cholera, and the Pathologies of English Masculinity," *Victorian Literature and Culture* 38: 2 (2010), 511–29; Helena Michie, *Victorian Honeymoons: Journeys to the Conjugal* (Cambridge University Press, 2007).

12 Raymond Williams, *The Country and the City*, 149. See also Jonathan Arac, *Commissioned Spirits*, on the relationship between Wordsworth's work and the panoramic overview in realist fiction at mid-century.

13 "sketch, n." in *Oxford English Dictionary*, 2nd edn, 1989. *OED Online*. Oxford University Press, Feb. 14, 2008 <http://dictionary.oed.com/cgi/entry/50226262>.

14 Richard Sha, *The Visual and Verbal Sketch in British Romanticism* (Philadelphia, PA: University of Pennsylvania Press, 1997), 14.

15 Martina Lauster, *Sketches of the Nineteenth Century: European Journalism and its Physiologies, 1830–50* (New York: Palgrave Macmillan, 2007), 20.

16 Though most of these illustrations were woodcuts and etchings, Thomson and Smith were among the first to use photographs to present the plight of the poor to a larger audience.

17 Blanchard Jerrold and Gustave Doré's *London: A Pilgrimage* [1872] (New York: Dover, 1970), xxxiii.

18 Sean Shesgreen, in *Images of the Outcast: The Urban Poor in the Cries of London* (New Brunswick, NJ: Rutgers University Press, 2002), argues that Marcellus Laroon, one of the most successful creators of the Cries, drew upon the methodology of natural history, providing a "visual encyclopedia" of the proliferation of social types and laborers in the fast-changing urban landscape while also documenting "what was local about this or that city" (2).

19 Shesgreen, *Images of the Outcast*, 34.

20 *Ibid.*, 36.

21 Cited in *ibid.*, 3.

22 Katie Trumpener, "City Scenes: Commerce, Utopia, and the Birth of the Picture-Book" in Richard Maxwell, ed., *The Victorian Illustrated Book* (Charlottesville, VA: University of Virginia Press, 2002), 349–50.

23 Alexander Welsh, *The City of Dickens* (Oxford: Clarendon Press, 1971), 23.

24 Timothy Barringer, "Representations of Labour in British Visual Culture, 1850–1875" (D. Phil. dissertation, University of Sussex, 1994), 288.

25 Henry Mayhew, *London Labour and the London Poor* 1865 (New York: Penguin, 1985), 263.

26 *Ibid.*, 262.

27 Maxwell, *Mysteries of Paris and London*, 14.

28 M. H. Abrams, *Natural Supernaturalism* (New York: W. W. Norton & Co., 1971), 65.

29 Lauster, *Sketches of the Nineteenth Century*, 42.

30 *Ibid.*, 43.

31 *Ibid.*, 134.

32 *Ibid.*, 134. For more on the Asmodean tradition, see also David Pike, *Metropolis on the Styx.*

33 George Sala, "The Streets of the World" in *Temple Bar*, vol. 10 (March 1864), 335.

34 *Ibid.*, 6.

35 *Ibid.*, 7.

36 *Ibid.*, 496.

37 Alison Byerly, "Effortless Art: the Sketch in Nineteenth-Century Painting and Literature," *Criticism* 41: 3 (Summer 1999), 352.

38 Sha, *The Visual and Verbal Sketch*, 152.

39 Dickens, *Sketches by Boz* [1836] (New York and Boston: Books, Inc., 1968), 176.

40 Mary Cowling, *The Artist as Anthropologist: Type and Character in Victorian Art* (New York: Cambridge University Press, 1989). In describing the disciplinary frameworks of cosmopolitan realism, I refer to both its proto-sociological and anthropological components. The difference between the

two is best encapsulated by James Buzard when he speaks of the "disabling institutional schism between sociology (for 'us') and anthropology (for others)" (*Disorienting Fiction*, 38).

41 See Barringer, "Representations of Labour" for a fuller account of Pritchard's influence on Mayhew.

42 Cited in *ibid.*, 37.

43 Cited in Cowling, *The Artist as Anthropologist*, 189.

44 On the racializing of class in urban investigation, see especially the chapter on "Urban Spectatorship" in Judith Walkowitz's *City of Dreadful Delight: Narratives of Sexual Danger in Late-Victorian London* (Chicago University Press, 1992). The degree to which racial typing took place in urban investigation varied enormously – Mayhew, for instance, goes to lengths to debunk some anti-Semitic stereotypes despite the fact that he singles out Jewish trade for particular attention – "Concerning the street-trades pursued by the Jews, I believe there is not at present a single one of which they can be said to have a monopoly" (194).

45 David Cannadine, *Ornamentalism* (New York: Oxford University Press, 2001), xix.

46 On the subject of time in Dickens' sketches in particular, see Amanpal Garcha, "Styles of Stillness and Motion: Market Culture and Narrative Form in *Sketches by Boz*," *Dickens Studies Annual* 30 (2001): 1–22 and Chapter 2 of Deborah Epstein Nord's *Walking the Victorian Streets* (Ithaca, NY: Cornell University Press, 1995).

47 Dickens, *Sketches by Boz*, 70–71.

48 Gillian Forrester, "Mapping a New Kingston: Belisario's Sketches of Character" in Tim Barringer, Gillian Forrester, and Barbara Martinez-Ruiz, *Art and Emancipation in Jamaica: Isaac Mendes Belisario and His Worlds* (New Haven, CT: Yale Center for British Art and Yale University Press, 2008), 71.

49 Forrester, "Mapping a New Kingston," 80.

50 For more on Levy's ethnographic project, see Susan Bernstein's introduction to the Broadview edition of *Reuben Sachs*.

51 Lauster's critique of Benjamin emphasizes the ideological flexibility of the sketch tradition. Arguing that Benjamin's reading of the sketch is overly reductive, she notes that he ignores the importance of sketches to bourgeois self-understanding, alongside the understanding of other classes.

52 Richard Altick, *The Shows of London* (Cambridge, MA: Belknap, 1978), 475.

53 Gillen d'Arcy Wood, in *The Shock of the Real: Romanticism and Visual Culture* (New York: Palgrave, 2001), points out that the panorama was "from the first, an international phenomenon. Barker filed a patent for his invention in 1787, and the technology crossed the Atlantic as early as 1794, when a 'Panorama of London and Westminster' opened in New York City" (101).

54 Philip Shaw's "'Mimic Sights': A Note on Panorama and Other Indoor Displays in Book VII of *The Prelude*," *Notes and Queries* 40 (1993), 462–4, argues that Wordsworth is most likely to have seen Robert Barker's *London from the Roof of the Albion Mills* (1791), another popular London work, but that he might also have visited Girtin's *Eidometropolis*.

55 Joss Marsh, "Spectacle" in *A Companion to Victorian Literature and Culture*, ed. Herbert Tucker (Malden: Blackwell, 1999), 281.

56 Wood, *Shock of the Real*, 103.

57 In Stephen Oettermann, *The Panorama: History of a Mass Medium* (New York: Zone, 1997); Jonathan Crary, *Techniques of the Observer*; and Bernard Comment, *The Panorama*, trans. Ann-Marie Glasheen (London: Reaktion Books, 1999). On the relationship between the rise of the panorama and that of the panopticon, see Oettermann, 41.

58 Crary, *Techniques*, 22.

59 *Ibid.*, 21.

60 Oettermann, *The Panorama*, 45–7.

61 Comment, *The Panorama*, 19.

62 Thomas Richards, *The Imperial Archive* (New York: Verso, 1993). Writing in particular of Burford's Leicester Square panoramas, Altick states that "India figured in half a dozen other Leicester Square shows: Calcutta (1830), Bombay (1831), Benares (1840), the Himalayas (1847), and two focal points of the Sepoy Mutiny, Delhi and Lucknow (1857–58) ... Another topic that repeatedly found its way onto Burford's canvases was the British campaign to open China to western trade" (177).

63 Robert Burford, *Description of a view of the city of Calcutta; now exhibiting at the Panorama, Leicester Square* (London: J. & C. Adlard, 1830) and *Description of the Panorama of the Superb City of Mexico, and the Surrounding Scenery* (Washington, 1832). For an incisive reading of the role of panoramas in imperial relations with Mexico, see Robert D. Aguirre, "Annihilating the Distance: Panoramas and the Conquest of Mexico, 1822–1848," *Genre* 35. 1 (Spring 2002), 25–54.

64 Crary, *Techniques*, 113.

65 On the variety of three-dimensional panoramic spectacles such as the "Great Globe," see Oettermann, *The Panorama*, 90–92.

66 William Galperin, *The Return of the Visible in British Romanticism* (Baltimore, MD: Johns Hopkins University Press, 1993), 51.

67 *Ibid.*, 40.

68 March 12, 1859, cited. in Altick, *The Shows of London*, 482.

69 Notices for the spectacles, for example, appeared in the *Morning Chronicle* (Galperin, *Return of the Visible*, 39) and in the *News of the World*, newspapers that sold to a wide and varied demographic.

70 J. R. Smith, *Descriptive Book of the Tour of Europe: The Largest Moving Panorama in the World* (New York: Pettinger & Gray, 1855), 4.

71 This and all subsequent references to *The Prelude* are to the 1850 version of the poem which appears in William Wordsworth, *The Prelude 1799, 1805, 1850*, ed. Jonathan Wordsworth, M. H. Abrams, and Stephen Gill (New York: Norton, 1979).

72 Wood, *Shock of the Real*, 120.

73 Comment, *The Panorama*, 80.

74 J. Burford, *Description of a view of the city of Edinburgh and surrounding country, now exhibiting in the Panorama Leicester Square* (London: J. & C. Adlard, 1825).

75 John Britton, *A brief account of the Colosseum, in the Regent's Park, London: Comprising a description of the building; the panoramic view from the top of St. Paul's Cathedral; the conservatory, &c.* (London: T. Bensley, 1829), 1.

76 In *The Victorians and the Visual Imagination* (New York: Cambridge University Press, 2000), Kate Flint offers readings of the horizon as both a limitation and a symbol of infinity in a variety of nineteenth-century literary and visual texts.

77 Reprinted in Maureen Gillespie Andrews (ed.), *William Wordsworth's "The Sublime in Landscape"* (University of Rochester Department of English, 1972), 118.

78 Albert O. Wlecke, *Wordsworth and the Sublime* (Berkeley, CA: University of California Press, 1973), 50.

79 Oettermann, *The Panorama*, 15.

80 *The Prelude*, n. 7, 238.

81 See *London Labour and the London Poor*, vol. 4, "Those that will not work."

82 Lindenberger mentions that Coleridge called Wordsworth "spectator ab extra" in relation to the city (206); see Herbert Lindenberger, *On Wordsworth's Prelude* (Princeton University Press, 1963).

83 Galperin, *The Return of the Visible*, 124.

84 In *Unreal Cities* William Chapman Sharpe skillfully describes the ways in which three biblical cities – Babel, Babylon, and Jerusalem – overlay the "hallucinatory unreality of contemporary urban life" in Wordsworth's poem (15).

85 Cited in Lindenberger, *On Wordsworth's Prelude*, 33.

86 William Wordsworth, *A Guide Through the District of the Lakes in the North of England* [1822] (Malvern: Tantivy Press, 1948), 55.

87 John Plotz, *The Crowd: British Literature and Public Politics* (Berkeley, CA: University of California Press, 2000), 35.

88 Edward Said, *Culture and Imperialism* (New York: Knopf, 1993), 66.

89 Buzard, *Disorienting Fiction*, 107.

90 See Chapter 1.

91 Charles Dickens, *Bleak House*, ed. Norman Page (Harmondsworth: Penguin, 1971), 307. All subsequent references to *Bleak House* appear parenthetically.

92 For a sustained reading of Dickens' engagement with cosmopolitan ideals and his critique of global capital, see Amanda Anderson's chapter on *Little Dorritt* in *The Powers of Distance*, and James Buzard's essay "The Country of the Plague," 413–21.

93 While numerous critics have pointed to the problem of representation in *Bleak House*, J. Hillis Miller's essay "Interpretation in *Bleak House*" in *Bleak House: Charles Dickens*, ed. Jeremy Tambling (New York: St. Martin's Press, 1998), 29–53, offers perhaps the most thorough and convincing scrutiny of this theme.

94 Charles Dickens, *Master Humphrey's Clock and A Child's History of England* (Philadephia, PA: Jesper Harding, 1847), 240.

95 *Ibid.*

96 Michael Slater, ed., *Dickens' Journalism*, Vol. 1. *The Amusements of the People and Other Papers: Reports, Essays, and Reviews, 1834–51* (Columbus, OH: Ohio University Press, 1996), 136.

97 *Household Words*, April 20, 1850; reprinted in Slater, *Dickens' Journalism*, 201–12.

98 In Buzard's reading, the novel's investment in its characters is part of its aspiration to portray "a new Britain in which every former nobody will be granted recognition and consequence" (151).

99 William Wordsworth, Preface to *Lyrical Ballads* (1802), in William Wordsworth and Samuel Taylor Coleridge, *Lyrical Ballads*, ed. R. L. Brett and A. R. Jones (London: Methuen 1978), 259.

CHAPTER 3: THE REALIST SPECTATOR AND THE ROMANCE PLOT

1 Henry James, "Letter to Grace Norton" (January 24, 1885) in Percy Lubbock, ed., *The Letters of Henry James*, vol. I (New York: Charles Scribner's Sons, 1920), 114.

2 See Gandhi, *Affective Communities*, 8–9, on the growing internationalism of British socialism over the course of the nineteenth century.

3 Recent works in which this definition of cosmopolitanism has been articulated include Cheah and Robbins' collection *Cosmopolitics*: see, in particular, Amanda Anderson's essay, "Cosmopolitanism, Universalism, and the Divided Legacies of Modernity in *Cosmopolitics*." K. Anthony Appiah's essay "Cosmopolitan Patriots" in Martha Nussbaum and Joshua Cohen, eds., *For Love of Country? Debating the Limits of Patriotism* (Boston: Beacon Press, 1996) also distinguishes between cosmopolitanism and humanism: "The cosmopolitan ... celebrates the fact that there are different local human ways of being, while humanism is consistent with the desire for global homogeneity" (25). See also Carol Breckenridge, Sheldon Pollock, Homi Bhabha, and Dinesh Chakrabarty, eds., *Cosmopolitanism* (Durham, NC: Duke University Press, 2002); and Ross Posnock, "The Dream of Deracination: the Uses of Cosmopolitanism," *American Literary History* 12: 4 (Fall 2000): 802–18.

4 Arthur Conan Doyle, *A Study in Scarlet* (New York: Oxford University Press, 1994). All further references to this text will appear parenthetically.

5 McLaughlin, *Writing the Urban Jungle*, 6.

6 Among other cultural phenomena, the pervasiveness of these ideas accounts for the "thin veneer" plot of a variety of *fin-de-siècle* novels, such as *Dr Jekyll and Mr Hyde* and *Heart of Darkness*. *A Study in Scarlet*'s use of degeneration discourse in its representation of London as an imperial "cesspool" suggests that it, too, understands culture according to this model.

7 Arthur Conan Doyle, *The Sign of Four* in *The Original Illustrated 'Strand' Sherlock Holmes* (Hertfordshire: Wordsworth Editions, 1989), 65.

8 John McClure, *Late Imperial Romance* (New York: Verso, 1994), 3.

9 Gillian Beer, *The Romance* (London: Methuen, 1970), 5.

10 Doyle's choice of America as the site of his novel was both commercially canny and politically expedient. Interest in American frontier tales in the late

nineteenth century was at a height; popular exhibitions in the 1880s, such as Buffalo Bill's Wild West Show, "only confirmed the image of Americans as reassuringly barbarian" (Alexander Zwerdling, *Improvised Europeans: American Literary Expatriates and the Siege of London* [New York: Basic Books, 1998], 143). Richard Burton's 1861 travel narrative, *The City of the Saints* (obviously a central influence on Doyle, who riffs on its title in the second half of his novel), had piqued curiosity about the parts of America represented in *A Study in Scarlet*. The novel's exoticism also allows Doyle to reflect on contemporary colonial issues circumspectly. By bringing into critical focus Mormon, rather than British, imperialism, Doyle can explore the excesses of colonial rule (such as genocide and rape, both of which are hinted at in the novel) at a remove.

11 The sheer number of far-ranging geographical references in Doyle's detective fiction is a noteworthy aspect of his cosmopolitan imaginary. "The Sherlock Holmes Atlas," a useful website that maps out all geographical references in the Sherlock Holmes canon (www.sherlock-holmes.org/atlas/), tells us that *A Study in Scarlet* alone contains references to Afghanistan, India, Denmark, Russia, France, South America, Spain, the Netherlands, and several locations in the United States and Britain.

12 See Stephen Arata, *Fictions of Loss in the Victorian Fin-de-Siècle* (New York: Cambridge University Press, 1996), 144.

13 Arthur Conan Doyle, "The Adventure of the Engineer's Thumb" in *The Original Illustrated 'Strand' Sherlock Holmes* (Hertfordshire: Wordsworth Editions, 1989), 232.

14 Sometimes the knowledge he accumulates is not even accounted for within the plot of a given novel. The importance of his expertise in singlestick playing, for instance (*Study in Scarlet*, 16), is not revealed here though we learn in subsequent stories that it is an effective way to fight criminals.

15 Arthur Conan Doyle, "The Adventure of the Speckled Band" in *The Original Illustrated 'Strand' Sherlock Holmes* (Hertfordshire: Wordsworth Editions, 1989), 214.

16 Coleridge describes the imagination as the "shaping spirit" and in *Biographia Literaria* asserts that poems derive organic unity from the poet's subjective imagination rather than from objective criteria (such as the strict conventions of earlier eighteenth-century poetry): "He diffuses a tone and spirit of unity that blends and (as it were) fuses, each into each, by that synthetic and magical power to which we have exclusively appropriated the name of imagination." While Coleridge was ultimately invested in the "magical" ability of the poetic mind to reflect absolute, objective truths, late-Victorian aesthetic theorists, such as Pater, saw perceptual knowledge as inherently relativistic, since the "shaping spirit" of the mind removes its object from a dynamic context in order to contemplate it.

17 Matthew Arnold, "Preface to Poems" in A. Dwight Culler, ed., *Poetry and Criticism of Matthew Arnold* (Boston: Houghton Mifflin, 1961), 212.

18 Matthew Arnold, "The Function of Criticism at the Present Time" in Culler, ed., *Poetry and Criticism of Matthew Arnold*, 258.

19 McLaughlin notes, for example, that "The socially marginal Holmes is the protector of the 'home'-land" (30).

20 Arthur Conan Doyle, *The Sign of Four*, 71.

21 Doyle, "The Adventure of the Cardboard Box" in *The Original Illustrated 'Strand' Sherlock Holmes* (Hertfordshire: Wordsworth Editions, 1989), 307.

22 For a detailed discussion of web imagery in Victorian discourse, see Gillian Beer, *Darwin's Plots: Evolutionary Narrative in Darwin, George Eliot and Nineteenth-Century Fiction* (Boston: Arc Paperbacks, 1983).

23 Cited in Beer, *Darwin's Plots*, 155.

24 Walter Pater, "Conclusion," *The Renaissance: Studies in Art and Poetry* in William E. Buckler, ed., *Walter Pater: Three Major Texts* (New York University Press, 1986), 218.

25 Political intrigue and bombings in Britain at the time the novel was published had largely to do with the struggle for Home Rule, and the novel exploits this context for the titillating effects that references to terrorism would have had on its contemporary readers.

26 For a discussion of Doyle's growing interest in the occult during this period, see Lydia Alix Fillingham, "'The Colorless Skein of Life': Threats to the Private Sphere in Conan Doyle's *A Study in Scarlet*," *English Literary History* 56: 3 (1989), 667–88. Doyle's obituary in the *New York Times* (July 8, 1930) is also worth reading; it notes that the writer considered his work on spiritualism to be far more important than his invention of Sherlock Holmes; in seeming deference to this view, the column devotes as much space to discussion of Doyle's involvement with psychical research as it does to his fiction.

27 The Cottingly fairy photographs, taken in 1917 by two girls who claimed to commune with fairies at the bottom of their garden, were considered fakes by many (the photographers confessed to their forgery in the 1980s), but Doyle was among those who upheld their authenticity. Silver states that "Doyle's name and belief made the fairies famous; he was associated in the public mind with the quintessentially rational, supremely scientific and essentially untrickable master sleuth, Sherlock Holmes – the man who knew everything" (190).

28 Patrick Brantlinger, *Rule of Darkness: British Literature and Imperialism, 1830–1914* (Ithaca, NY: Cornell University Press, 1988), 252.

29 Henry James, *The Princess Casamassima* (New York: Penguin, 1987). All further references to this edition will appear parenthetically.

30 Henry James, "The Art of Fiction" in Morton Dauwen Zabel, ed., *The Portable Henry James* (New York: Penguin, 1977), 394.

31 Henry James, "London" in Zabel, ed., *The Portable Henry James*, 529.

32 Jonathan Freedman, *Professions of Taste: Henry James, British Aestheticism and Commodity Culture* (Stanford University Press, 1990).

33 Walkowitz, *City of Dreadful Delight*, 16.

34 Henry James, *Letters*, ed. Leon Edel (Cambridge, MA: Harvard University Press, 1974–84), vol. III, 244.
35 See Zwerdling, *Improvised Europeans*.
36 Leon Edel and Lyall H. Powers, eds., *The Complete Notebooks of Henry James* (New York: Oxford University Press, 1987), 218.
37 James, "London," 522.
38 *Ibid.*
39 *Ibid.*, 519.
40 Doyle, "The Adventure of the Cardboard Box," 319.
41 See, for example, Mark Seltzer, "*The Princess Casamassima*: Realism and the Fantasy of Surveillance," *Nineteenth-Century Fiction* 35: 4 (1981), 506–34. Seltzer argues that the novel participates in the policing function of culture that it diagnoses and suggests that "it is the incompatibility of aesthetic and political claims that leads to Hyacinth's suicide" (533).
42 James, "Art of Fiction," 390.
43 Lionel Trilling, "The Princess Casamassima" in J. Don Vann, ed., *Critics on Henry James* (University of Miami Press, 1972), 71.
44 *Ibid.*, 73.
45 Ross Posnock, *The Trial of Curiosity: Henry James, William James and the Challenge of Modernity* (New York: Oxford University Press, 1991), 67.
46 *Ibid.*, 71.

CHAPTER 4: ETHNOGRAPHY AND ALLEGORY

1 Oscar Wilde, "The Soul of Man under Socialism" in *The Complete Works of Oscar Wilde* (New York: Harper & Row, 1989), 1079.
2 See Matthew Beaumont's *Utopia, Ltd.: Ideologies of Social Dreaming in England, 1870–1900* (Boston and Leiden: Brill, 2005) for an account of "late nineteenth-century utopianism in its historical and ideological context" (5). In his chapter on Morris, Beaumont points to the importance of the "here and now" for Morris, as indicated by the word "Nowhere." For Beaumont, the novel is a struggle to depict a present that is "present to itself" (172).
3 William Booth, *In Darkest England and the Way Out* (London: McCorquo-dale & Co., 1890), 16. All subsequent references to this text will appear parenthetically.
4 In *Outcast London* (New York: Pantheon, 1971), Gareth Stedman Jones uses the term "social imperialist" to link Booth to other writers of the period who advocated colonization as a solution to England's class problems (308).
5 See Gikandi, "Race and Cosmopolitanism" and Peter Van der Veer, "Colonial Cosmopolitanism" in Steven Vertovec and Robin Cohen, eds., *Conceiving Cosmopolitanism: Theory, Context and Practice* (Oxford: Oxford University Press, 2005), 165–80.
6 Regenia Gagnier, "Good Europeans and Neo-liberal Cosmopolitans: Ethics and Politics in Late Victorian and Contemporary Cosmopolitanism," *Victorian Literature and Culture* 38: 2 (2010), 591–615.

7 See Gandhi, *Affective Communities*, on the internationalism of British social-ism at the *fin de siècle* and its relation to sexual politics. Though the most avant-garde work of this period dealt with sexuality, I do not treat this subject substantially in this book because many of the queer and feminist writers of the *fin de siècle* explicitly shunned totalizing views of the city as part of their critique of normativity.

8 Levine, *The Realistic Imagination*, 8.

9 Ruth Livesey, *Socialism, Sex, and the Culture of Aestheticism in Britain, 1880–1914* (Oxford University Press, 2007), 92, 97.

10 On the intersection between religious thought and cosmopolitanism in the contemporary context, see Srinivas Aravamudan's *Guru English: South Asian Religion in a Cosmopolitan Language* (Princeton University Press, 2005).

11 Northrop Frye, *Anatomy of Criticism* (Princeton University Press, 1957), 90.

12 Barry Qualls, *The Secular Pilgrims of Victorian Fiction* (Cambridge University Press, 1982), 12.

13 *Ibid.*, 15.

14 Stocking, *Victorian Anthropology*, 47–8.

15 Buzard and Childers, "Introduction: Victorian Ethnographies," 351.

16 Buzard, *Disorienting Fiction*, 8.

17 James Clifford, "On Ethnographic Allegory" in James Clifford and George Marcus, eds., *Writing Culture: The Poetics and Politics of Ethnography* (Berkeley, CA: University of California Press, 1986), 101.

18 William Morris, *News from Nowhere* [1890] (London: Penguin, 1993), 117. All subsequent references to this edition will appear parenthetically.

19 *Commonweal* (June 7, 1890), 184.

20 The Crane illustration appeared in *Commonweal* 6: 228 (May 24, 1890).

21 For an extended analysis of *News from Nowhere* as a critique of the realist novel, see Patrick Brantlinger, "*News from Nowhere*: Morris's Socialist Anti-Novel," *Victorian Studies* 19 (1975), 35–49.

22 Buzard, *Disorienting Fiction*, 303.

23 *Ibid.*, 313.

24 See Morris, *News from Nowhere*, 126.

25 David J. Nicoll, "Stanley's Exploits: or, Civilizing Africa," *Commonweal* (April 26, 1890).

26 *Ibid.*

27 Raymond Williams' *The Country and the City* makes this point about many nineteenth-century works and maps out more generally the literary history of the relationship between the "country" and national identity.

28 Cited in Nicholas Salmon, ed., *William Morris on History* (Sheffield: Academic Press, 1996), 12.

29 On Morris' preoccupation with "manliness," see Ruth Livesey's chapter on "William Morris and the Aesthetics of Manly Labour" in her *Socialism, Sex, and the Culture of Aestheticism in Britain*.

30 William Peterson argues that the non-transparency of Kelmscott books always emphasized the materialist presence of the book itself so as to convey

the materializable possibilities of utopian belief. See *The Kelmscott Press: A History of William Morris's Typographical Adventure* (Oxford and New York: Oxford University Press, 1991).

31 This interpretation is also supported by the fact that neither the workers to whom the book was supposedly directed, nor the middle classes, would have been able to buy it in Morris' time. In the utopic future, however, it would presumably be free or accessible to all at the British Library. Kelmscott Press editions were expensive and rare and thus quickly snapped up by collectors – even middle-class readers would have had difficulty getting access to them; *Commonweal*, on the other hand, was reasonably affordable at a penny an issue.

32 David Trotter, *The English Novel in History* (New York: Routledge, 1993), 28.

33 On Dickens' critique of what he calls "telescopic philanthropy" in *Bleak House*, see Chapter 2.

34 Troy Boone, "Remaking 'Lawless Lads and Licentious Girls': The Salvation Army and the Regeneration of Empire" in John Hawley, ed., *Christian Encounters with the Other* (New York: Macmillan, 1998), 117.

35 See Arnold's "The Function of Criticism at the Present Time."

36 See Qualls, *Secular Pilgrims*.

37 Cited in Clifford, "On Ethnographic Allegory," 101.

CHAPTER 5: THE MOMENT AND THE END OF TIME

1 E. M. Forster, *Howard's End* [1910] (New York: Bantam, 1985), 221–2.

2 For Forster, Orwell, and Woolf, I have in mind *Passage to India, Burmese Days,* and *The Voyage Out* respectively.

3 See Ian Baucom, *Out of Place*, on the change in conceptions of British identity "from place to race" in the wake of twentieth-century immigration from the former spaces of empire.

4 In *Modernist Fiction, Cosmopolitanism, and the Politics of Community* (Cambridge University Press, 2001), Jessica Berman makes a well-researched and powerful case for Woolf's commitment to internationalism in her political activism as well as in her literary writing. See in particular Chapter 1 on Woolf's relationship to the Women's Cooperative Guild.

5 Brent Edwards, *The Practice of Diaspora* (Cambridge, MA: Harvard University Press, 2003); Laura Winkiel, *Modernism, Race and Manifestos* (Cambridge University Press, 2008); and Laura Doyle and Laura Winkiel, eds., *Geomodernisms: Race, Modernism, Modernity* (Bloomington, IN: Indiana University Press, 2005).

6 In Berman, *Modernist Fiction, Cosmopolitanism, and the Politics of Community*; Deborah Parsons, *Streetwalking the Metropolis* (Oxford University Press 2000); and Holly Henry, *Virginia Woolf and the Discourse of Science* (Cambridge University Press, 2003). "Global aesthetics" is a phrase used by Henry to describe the relation between Woolf's cosmopolitanism and her interest in astronomy; Henry argues, as I do, that Woolf's idealism is closely

connected to her imagination of the world, though Henry's work highlights the role of her literal contemplation of the globe through astronomical instruments.

7 Berman, *Modernist Fiction*, 15.

8 Walkowitz, *Cosmopolitan Style*, 6.

9 See Chapter 2.

10 Fredric Jameson "Modernism and Imperialism" in Terry Eagleton, Fredric Jameson, and Edward W. Said, *Nationalism, Colonialism and Literature* (Minneapolis, MN: University of Minnesota Press, 1990), 51.

11 Jameson, "Modernism and Imperialism," 58.

12 Forster, *Howard's End*, 248.

13 *Ibid.*, 205.

14 See *The Secret Agent*, ed. Roger Tennant [1907] (New York: Oxford University Press, 1983), 303–5. All subsequent references will appear parenthetically.

15 *Ibid.*, 147.

16 *Mrs. Dalloway* [1925] (New York: Harcourt Brace, 1981), 16. All subsequent references will appear parenthetically.

17 David Glover, "Aliens, Anarchists and Detectives: Legislating the Immigrant Body," *New Formations* 32 (1997), 23. Interestingly, and perhaps not surprisingly, Arthur Conan Doyle was one of those who supported the anti-alien movement (see Glover, "Aliens, Anarchists and Detectives," 25).

18 Sally Ledger and Roger Luckhurst, *The Fin-de-Siécle Reader: A Reader in Cultural History c.1880–1900* (New York: Oxford University Press, 2000), 199.

19 See Holly Henry, *Virginia Woolf and the Discourse of Science*.

20 See Georg Simmel, "The Metropolis and Modern Life" in Kurt H. Wolff, ed., *The Sociology of Georg Simmel* (Glencoe, IL: Free Press, 1964).

21 On degeneration and urban writing, see especially McLaughlin, *Writing the Urban Jungle* and Judith Walkowitz, *City of Dreadful Delight*.

22 Peter Galison, *Einstein's Clocks, Poincaré's Maps: Empires of Time* (New York: W. W. Norton, 2003), 14.

23 *Ibid.*, 85.

24 *Ibid.*, 225

25 *Ibid.*, 327.

26 See Anderson, *Imagined Communities*.

27 Rebecca Walkowitz points out in *Cosmopolitan Style* that *The Secret Agent*'s cosmopolitan subject matter also "helped to shape Conrad's cosmopolitan reputation among early readers," 38.

28 Hermia Oliver, *The International Anarchist Movement in Late Victorian London* (London: Croom Helm/St. Martin's, 1983), 101.

29 George Woodcock, *Anarchism: A History of Libertarian Ideas and Movements* (Cleveland, OH: Meridian, 1962), 371.

30 Bernard Gainer, *The Alien Invasion: The Origins of the Aliens Act of 1905* (London: Heinemann, 1972), 101.

31 Glover, "Aliens, Anarchists and Detectives," 23.

32 See Mark Conroy, "The Panoptical City: the Structure of Suspicion in *The Secret Agent,*" *Conradiana* 15: 3 (1983), 203–17; Alex Houen, "*The Secret Agent*: Anarchism and the Thermodynamics of Law," *English Literary History* 65: 4 (1998): 995–1016; and Michael Whitworth, "Inspector Heat Inspected: *The Secret Agent* and the Meanings of Entropy," *Review of English Studies* 49: 193 (1998): 40–59.

33 See McLaughlin, *Writing the Urban Jungle,* for a book-length study of the urban jungle motif.

34 Donna Haraway, "A Manifesto for Cyborgs: Science, Technology, and Socialist Feminism in the 1980s," *Socialist Review* 80: 15 (1985), 67, 72.

35 Roger Hampson tracks Verloc's perambulations and details which streets in the novel exist, or existed, and which are fictional; see "'Topographical Mysteries': Conrad and London" in *Conrad's Cities,* ed. Gene Moore (Amsterdam and Atlanta: Rodopi, 1992), 159–75.

36 Martin Ray, "The Landscape of *The Secret Agent*" in *Conrad's Cities,* ed. Gene Moore, 97–125.

37 Conroy, in "The Panoptical City," argues that the novel is obsessed with the inescapability of panoptical power, and focuses in particular on the prevalence of metaphors of entrapment and imprisonment.

38 Wolff, *The Sociology of Georg Simmel,* 413.

39 Roger Tennant, Introduction to *The Secret Agent,* xiii.

40 Jonathan Arac, "Romanticism, the Self and the City: *The Secret Agent* in Literary History," *Boundary 2* 9: 1 (1980), 80.

41 Joseph Conrad, "Autocracy and War" in *Notes on Life and Letters* (Charleston, SC: BiblioBazaar, 2006), 75–6.

42 See, for example, Jessica Berman, *Modernist Fiction*; Kathy J. Phillips, *Virginia Woolf against Empire* (Knoxville, TN: University of Tennessee Press, 1994); and Susan M. Squier, *Virginia Woolf and London* (Chapel Hill, NC: Univeristy of North Carolina Press, 1985).

43 Virginia Woolf, "Modern Fiction" in *The Common Reader* (New York: Harcourt, Brace & Co., 1953), 154.

44 Conrad, *The Secret Agent,* 9.

45 Susan Stanford Friedman, "Uncommon Readings: Seeking the Geopolitical Woolf," *South Carolina Review* 29: 1 (1996).

46 Ann Banfield, *Unspeakable Sentences: Narration and Representation in the Language of Fiction* (Boston: Routledge & Kegan Paul, 1982), 316.

47 See Chapter 2.

48 Gillian Beer, "The Island and the Aeroplane: the Case of Virginia Woolf" in Homi Bhabha, ed., *Nation and Narration* (New York: Routledge, 1990), 272.

49 See Beer, "Virginia Woolf and Pre-History" in *Virginia Woolf: The Common Ground* (Ann Arbor, MI: University of Michigan Press, 1996) on the importance of prehistory and the primeval in Woolf's work.

50 "Flying over London," *Vogue,* March 1, 1950: 132.

51 Haraway, "A Manifesto for Cyborgs," 72.

CONCLUSION

1 Colin McCabe *et al.*, "Interview: Salman Rushdie talks to the London Consortium about *The Satanic Verses*," *Critical Quarterly* 38: 1 (1996), 68.

2 John Clement Ball, *Imagining London* (University of Toronto Press, 2004), 5, 7.

3 *Ibid.*, 4–5.

4 See Gillian Gane, "Migrancy, the Cosmopolitan Intellectual and the Global City in *The Satanic Verses*," *Modern Fiction Studies* 48: 1 (Spring 2002), 18–49. Gane argues that the novel reflects a central tension in postcolonial theory by creating an aporia between the claims of authenticity and the liberating energies of mobility, migrancy, and hybridity.

5 This comment is on the commentary track to the DVD version and is cited by Ted Hovet in "The Invisible London of *Dirty Pretty Things*, or Dickens, Frears, and Film Today," *Literary London: Interdisciplinary Studies in the Representation of London* 4: 2 (2006); www.literarylondon.org/London-journal/september 2006/hovet.html, 17 paragraphs (3). See Hovet for an extended comparison of Frears to Dickens.

6 On the relationship between British identity and its oratic places, see Baucom, *Out of Place*.

7 Saskia Sassen, *Cities in a World Economy* (London: Pine Forge Press, 1994), 5.

8 For a full exploration of the twinned themes of bodily violation and economic exploitation, see Emily Davis, "The Intimacies of Globalization: Bodies and Borders On-Screen," *Camera Obscura* 21.62 [2] (2006): 33–73.

9 Ball, *Imagining London*, 245.

10 Kevin Robins, "To London: The City Beyond the Nation" in David Morley and Kevin Robins, eds., *British Culture Studies* (Oxford and New York: Oxford University Press, 2001), 492.

Bibliography

Abrams, M. H. *Natural Supernaturalism*. New York: W. W. Norton & Co., 1971.
    "The Design of *The Prelude*: Wordsworth's Long Journey Home" in *The Prelude 1799, 1805, 1850*, ed. Jonathan Wordsworth, M. H. Abrams, and Stephen Gill, 585–98. New York: Norton, 1979.

Adams, Hazard, ed. *Critical Theory Since Plato*. New York: Harcourt, 1971.

Agathocleous, Tanya. "Cosmopolitanism and Literary Form" *Literature Compass* 7: 6 (June 2010), 452–66.

Aguirre, Robert D. "Annihilating the Distance: Panoramas and the Conquest of Mexico, 1822–1848," *Genre* 35. 1 (Spring 2002), 25–54.

Albert (Prince Consort) and Sir Arthur Helps. *The Principal Speeches and Address of His Royal Highness, The Prince Consort*. London: John Murray, 1862.

Allen, Rick. *The Moving Pageant: A Literary Sourcebook on London Street Life, 1700–1914*. London: Routledge, 1998.

Altick, Richard. *The Shows of London*. Cambridge, MA: Belknap Press, 1978.

Anderson, Amanda. "Cosmopolitanism, Universalism, and the Divided Legacies of Modernity" in *Cosmopolitics: Thinking and Feeling Beyond the Nation*, ed. Pheng Cheah and Bruce Robbins, 265–90. Minneapolis, MN: University of Minnesota Press, 1998.
    The Powers of Distance: Cosmopolitanism and the Cultivation of Detachment. Princeton University Press, 2001.
    The Way We Argue Now. Princeton University Press, 2005.

Anderson, Benedict. *Imagined Communities*. New York: Verso, 1983.
    "Exodus," *Critical Inquiry* 20. 2 (Winter 1994), 314–27.
    "Nationalism, Identity, and the World-in-Motion: On the Logics of Seriality" in *Cosmopolitics: Thinking and Feeling Beyond the Nation*, ed. Pheah Cheng and Bruce Robbins, 117–34. Minneapolis, MN: University of Minnesota Press, 1998.

Anderson, Gregory. *Victorian Clerks*. Manchester University Press, 1976.

Andrews, Maureen Gillespie, ed. *William Wordsworth's "The Sublime in Landscape": Text and Critical Introduction*. University of Rochester Department of English, 1972.

Appiah, Kwame Anthony. "Cosmopolitan Patriots" in Martha Nussbaum and Joshua Cohen, eds., *For Love of Country? Debating the Limits of Patriotism*. Boston: Beacon Press, 1996.

Cosmopolitanism. New York: W.W. Norton & Co., 2006.

Arac, Jonathan. "Romanticism, Self and the City: The Secret Agent in Literary History," *Boundary* 29 (1980), 75–90.

Critical Genealogies: Historical Situations for Postmodern Literary Studies. New York: Columbia University Press, 1987.

Commissioned Spirits: The Shaping of Social Motion in Dickens, Carlyle, Melville, and Hawthorne. New York: Columbia University Press, 1989.

Arata, Stephen. *Fictions of Loss in the Victorian Fin-de-Siècle.* New York: Cambridge University Press, 1996.

Aravamudan, Srinivas. *Guru English: South Asian Religion in a Cosmopolitan Language.* Princeton University Press, 2005.

Arendt, Hannah. *The Origins of Totalitarianism.* San Diego, CA: Harcourt Brace Jovanovich, 1994.

Arnold, Matthew. "The Function of Criticism at the Present Time" in *Poetry and Criticism of Matthew Arnold,* ed. A. Dwight Culler, 237–59. Boston: Houghton Mifflin, 1961.

"Preface to Poems" in *Poetry and Criticism of Matthew Arnold,* ed. A. Dwight Culler, 203–15. Boston: Houghton Mifflin, 1961.

Auerbach, Jeffrey A. *The Great Exhibition of 1851: A Nation of Display.* New Haven, CT: Yale University Press, 1999.

and Peter H. Hoffenberg, eds. *Britain, the Empire, and the World at the Great Exhibition of 1851.* Aldershot: Ashgate, 2008.

Ball, John Clement. *Imagining London.* University of Toronto Press, 2004.

Banfield, Ann. *Unspeakable Sentences: Narration and Representation in the Language of Fiction.* Boston: Routledge & Kegan Paul, 1982.

The Phantom Table. New York: Cambridge University Press, 2000.

Barringer, Tim, Gillian Forrester, and Barbara Martinez-Ruiz. *Art and Emancipation in Jamaica: Isaac Mendes Belisario and His Worlds.* New Haven, CT: Yale Center for British Art and Yale University Press, 2008.

Baucom, Ian. *Out of Place: Englishness, Empire, and the Locations of Identity.* Princeton University Press, 1999.

Beaumont, Matthew. *Utopia Ltd.: Ideologies of Social Dreaming in England 1870–1900.* Boston and Leiden: Brill, 2005.

Beer, Gillian. *The Romance.* London: Methuen, 1970.

Darwin's Plots: Evolutionary Narrative in Darwin, George Eliot and Nineteenth-Century Fiction. Boston: Arc Paperbacks, 1983.

"The Island and the Aeroplane: the Case of Virginia Woolf" in *Nation and Narration,* ed. Homi Bhabha, 265–90. New York: Routledge, 1990.

Virginia Woolf: The Common Ground. Ann Arbor, MI: University of Michigan Press, 1996.

"Virginia Woolf and Pre-History'" in *Virginia Woolf: the Common Ground.* Ann Arbor, MI: University of Michigan Press, 1996.

Bell, Duncan. *The Idea of Greater Britain: Empire and the Future of World Order: 1860–1900.* Princeton University Press, 2007.

ed. *Victorian Visions of Global Order.* Cambridge University Press, 2007.

Bellamy, Edward. *Looking Backward.* New York: Dover Publications, 1996.

Benjamin, Walter. *Charles Baudelaire: A Lyric Poet in the Era of High Capitalism,* trans. Harry Zohn. London: New Left Books, 1973.

Berman, Jessica. *Modernist Fiction, Cosmopolitanism, and the Politics of Community.* Cambridge University Press, 2001.

Bhabha, Homi, ed. *Nation and Narration.* New York: Routledge, 1990.

Bindé, Jérôme. "Towards an Ethics of the Future" in *Globalization,* ed. Arjun Appadurai, 90–114. Durham, NC: Duke University Press, 2001.

Binnie, Jon *et al.,* eds. *Cosmopolitan Urbanism.* New York: Routledge, 2006.

Bohman, James and Matthias Lutz-Bachmann. "Introduction" in *Perpetual Peace: Essays on Kant's Cosmopolitan Ideal,* ed. James Bohman and Matthias Lutz-Bachmann. Cambridge, MA: MIT Press, 1997.

Boone, Troy. "Remaking 'Lawless Lads and Licentious Girls': The Salvation Army and the Regeneration of Empire" in *Historicizing Christian Encounters with the Other,* ed. John Hawley, 103–21. New York: Macmillan, 1998.

Booth, Charles. *Life and Labour of the People in London.* New York: AMS, 1970.

Booth, William. *In Darkest England and the Way Out.* London: McCorquodale & Co., 1890.

Brantlinger, Patrick. "*News from Nowhere*: Morris's Socialist Anti-Novel," *Victorian Studies* 19 (1975), 35–49.

  Rule of Darkness: British Literature and Imperialism 1830–1914. Ithaca, NY: Cornell University Press, 1988.

Breckenridge, Carol A., Sheldon Pollock, Homi K. Bhabha, and Dinesh Chakrabarty, eds. *Cosmopolitanism.* Durham, NC: Duke University Press, 2002.

Brennan, Timothy. *At Home in the World: Cosmopolitanism Now.* Cambridge, MA: Harvard University Press, 1997.

Brewster, Dorothy. *Virginia Woolf's London.* New York University Press, 1960.

Briggs, Asa. *1851.* London: Historical Association, 1951.

  Victorian Cities. London: Penguin, 1990.

Britton, John. *A brief account of the Colosseum, in the Regent's Park, London: Comprising a description of the building: The panoramic view from the top of St. Paul's Cathedral; the conservatory, &c.* London: T. Bensley, 1829.

Brown, William Wells. *An American Fugitive in Europe: Sketches of Places and People Abroad.* Boston: J. P. Jewett, 1854.

Burford, J. *Description of a view of the city of Edinburgh and surrounding country, now exhibiting in the Panorama Leicester Square.* London: J. & C. Adlard, 1825.

Burford, Robert. *Description of a View of the City of Calcutta; now Exhibiting at the Panorama, Leicester Square.* London: J. & C. Adlard, 1830.

  Description of the view of the City of Mexico, and surrounding country, now exhibiting in the Panorama, Leicester Square. London: J. & C. Adland, 1826.

Burton, Antoinette M. *At the Heart of the Empire: Indians and the Colonial Encounter in Late-Victorian Britain.* Berkeley, CA: University of California Press, 1998.

Buzard, James. "'Anywhere's Nowhere': *Bleak House* as Metropolitan Autoethnography," *Yale Journal of Criticism* 12: 1 (1999), 7–39.

Disorienting Fiction: The Autoethnographic Work of Nineteenth-Century British Novels. Princeton University Press, 2005.

"'The Country of the Plague': Anticulture and Autoethnography in Dickens's 1850s," *Victorian Literature and Culture* 38: 2 (2010), 413–21.

and Joseph Childers. "Introduction: Victorian Ethnographies," *Victorian Studies* 41: 3 (Spring 1998), 351–3.

Buzard, James, Joseph W. Childers, and Eileen Gillooly, eds. *Victorian Prism: Refractions of the Crystal Palace.* Charlottesville, VA: University of Virginia Press, 2007.

Byerly, Alison. "Effortless Art: the Sketch in Nineteenth-Century Painting and Literature," *Criticism* 41: 3 (Summer 1999), 349–64.

Cain, P. J. "Economics and Empire: the Metropolitan Context" in *The Oxford History of the British Empire, Vol. III: The Nineteenth Century,* ed. Andrew Porter. Oxford and New York: Oxford University Press, 2001.

Cannadine, David. *Ornamentalism.* New York: Oxford University Press, 2001.

Carpenter, Mary Wilson. "Medical Cosmopolitanism: *Middlemarch,* Cholera, and the Pathologies of English Masculinity," *Victorian Literature and Culture* 38: 2 (2010), 511–29.

Casanova, Pascale. *The World Republic of Letters.* Cambridge, MA: Harvard University Press, 2004.

Certeau, Michel de. *The Practice of Everyday Life.* Berkeley, CA: University of California Press, 1984.

Chakrabarty, Dipesh. *Provincializing Europe.* Princeton University Press, 2000.

Chamberlin, J. Edward and Sander L. Gilman. *Degeneration: the Dark Side of Progress.* New York: Columbia University Press, 1995.

Chase, Karen and Michael Levenson. "Mayhew, the Prince and the Poor" in *Victorian Prism: Refractions of the Crystal Palace,* ed. James Buzard, Joseph W. Childers, and Eileen Gillooly. Charlottesville, VA: University of Virginia Press, 2007.

Cheah, Pheng. *Inhuman Conditions: On Cosmopolitanism and Human Rights.* Cambridge, MA: Harvard University Press, 2007.

Cheah, Pheng and Bruce Robbins, eds. *Cosmopolitics: Thinking and Feeling Beyond the Nation.* Minneapolis, MN: University of Minnesota Press, 1998.

Cheyette, Bryan. *Constructions of "the Jew" in English Literature and Society.* Cambridge University Press, 1993.

Claybaugh, Amanda. *The Novel of Purpose: Literature and Social Reform in the Anglo-American World.* Ithaca, NY: Cornell University Press, 2006

Clifford, James. "On Ethnographic Allegory" in *Writing Culture: The Poetics and Politics of Ethnography,* ed. James Clifford and George Marcus, 98–121. Berkeley, CA: University of California Press, 1986.

Cohen, Margaret and Carolyn Dever, eds. *The Literary Channel: the Inter-National Invention of the Novel.* Princeton University Press, 2002.

Cole, Henry. *On the International Results of the Exhibition of 1851.* London: David Bogue, 1852.

Comment, Bernard. *The Panorama*, trans. Ann-Marie Glasheen. London: Reaktion Books, 1999.

Conrad, Joseph. "Autocracy and War" in *Notes on Life and Letters.* Charleston, NC: BiblioBazaar, 2006.

The Secret Agent, ed. Roger Tennant [1907]. New York: Oxford University Press, 1983.

Conroy, Mark. "The Panoptical City: The Structure of Suspicion in *The Secret Agent*," *Conradiana* 15: 3 (1983), 203–17.

Crary, Jonathan. *Techniques of the Observer.* Boston: MIT Press, 1992.

Curtis, L. Perry. *Apes and Angels: The Irishman in Victorian Caricature.* Washington: Smithsonian Institution Press, 1971.

Davis, Emily. "The Intimacies of Globalization: Bodies and Borders On-Screen," *Camera Obscura* 62 21:62[2] (2006), 33–73.

Davis, John R. *The Great Exhibition.* Stroud: Sutton, 1999.

Derrida, Jacques, *On Cosmopolitanism and Forgiveness.* New York: Routledge, 2001.

Dicey, Edward. "Why England is Unpopular," *Cosmopolis* 4 (December 1896).

Dickens, Charles. *Master Humphrey's Clock.* Philadelphia, PA: Jesper Harding, 1847.

Sketches by Boz. New York and Boston: Books Inc., 1968.

Bleak House, ed. Norman Page. Harmondsworth: Penguin, 1971.

Don Vann, J. and Rosemary T. VanArsdel, eds. *Periodicals of Queen Victoria's Empire: An Exploration.* University of Toronto Press, 1996.

Doyle, Arthur Conan. "The Adventure of the Cardboard Box" in *The Original Illustrated 'Strand' Sherlock Holmes*, 307–30. Ware, Hertfordshire: Wordsworth Editions, 1989.

"The Adventure of the Engineer's Thumb" in *The Original Illustrated 'Strand' Sherlock Holmes*, 230–43. Ware, Hertfordshire: Wordsworth Editions, 1989.

"The Adventure of Speckled Band" in *The Original Illustrated 'Strand' Sherlock Holmes*, 214–30. Ware, Hertfordshire: Wordsworth Editions, 1989.

"The Sign of Four" in *The Original Illustrated 'Strand' Sherlock Holmes*, 64–117. Ware, Hertfordshire: Wordsworth Editions, 1989.

A Study in Scarlet. New York: Oxford University Press, 1994.

Doyle, Laura and Laura Winkiel, eds. *Geomodernisms: Race, Modernism, Modernity.* Bloomington, IN: Indiana University Press, 2005.

Eagleton, Terry, Fredric Jameson, and Edward W. Said. *Nationalism, Colonialism and Literature.* Minneapolis, MN: University of Minnesota Press, 1990.

Edel, Leon and Lyall H. Powers, eds. *The Complete Notebooks of Henry James.* New York: Oxford University Press, 1987.

Edwards, Brent. *The Practice of Diaspora.* Cambridge, MA: Harvard University Press, 2003.

Epstein, Hugh. "A Pier-Glass in the Cavern: London in *The Secret Agent*" in *Conrad's Cities*, ed. Gene Moore, 175–97. Amsterdam and Atlanta, GA: Rodopi, 1992.

Esty, Jed. *A Shrinking Island: Modernism and National Culture in England.* Princeton University Press, 2004.

Fabian, Johannes. *Time and the Other.* New York: Columbia University Press, 2002.

Fillingham, Lydia Alix. "'The Colorless Skein of Life': Threats to the Private Sphere in Conan Doyle's *A Study in Scarlet*," *English Literary History* 56: 3 (1989), 667–88.

Fleishman, Avrom. "The Symbolic World of *The Secret Agent*," *ELH* 32: 2 (1965), 196–219.

Flint, Kate. *The Victorians and the Visual Imagination.* New York: Cambridge University Press, 2000.

Forrester, Gillian. "Mapping a New Kingston: Belisario's Sketches of Character" in Tim Barringer, Gillian Forrester, and Barbara Martinez-Ruiz, *Art and Emancipation in Jamaica: Isaac Mendes Belisario and His Worlds* New Haven: Yale Center for British Art and Yale University Press, 2008.

Forster, E. M. *Howard's End* [1910]. New York: Bantam, 1985.

Foucault, Michel. *Discipline and Punish: The Birth of the Prison.* New York: Vintage, 1995.

Freedman, Jonathan L. *Professions of Taste: Henry James, British Aestheticism and Commodity Culture.* Stanford University Press, 1990.

Friedman, Susan Stanford, "Uncommon Readings: Seeking the Geopolitical Woolf," *South Carolina Review* 29: 1 (1996), 24–44.

Frye, Northrop. *Anatomy of Criticism.* Princeton University Press, 1957.

"Varieties of Literary Utopias," *Daedalus* 94 (1965), 323–47.

Gainer, Bernard. *The Alien Invasion: The Origins of the Aliens Act of 1905.* London: Heinemann, 1972.

Gagnier, Regenia. "Good Europeans and Neo-liberal Cosmopolitans: Ethics and Politics in Late Victorian and Contemporary Cosmopolitanism," *Victorian Literature and Culture* 38: 2 (2110).

Galison, Peter. "Einstein's Clocks: the Place of Time," *Critical Inquiry* 26: 2 (Winter 2000), 355–89.

Einstein's Clocks, Poincaré's Maps: Empires of Time. New York: W. W. Norton, 2003.

Galperin, William. *The Return of the Visible in British Romanticism.* Baltimore, MD: Johns Hopkins University Press, 1993.

Gandhi, Leela. *Affective Communities: Anticolonial Thought, Fin-de-Siècle Radicalism, and the Politics of Friendship.* Durham, NC: Duke University Press, 2006.

Gane, Gillian. "Migrancy, the Cosmopolitan Intellectual and the Global City in *The Satanic Verses*," *Modern Fiction Studies* 48: 1 (Spring 2002), 18–49.

Garcha, Amanpal, "Styles of Stillness and Motion: Market Culture and Narrative Form in *Sketches by Boz*," *Dickens Studies Annual* 30 (2001), 1–22.

Gerzina, Gretchen. *Black London: Life Before Emancipation.* London: John Murray, 1995.

Gibbs-Smith, C. H., ed. *The Great Exhibition of 1851: A Commemorative Album.* London: HMSO, 1950.

Gidal, Eric. *Poetic Exhibitions: Romantic Aesthetics and the Pleasures of the British Musuem*. Lewisburg: Bucknell University Press, 2001.

Gikandi, Simon. "Race and Cosmopolitanism," *American Literary History* 14: 3 (2002), 593–615.

Gilbert, Pamela K., ed. *Imagined Londons*. Albany, NY: State University of New York Press, 2002.

Mapping the Victorian Social Body. Albany, NY: State University of New York Press, 2004.

Gilroy, Paul. *Against Race*. Cambridge, MA: Harvard University Press, 2002.

Postcolonial Melancholia. New York: Columbia University Press, 2007.

Glover, David. "Aliens, Anarchists and Detectives: Legislating the Immigrant Body," *New Formations* 32 (1997), 22–32.

Gogwilt, Christopher. *The Fiction of Geopolitics: Afterimages of Culture, from Wilkie Collins to Alfred Hitchcock*. Stanford University Press, 2000.

Goodlad, Lauren M. E. "Trollopian 'Foreign Policy': Rootedness and Cosmopolitanism in the Mid-Victorian Global Imaginary," *PMLA* 124: 2 (March 2009), 437–54.

"Cosmopolitanism's Actually Existing Beyond: Towards a Victorian Geopolitical Aesthetic," *Victorian Literature and Culture* 38: 2 (2010), 399–413.

Goodlad, Lauren M. E. and Julia M. Wright. "Introduction and Keywords." Special Issue on "Victorian Internationalisms." *Romanticism and Victorianism on the Net* 48 (2007).

Greenwood, Frederick. "The Safeguards of Peace," *Cosmopolis* 2 (May 1896).

Gurney, Peter. "An Appropriated Space: the Great Exhibition, the Crystal Palace and the Working Class" in *The Great Exhibition of 1851: New Interdisciplinary Essays*, ed. Louise Purbrick. Manchester University Press, 2001.

Hall, Stuart. "The Local and the Global: Globalization and Ethnicity" in *Culture, Globalization, and the World-System: Contemporary Conditions for the Representation of Identity*, ed. Anthony D. King. Minneapolis, MN: University of Minnesota Press, 1997.

Hampson, Roger. "'Topographical Mysteries': Conrad and London" in *Conrad's Cities*, ed. Gene Moore, 159–75. Amsterdam and Atlanta, GA: Rodopi, 1992.

Hanley, Keith and Greg Kucich. "Introduction: Global Formations and Recalcitrances," *Nineteenth-Century Contexts* 29: 2 (2007), 73–88.

Haraway, Donna. "A Manifesto for Cyborgs: Science, Technology, and Socialist Feminism in the 1980s," *Socialist Review* 80: 15 (1985), 65–107.

Hardt, Michael and Antonio Negri. *Empire*. Cambridge, MA: Harvard University Press, 2000.

Harrison, Frederic. "The True Cosmopolis," *Cosmopolis* 3 (August 1896).

Harvey, David. "Cosmopolitanism and the Banality of Geographical Evils," *Public Culture* 12: 2[31] (Spring, 2000), 529–64.

Spaces of Hope. Berkeley, CA: University of California Press, 2000.

"The Cartographic Imagination: Balzac in Paris" in *Cosmopolitan Geographies: New Locations in Literature and Culture*, ed. Vinay Dharwadker, 63–87. New York: Routledge, 2001.

Cosmopolitanism and the Geographies of Freedom. New York: Columbia University Press, 2009.

Hayles, N. Katherine. *The Cosmic Web: Scientific Field Models and Literary Strategies in the Twentieth Century.* Ithaca, NY: Cornell University Press, 1984.

How We Became Posthuman: Virtual bodies in Cybernetics, Literature, and Informatics. University of Chicago Press, 1999.

Henry, Holly. *Virginia Woolf and the Discourse of Science.* Cambridge University Press, 2003.

Henson, Louise, *et al. Culture and Science in the Nineteenth-Century Media.* Aldershot: Ashgate, 2004.

Herbert, Christopher. *Culture and Anomie.* University of Chicago Press, 1991.

Hertz, Neil. *The End of the Line: Essays on Psychoanalysis and the Sublime.* New York: Columbia University Press, 1985.

Hoffenberg, Peter H. *An Empire on Display.* Berkeley, CA, University of California Press, 2001.

Holton, Robert John. "Cosmopolitanism or Cosmopolitanisms? The Universal Races Congress of 1911," *Global Networks* 2 (2002), 153–70.

Houen, Alex. "*The Secret Agent*: Anarchism and the Thermodynamics of Law," *English Literary History* 65: 4 (1998), 995–1016.

Hovet, Ted. "The Invisible London of *Dirty Pretty Things*; or Dickens, Frears, and Film Today," *Literary London: Interdisciplinary Studies in the Representation of London* 4: 2 (2006); www.literarylondon.org/london-journal/september2006/hovet.html, 17 paragraphs.

Howe, Anthony. "Free Trade and Global Order" in Duncan Bell, ed., *Victorian Visions of Global Order.* Cambridge University Press, 2007.

Humpherys, Anne. *Henry Mayhew.* Boston: Twayne Publishers, 1984.

Hutton, Sean. "The Irish in London" in Nick Merriman, ed., *The Peopling of London.* Museum of London, 1993.

Innes, C. L. *A History of Black and Asian Writing in Britain.* Cambridge University Press, 2008.

Jacobs, Jane. *The Death and Life of Great American Cities.* New York: Vintage, 1992.

James, Henry. *Letters*, ed. Leon Edel. 3 vols. Cambridge, MA: Harvard University Press, 1974–84.

"Art of Fiction" in *The Portable Henry James*, ed. Morton Dauwen Zabel, 387–414. New York: Penguin, 1977.

"London" in *The Portable Henry James*, ed. Morton Dauwen Zabel, 513–32. New York: Penguin, 1977.

The Princess Casamassima. New York: Penguin, 1987.

Jameson, Fredric. *The Political Unconscious: Narrative as a Socially Symbolic Act.* Ithaca, NY: Cornell University Press, 1981.

"Modernism and Imperialism" in Terry Eagleton, Fredric Jameson, and Edward W. Said, *Nationalism, Colonialism and Literature.* Minneapolis, MN: University of Minnesota Press, 1990.

Postmodernism, or The Cultural Logic of Late Capitalism. Durham, NC: Duke University Press, 1992.

"Cognitive Mapping" in *Marxism and the Interpretation of Culture*, ed. Cary Nelson and Larry Grossberg, 347–57. Urbana, IL: University of Illinois Press, 1998.

Archaeologies of the Future. New York: Verso, 2005.

Jay, Martin. *Downcast Eyes*. Berkeley, CA: University of California Press, 1994.

Jerrold, Blanchard and Gustave Doré. *London: a Pilgrimage* [1872]. New York: Dover, 1970.

Joshi, Priya. *In Another Country: Colonialism, Culture, and the English Novel in India*. New York: Columbia University Press, 2002.

Joyce, Simon. *Capital Offenses: Geographies of Class and Crime in Victorian London*. Charlottesville, VA: University of Virginia Press, 2003.

Kant, Immanuel. "To Perpetual Peace: a Philosophical Sketch" in *Perpetual Peace and Other Essays on Politics, History, and Morals*, trans. Ted Humphrey. Indianapolis, IN: Hackett, 1983.

Keirstead, Christopher. "A 'Bad Patriot'?: Elizabeth Barrett Browning and Cosmopolitanism," *Victorians Institute Journal* 33 (2005), 69–95.

"Stranded at the Border: Browning, France, and the Challenge of Cosmopolitanism in Red Cotton Night-Cap Country," *Victorian Poetry* 43: 4 (Winter 2005), 411–34.

Keith, Michael. *After the Cosmopolitan? Multicultural Cities and the Future of Racism*. London and New York: Routledge, 2005.

Kelley, Theresa. *Wordsworth's Revolutionary Aesthetics*. New York: Cambridge University Press, 1988.

Kern, Stephen. *The Culture of Space and Time 1880–1918*. Cambridge, MA: Harvard University Press, 1983.

King, Ross. "Wordsworth, Panoramas, and the Prospect of London," *Studies in Romanticism* 32: 1 (1993), 57–73.

Koenigsberger, Kurt. *The Novel and the Menagerie: Totality, Englishness, and Empire*. Columbus, OH: Ohio University State Press, 2007.

Kriegel, Lara. "Narrating the Subcontinent in 1851: India at the Crystal Palace" in *The Great Exhibition of 1851: New Interdisciplinary Essays*, ed. Louise Purbrick. New York: Manchester University Press, 2001.

Lauster, Martina. *Sketches of the Nineteenth Century: European Journalism and its Physiologies, 1830–50*. New York: Palgrave, Macmillan 2007.

Ledger, Sally and Roger Luckhurst. *The Fin-de-Siècle Reader: A Reader in Cultural History c.1880–1900*. New York: Oxford University Press, 2000.

Levine, Caroline. "Strategic Formalism: Toward a New Method in Cultural Studies," *Victorian Studies* 48: 4 (Summer 2006), 625–57.

"Scaled up, Writ Small: a Response to Carolyn Dever and Herbert F. Tucker," *Victorian Studies* 49: 1 (Autumn 2006), 100–105.

Levine, George. *The Realistic Imagination: English Fiction from Frankenstein to Lady Chatterley*. University of Chicago Press, 1981.

Lindenberger, Herbert. *On Wordsworth's Prelude*. Princeton University Press, 1963.

Liu, Alan. *The Sense of History*. Stanford University Press, 1989.

Livesey, Ruth. *Socialism, Sex, and the Culture of Aestheticism in Britain, 1880–1914.* Oxford University Press, 2007.

Lukács, Georg. *The Theory of the Novel,* trans. Anna Bostock. Boston, MA: MIT Press, 1971.

Studies in European Realism. London, Merlin Press, 1972.

Mackenzie, John M. "Empire and Metropolitan Cultures" in *The Oxford History of the British Empire.* Vol. III: *The Nineteenth Century,* ed. Andrew Porter. Oxford and New York: Oxford University Press, 2001.

Marcus, Sharon. "Same Difference? Transnationalism, Comparative Literature, and Victorian Studies," *Victorian Studies* 45: 4 (2003), 677–86.

Mare, Eric de. *Victorian London Revealed: Gustav Doré's Metropolis.* London: Penguin, 2001.

Marin, Louis. *Utopics: Spatial Play.* Atlantic Highlands, NJ: Humanities Press, 1984.

Marsh, Joss. "Spectacle" in *A Companion to Victorian Literature and Culture,* ed. Herbert Tucker, 276–87. Malden: Blackwell, 1999.

Marx, Karl and Friedrich Engels, *The Communist Manifesto* [1848], ed. Frederic L. Bender. New York: Norton, 1988.

Masterman, Charles Frederick Gurney. *The Heart of the Empire.* London: T. Fisher Unwin, 1901.

Maxwell, Richard. *The Mysteries of Paris and London.* Charlottesville, VA: University of Virginia Press, 1992.

Mayhew, Henry. *London Labour and the London Poor* [1865]. New York: Penguin, 1985.

Mayhew, Henry and John Binny. *The Criminal Prisons of London and Scenes of Prison Life.* London: Cass, 1968.

McCabe, Colin, *et al.* "Interview: Salman Rushdie talks to the London Consortium about *The Satanic Verses,*" *Critical Quarterly* 38: 1 (1996), 50–70.

McClintock, Anne. *Imperial Leather.* New York: Routledge, 1995.

McClure, John A. *Late Imperial Romance.* New York: Verso, 1994.

McLaughlin, Joseph. *Writing the Urban Jungle: Reading Empire in London from Doyle to Eliot.* Charlottesville, VA: University Press of Virginia, 2000.

Menke, Richard. *Telegraphic Realism: Victorian Fiction and Other Information Systems.* Stanford University Press, 2008.

Merriman, Nick, ed. *The Peopling of London: Fifteen Thousand Years of Settlement from Overseas.* Museum of London, 1993.

Merriman, Nick, and Rozina, Visram. "The World in a City" in Nick Merriman, ed., *The Peopling of London.* Museum of London, 1993.

Message, Kylie and Ewan Johnston. "The World within the City: The Great Exhibition, Race, Class and Social Reform" in Jeffrey A. Auerbach and Peter H. Hoffenberg, eds. *Britain, the Empire, and the World at the Great Exhibition of 1851.* Aldershot: Ashgate, 2008.

Michie, Helena. *Victorian Honeymoons: Journeys to the Conjugal.* Cambridge University Press, 2007.

Mignolo, Walter D. "The Many Faces of Cosmo-polis: Border Thinking and Critical Cosmopolitanism" in *Cosmopolitanism,* ed. Carol A. Breckenridge,

Sheldon Pollock, Homi K. Bhabha, and Dinesh Chakrabarty, 157–89. Durham, NC: Duke University Press, 2002.

Miller, J. Hillis. "Interpretation in Bleak House" in *Bleak House: Charles Dickens*, ed. Jeremy Tambling, 29–53. New York: St. Martin's Press, 1998.

Mitchell, Timothy. *Colonising Egypt*. New York: Cambridge University Press, 1988.

"The World as Exhibition," *Comparative Studies in Society and History*, 31: 2 (April 1989), 217–36.

Moore, Gene M., ed. *Conrad's Cities*. Amsterdam and Atlanta, GA: Rodopi, 1992.

Morris, William. *News from Nowhere* [1890]. London: Penguin, 1993.

Nagel, Thomas. *The View from Nowhere*. New York: Oxford University Press, 1986.

Nord, Deborah Epstein. *Walking the Victorian Streets*. Ithaca, NY: Cornell University Press, 1995.

Oetermann, Stefan. *The Panorama: History of a Mass Medium*. New York: Zone, 1997.

Oliver, Hermia. *The International Anarchist Movement in Late Victorian London*. London: Croom Helm/St. Martin's, 1983.

Parsons, Deborah. *Streetwalking the Metropolis*. Oxford University Press, 2000.

Pater, Walter. "Coleridge" in *Selected Writings of Walter Pater*, ed. Harold Bloom. New York: Columbia University Press, 1982.

The Renaissance: Studies in Art and Poetry in Walter Pater: Three Major Texts, ed. William E. Buckler. New York University Press, 1986.

Pearson, Ronald. "Thackeray and Punch at the Exhibition: Authority and Ambivalence in Verbal and Visual Caricatures" in *The Great Exhibition of 1851*, ed. Louise Purbrick, Manchester University Press, 2001.

Pecora, Vincent. *Secularization and Cultural Criticism: Religion, Nation, and Modernity*. University of Chicago Press, 2006.

Peters, John G. "Joseph Conrad's 'Sudden Holes' in Time: the Epistemology of Temporality," *Studies in the Novel* 32: 4 (2000), 420–41.

Peterson, William. *The Kelmscott Press: A History of William Morris's Typographical Adventure*. Oxford and New York: Oxford University Press, 1991.

Phillips, Kathy J. *Virginia Woolf against Empire*. Knoxville, TN: University of Tennessee Press, 1994.

Pick, Daniel. *Faces of Degeneration: A European Disorder*. Cambridge University Press, 1989.

Pike, David. *Metropolis on the Styx: The Underworlds of Modern Urban Culture, 1800–2001*. Ithaca, NY: Cornell University Press, 2007.

Plotz, John. *The Crowd: British Literature and Public Politics*. Berkeley, CA: University of California Press, 2000.

Posnock, Ross. *The Trial of Curiosity: Henry James, William James, and the Challenge of Modernity*. New York: Oxford University Press, 1991.

"The Dream of Deracination: The Uses of Cosmopolitanism," *American Literary History* 12: 4 (2000), 802–18.

Pubrick, Louise, ed. *The Great Exhibition of 1851*. Manchester University Press, 2001.

Puchner, Martin. *Poetry of the Revolution: Marx, Manifestoes and the Avant-Garde*. Princeton University Press, 2006.

Pugh, Simon. *Reading Landscape: Country, City, Capital.* Manchester and New York: Manchester University Press, 1990.

Pykett, Lynn, ed. *Reading Fin-de-siècle Fictions.* New York: Longman, 1996.

Qualls, Barry, *The Secular Pilgrims of Victorian Fiction.* Cambridge University Press, 1982.

Ray, Martin. "The Landscape of *The Secret Agent*" in *Conrad's Cities*, ed. Gene Moore, 97–125. Amsterdam and Atlanta, GA: Rodopi, 1992.

Reid, Julia. "*The Academy* and *Cosmopolis*: Evolution and Culture in Robert Louis Stevenson's Periodical Encounters" in Louise Henson *et al.*, *Culture and Science in the Nineteenth-Century Media.* Aldershot: Ashgate, 2004.

Richards, Thomas. *The Imperial Archive.* New York: Verso, 1993.

Robbins, Bruce. "Telescopic Philanthropy: Professionalism and Responsibility in *Bleak House*" in *Nation and Narration*, ed. Homi Bhabha, 213–30. London: Routledge, 1990.

  "Introduction Part I: Actually Existing Cosmopolitanisms" in *Cosmopolitics: Thinking and Feeling Beyond the Nation*, ed. Pheng Cheah and Bruce Robbins, 1–20. Minneapolis, MN: University of Minnesota Press, 1998.

  Feeling Global: Internationalism in Distress. New York University Press, 1999.

  "Victorian Cosmopolitanism, Interrupted," *Victorian Literature and Culture* 38: 2 (2010), 421–7.

Robertson, Roland. *Globalization: Social Theory and Global Culture.* London: Sage, 1991.

Robins, Kevin. "To London: the City Beyond the Nation" in *British Cultural Studies*, ed. David Morley and Kevin Robins, 473–95. Oxford and New York: Oxford University Press, 2001.

Said, Edward W. *Culture and Imperialism.* New York: Knopf, 1993.

Sala, George. "The Streets of the World." *Temple Bar* 10 (March 1864).

Salmon, Nicholas, ed. *William Morris on History.* Sheffield Academic Press, 1996.

Sandhu, Sukhdev. *London Calling: How Black and Asian Writers Imagined a City.* London: Harper Perennial, 2004.

Sassen, Saskia. *Cities in a World Economy.* London: Pine Forge Press, 1994.

  Globalization and its Discontents. New York: New Press, 1998.

Schlereth, Thomas J. *The Cosmopolitan Ideal in Enlightenment Thought, Its Form and Function in the Ideas of Franklin, Hume, and Voltaire, 1694–1790.* University of Notre Dame Press, 1977.

Schneer, Jonathan. *London 1900.* New Haven, CT: Yale University Press, 2000.

Seltzer, Mark. "*The Princess Casamassima*: Realism and the Fantasy of Surveillance," *Nineteenth-Century Fiction* 35: 4 (1981), 506–34.

Sha, Richard. *The Visual and Verbal Sketch in British Romanticism.* Philadelphia, PA: University of Pennsylvania Press, 1997.

Sharpe, William Chapman. *Unreal Cities: Urban Figuration in Wordsworth, Baudelaire, Whitman, Eliot, and Williams.* Baltimore, MD, and London: Johns Hopkins University Press, 1990.

Shaw, Philip. "'Mimic Sights': A Note on Panorama and other Indoor Displays in Book VII of *The Prelude*," *Notes and Queries* 40 (1993), 462–4.

"Romantic Space: Topo-analysis and Subjectivity in *The Prelude*" in *The Prelude: Theory in Practice*, ed. Nigel Wood. Buckingham and Philadelphia: Open University Press, 1993.

Shesgreen, Sean. *Images of the Outcast: the Urban Poor in the Cries of London.* New Brunswick, NJ: Rutgers University Press, 2002.

Silver, Carole. *Strange and Secret People: Fairies and Victorian Consciousness.* New York: Oxford University Press, 1999.

Simmel, Georg. "The Metropolis and Modern Life" in Kurt Wolff, ed., *The Sociology of Georg Simmel.* Glencoe, IL: Free Press, 1964.

Slater, Michael, ed. *Dickens' Journalism.* Vol. I. *The Amusements of the People and Other Papers: Reports, Essays, and Reviews, 1834–51.* Columbus, OH: Ohio University Press, 1996.

Smith, Charles Manby. *The Little World of London: or, Pictures in Little of London Life.* London: Arthur Hall, Virtue, & Co., 1857.

Smith, J. R. *Descriptive Book of the Tour of Europe: the Largest Moving Panorama in the World.* New York: Pettinger & Gray, 1855.

Snaith, Anna. *Public and Private Negotiations.* New York: St. Martin's Press, 2000.

Spivak, Gayatri Chakravorty. "Three Women's Texts and a Critique of Imperialism," *Critical Inquiry* 12 (1985), 243–61.

Squier, Susan M. *Virginia Woolf and London.* Chapel Hill, NC: University of North Carolina Press, 1985.

Stedman Jones, Gareth. *Outcast London.* New York: Pantheon, 1971.

Stocking, George. *Victorian Anthropology.* New York: Free Press, 1987.

Sullivan, Alvin, ed. *British Literary Magazines: The Victorian and Edwardian Age, 1837–1913.* Westport, CT: Greenwood Press, 1983–6.

Tamarkin, Elisa. "Black Anglophilia; or, the Sociability of Anti-Slavery," *American Literary History* 14: 3 (2002), 444–78.

Temple, Richard. *Cosmopolitan Essays.* London: Chapman & Hall, 1886.

Tobin, Thomas. "A Method and Formula for Quantifying Timeliness in Nineteenth-Century Periodicals." Unpublished conference paper.

Trilling, Lionel. "The Princess Casamassima" in *Critics on Henry James*, ed. J. Don Vann. University of Miami Press, 1972.

Trotter, David. *The English Novel in History.* New York: Routledge, 1993.

Trumpener, Katie. *Bardic Nationalism: the Romantic Novel and the British Empire.* Princeton University Press, 1997.

"City Scenes: Commerce, Utopia, and the Birth of the Picture Book" in *The Victorian Illustrated Book*, ed. Richard Maxwell, 332–84. Charlottesville, VA: University of Virginia Press, 2002.

"The World in Images: Nineteenth-Century Picture Worlds and Modernist Ways of Seeing." Unpublished essay.

Twitchell, James B. *Romantic Horizons: Aspects of the Sublime in English Poetry and Painting, 1770–1850.* Columbia: University of Missouri Press, 1983.

Tylor, E. B. *Primitive Culture*, 2 vols. [1871]. London: John Murray, 1873.

Usui, Masami. "The Female Victims of the War in Mrs. Dalloway" in *Virginia Woolf and War*, ed. Mark Hussey, 151–63. Syracuse University Press, 1991.

Van der Veer, Peter. "Colonial Cosmopolitanism" in Steven Vertovec and Robin Cohen, eds., *Conceiving Cosmopolitanism: Theory, Context and Practice.* Oxford University Press, 2005.

Vertovec, Steven and Robin Cohen, eds. *Conceiving Cosmopolitanism: Theory, Context and Practice.* Oxford and New York: Oxford University Press, 2002.

Visram, Rozina. "South Asians in London" in *The Peopling of London: Fifteen Thousand Years of Settlement from Overseas*, ed. Nick Merriman. Museum of London, 1993.

Vries, Leonard de. *Panorama 1842–1864: The World of the Early Victorians as Seen through the Eyes of the Illustrated London News.* London: Marshall, 1967.

Walkowitz, Judith. *City of Dreadful Delight: Narratives of Sexual Danger in Late-Victorian London.* University of Chicago Press, 1992.

"'The Vision of Salome': Cosmopolitanism and Erotic Dancing in Central London, 1908–1918," *American Historical Review* 108: 2 (April 2003), 337–76.

"Cosmopolitanism, Feminism and the Moving Body," *Victorian Literature and Culture* 38: 2 (2010), 427–51.

Walkowitz, Rebecca. *Cosmopolitan Style: Modernism Beyond the Nation.* New York: Columbia University Press, 2007.

Wellek, René. "The Concept of Realism in Literary Scholarship" in *René Wellek: Concepts of Criticism*, ed. Stephen G. Nichols, Jr., 223–54. New Haven, CT: Yale University Press, 1963.

Welsh, Alexander. *The City of Dickens.* Oxford: Clarendon Press, 1971.

Whewell, William. "The General Bearing of the Great Exhibition on the Progress of Art and Science" in *Lectures on the Results of the Exhibition, delivered before the Society of Arts, Manufactures and Commerce, at the suggestion of H.R.H. Prince Albert, President of the Society.* London: David Bogue, 1852, 1–34.

Whitworth, Michael. "Inspector Heat Inspected: *The Secret Agent* and the Meanings of Entropy," *Review of English Studies* 49: 193 (1998), 40–59.

"Woolf's Web: Telecommunications and Community" in *Virginia Woolf and Communities*, ed. Jeanette McVicker, Laura Davis, and Georgia Johnston, 162–67. New York: Pace University Press, 1999.

Wilde, Oscar. "The Soul of Man under Socialism" in *The Complete Works of Oscar Wilde*, 1079–105. New York: Harper & Row, 1989.

Wiley, Michael. *Romantic Geography: Wordsworth and Anglo-European Spaces.* New York: St. Martin's, 1998.

Williams, Raymond. *The Country and the City.* New York: Oxford University Press, 1973.

"Metropolitan Perceptions and the Emergence of Modernism" in *The Politics of Modernism: Against the New Conformists*, ed. Tony Pinkney, 37–48. New York: Verso, 1989.

Winkiel, Laura. *Modernism, Race and Manifestos.* Cambridge University Press, 2008.

Wlecke, Albert O. *Wordsworth and the Sublime.* Berkeley, CA: University of California Press, 1973.

Wolff, Kurt H., ed. *The Sociology of Georg Simmel.* Glencoe, IL: Free Press, 1964.

Wolfreys, Julian. *Writing London.* Vols. I–III. London: Macmillan, 1998–2004.

Wong, Edlie. "Anti-Slavery Cosmopolitanism in the Black Atlantic," *Victorian Literature and Culture* 38: 2 (2010), 451–67.

Wood, Gillen d'Arcy. *The Shock of the Real: Romanticism and Visual Culture.* New York: Palgrave, 2001.

Woodcock, George. *Anarchism: A History of Libertarian Ideas and Movements.* Cleveland, OH: Meridian, 1962.

Woolf, Virginia. *Mrs. Dalloway* [1925]. New York: Harcourt Brace, 1981.

Three Guineas [1938]. New York: Harcourt Brace, 1966.

"Flying over London," *Vogue* (March 1, 1950), 132–3.

Wordsworth, William. *A Guide Through the District of the Lakes in the North of England* [1822]. Malvern: Tantivy Press, 1948.

The Prelude 1799, 1805, 1850, ed. Jonathan Wordsworth, M. H. Abrams, and Stephen Gill. New York: W. W. Norton, 1979.

Wordsworth, William and Samuel Taylor Coleridge. *Lyrical Ballads,* ed. R. L. Brett and A. R. Jones. London: Methuen, 1978.

Young, Paul. "Mission Impossible: Globalization and the Great Exhibition" in *Britain, the Empire, and the World at the Great Exhibition of 1851,* ed. Jeffrey A. Auerbach and Peter H. Hoffenberg. Aldershot: Ashgate, 2008.

Globalization and the Great Exhibition. Houndsmills, Basingstoke: Palgrave Macmillan, 2009.

Zwerdling, Alexander. *Virginia Woolf and the Real World.* Berkeley, CA: University of California Press, 1986.

Improvised Europeans: American Literary Expatriates and the Siege of London. New York: Basic Books, 1998.

Index

CAMBRIDGE STUDIES IN NINETEENTH-CENTURY
LITERATURE AND CULTURE

General editor
Gillian Beer, *University of Cambridge*

Lightning Source UK Ltd.
Milton Keynes UK
UKOW06f1200210815

257300UK00010B/208/P